T4-AJF-719

LIFE AND VOYAGES OF LOUIS JOLLIET
(1645-1700)

INSTITUTE OF JESUIT HISTORY PUBLICATIONS

LIFE AND VOYAGES
OF LOUIS JOLLIET
(1645-1700)

By

JEAN DELANGLEZ, S. J., PH. D., LITT. D.

PROFESSOR OF HISTORY

LOYOLA UNIVERSITY, CHICAGO

CHICAGO
INSTITUTE OF JESUIT HISTORY
1948

FOREWORD

The first study of the career of Louis Jolliet is John G. Shea's short biographical sketch in his *Discovery and Exploration of the Mississippi Valley*. This sketch was reproduced in French and slightly augmented by Ferland in his *Notes sur les registres de Notre-Dame de Québec*, the first edition of which appeared in 1854, the second in 1863. Ten years later, Margry published four articles in the *Revue Canadienne* entitled "Louis Joliet." Between 1872 and 1900, those who concerned themselves with Jolliet made use of these articles and of a few documents which had come to light in the meantime. In 1900–1901, Gagnon published several articles on Jolliet, also in the *Revue Canadienne*. In 1902, these articles appeared in book form under the title *Louis Jolliet. Découvreur du Mississippi et du pays des Ilinois, premier seigneur de l'Ile d'Anticosti*. The book was reprinted in 1913 and again in 1926, with no changes in the text except for the correction of some errata. Some unimportant appendices of the original issue were omitted in the reprintings.

Since 1902, Gagnon's book has replaced what had been previously published on Jolliet. Between this date and 1946, when a fourth reprint appeared, several studies on some phase of Jolliet's career were printed. Among these two deserve a special mention: that of Amédée Gosselin, "Jean Jolliet et ses enfants," which threw new light on the family of Louis Jolliet; and that of Father Francis Borgia Steck, *The Jolliet–Marquette Expedition, 1673*, in which the authenticity of an account of the discovery of the Mississippi is discussed. *Né à Québec . . . Louis Jolliet*, by Alain Grandbois, is a work of imagination.

The 1946 reprint of Gagnon's book is called "Édition du Troisième Centenaire," because it was supposed to appear in 1945, the third centenary of the birth of Jolliet. This reprint differs from previous ones in the elimination of some notes, the addition of others, the insertion of a few paragraphs in the text and four new appendices. It is superior to its predecessors insofar as it contains photographic reproductions of maps and documents.

Gagnon did not attempt to evaluate the evidence, but ac-

cepted the documentation at its face value. For instance, he
had no doubt that the Jolliet who was sent to Lake Superior by
Talon in 1669 was Louis; according to him the "Récit des voyages et des découvertes du Père Jacques Marquette" was written by "Father Marquette himself"; the Saint-Sulpice document, he says, is "in the handwriting of Jolliet"; the anonymous map and that of Franquelin are also by Jolliet, the latter
being "probably the one" which Frontenac sent to France in
1674; the anonymous compilation entitled "Relation de la
Nouvelle France, 1673," seems "to have been written entirely
by Jolliet." Gagnon's account of the voyage of 1673 is a para-
phrase of Dablon's Récit, for as we have just said, he thought
that the document had Marquette for its author. Not having
access to the documents for Jolliet's voyages to Hudson Bay
and to Labrador, Gagnon made use of the résumé of these
documents as published by Margry in 1872.

The present book is a condensation of ten articles published
between July 1944 and October 1946. In the bibliography
the titles of these articles are asterisked.

In condensing these articles, the following procedure has
been adopted. All the biographical data have been kept. The
account of the expedition of 1673 (Chapter Six), by far the
most important of Jolliet's three great voyages for which we
have evidence, is based on six of the above-mentioned articles.
For a detailed discussion of many moot points concerning the
discovery of the Mississippi, the reader is referred to the articles themselves; only the conclusions have been set down in
this book. In the course of these articles, I have noted more
than once that because Marquette's journal and that of Jolliet
are lost, anyone wishing to study the voyage of 1673 must of
necessity begin by carefully analyzing the few primary sources
which we possess. The attempt to write an account of the
discovery of the Mississippi on any other basis will certainly
have the following result: either a mere repetition, with the
usual literary frills, of what has been in print for the past two
hundred years, or an elaboration of theories which are quite
unsupported by the meager evidence available.

The matter of Chapter Two, in which is ascertained what
was known in Canada about the Mississippi prior to 1673,

did not appear in the series of articles on Jolliet. The abridgment of Jolliet's report of his journey to Hudson Bay (Chapter Eight) and the journal of his voyage to Labrador (Chapter Ten), which were published in the original in these articles are here translated. Finally the Jolliet documentation is calendared in an appendix.

At the time when I wrote the series of articles on Jolliet, quite a few documents were known to me only through calendars and guides. Since the publication of the articles I have had occasion to examine the documents themselves in the Archives of the Province of Quebec, in the Judicial Archives of Quebec and of Three Rivers as well as in the Archives of the Séminaire of Quebec (Laval University); hence they are here referred to by their archival press marks instead of by references to the printed lists. I take this opportunity to express my gratitude to the archivist and staff of each of these various institutions for their gracious assistance and their many courtesies.

Of the various maps in this book, that of Randin was drawn by Mr. F. J. Reif, S.J., and has already appeared in *Mid-America;* all the others were drawn by the Rev. R. E. Tischler, S.J. To him and to Mr. Reif, I express my heartfelt thanks.

Finally, I wish to acknowledge my great obligations to the Rev. John J. Wellmuth, S.J., of Xavier University, Cincinnati, and to thank him for reading the manuscript, for criticizing it, and for suggesting important changes and revisions. It is due to him that the book is less imperfect than it would otherwise have been. All defects and errors which may still be noted in this book, however, are attributable solely to the author.

ABBREVIATIONS

Manuscript Material

AC, Archives des Colonies, Paris.

AJQ, Archives Judiciaires, Québec.

ASH, Archives du Service Hydrographique, Paris.

BN, Bibliothèque Nationale, Paris.

BN, Mss. fr., Manuscrits français.

BN, Mss. fr., n. a. Manuscrits français, nouvelles acquisitions.

Printed Material

BRH, *Bulletin des recherches historiques.*

JR, *The Jesuit Relations and Allied Documents*, R. G. Thwaites, ed.

Margry, *Découvertes et Établissements des Français dans l'Ouest et dans le Sud de l'Amérique Septentrionale*, P. Margry, ed.

MA, *Mid-America.*

NYCD, *Documents relative to the Colonial History of the State of New York*, E. B. O'Callaghan, ed.

RAPQ, *Rapport de l'Archiviste de la Province de Québec*, P.– G. Roy, ed.

CONTENTS

CHAPTER I

EARLY YEARS (1645-1672)

Louis Jolliet,[1] the third child of Jehan Jollyet,[2] and of Marie d'Abancourt *dite* La Caille,[3] was born at Beauport, near Quebec,[4] shortly before September 21, 1645,[5] on which day he was baptized by Father Barthélemy Vimont, S.J., in the upper story of the house of the Company of New France (the One Hundred Associates) which was then used as the church of the town of Quebec.[6] He lost his father before he was six years old;[7] and six months after the death of Jean Jolliet, his wife married Godefroid Guillot *dit* Lavallée.[8]

We do not know where Louis lived between the date of his father's death and the time when he began to attend the Jesuit

---

[1] In every extant genuine signature, Jolliet spells his name with two "l's."—Cf. E. Gagnon, " 'Jolliet' ou 'Joliet'," BRH, 12 (1906): 306–310.

[2] According to Amédée Gosselin, "Jean Jolliet et ses enfants," *Proceedings and Transactions* of the Royal Society of Canada, 3rd series, 14 (1921), section 1, 65, Jolliet's father signed his name as in the text.

[3] Father Vimont wrote her name with a "t" when he entered the baptism of her son Louis in the church register; this is also the spelling of her name in the census of 1666. The "dite" came from her father, Adrien d'Abancourt *dit* La Caille, "the quail." Cf. BRH, 21 (1915): 235; 22 (1916): 322.

[4] That Jolliet was born at Beauport rather than at Quebec or at Château–Richer seems now established. See A. Pouliot and T.-E. Giroux, "Où est né Louis Jolliet?" BRH, 51 (1945): 334–346, 359–363, 374. This article is reprinted as Appendix A in the fourth reprint of E. Gagnon's *Louis Jolliet*, 265–290. On the various reprints of this book see Foreword.

[5] A photographic reproduction of the baptismal entry is in RAPQ, 1925, 197; printed and translated into French in Gagnon, *Louis Jolliet*, 26.

[6] Cf. Gagnon, *op. cit.*, 26–28.

[7] Jean Jolliet died on April 23, 1651 (Gosselin, "Jean Jolliet et ses enfants," *loc. cit.*, 66); he was buried on the following day. C. Tanguay, *Dictionnaire généalogique des familles canadiennes* (7 vols., Montreal, 1871–1890), 1: 324.

[8] Gosselin, *loc. cit.*, 67; Tanguay, *Dictionnaire généalogique*, 1: 292. In the census of 1666 (RAPQ, 1936, 54), Marie d'Abancourt is listed as "vefve de Jean Guillot." Philéas Gagnon wrote: "Guillot (Godefroid) dit Lavallée, qui se marie à Québec, en 1651, ne signe pas; mais est toujours nommé dans les papiers du temps, *Gefroy* au lieu de *Godefroy*." "Noms propres au Canada–Français," BRH, 15 (1909): 92.

College of Quebec. His name does not appear in contemporary documents until August 10, 1662, when he received minor orders from Bishop Laval, "in the sodality chapel of the College of the Jesuits" in Quebec.[9]   It is legitimate to deduce, however, that by this time Jolliet had finished his classical course, which took from six to seven years, and hence that since 1655 or thereabouts, he had followed the courses at the college; but whether as a boarder or as a day student is not known.

The future discoverer of the Mississippi was a musician, and it may be that his talent helped him to "work his way through college." After he had become a cleric, Jolliet either played the organ in the Jesuit church or taught music in the college of Quebec. At any rate he is mentioned as "musician" in the entry dated January 1, 1665, in the Journal of the Jesuits: "We invited to supper Sieurs Morin and Jolliet, our musicians (nos officiers de musique)."[10]

Six months later, Godefroid Guillot, his step-father, was drowned in the St. Lawrence, and on November 8, 1665, four months after the accident, Jolliet's mother married Martin Prevost, her third husband.[11]

In the census of 1666, we find the following entry: "Monsieur Jolliet, clercq d'esglise."[12]   On July 2 of the same year, Father Le Mercier wrote in the Journal of the Jesuits: "The first disputations in philosophy were held in the [chapel of the] sodality, with success.   All the public officials were present.   M. the Intendant [Talon] among others, presented some very good arguments.   M. Jolliet and Pierre Francheville defended the whole of logic very well."[13]

In 1667, Jolliet left the seminary and went to France late in the autumn of the same year.   Gosselin comments as follows upon the date of his sailing:

In his book Ernest Gagnon asserts that Jolliet left Quebec on the *Saint-Sébastien*, August 28, 1667. Yet Jolliet himself dates his account

9 Auguste Gosselin, *Vie de Mgr de Laval, premier évêque de Québec et apôtre du Canada, 1622–1708* (2 vols., Quebec, 1890), 2: 689.
10 C. H. Laverdière and H. R. Casgrain, eds., *Le Journal des Jésuites* (Montreal, 1892), 330.
11 Gosselin, "Jean Jolliet et ses enfants," *loc. cit.*, 67.
12 RAPQ, 1936, 3.
13 *Journal des Jésuites*, 345.

from the month of October. The census in which he is still said to be *clerc*[14] was taken in September and in October [1667]. This can readily be ascertained by comparing the age of young children [given in the census] with the date of their baptism as found in the church registers.[15]

While Gosselin is quite right in basing his argument on the account of October 14, 1668, his reasoning based on the census of 1667 does not prove all that he supposes, in particular we cannot deduce from the entry referred to the date when Jolliet decided to leave the seminary. First of all, the ages given in the nominal censuses are often approximate or quite erroneous.[16] As a matter of fact, the nominal census of 1667 seems to have been completed in August.[17] Secondly, Jolliet may well have been listed as *clerc* in September 1667, even though he had ceased being a seminarist, because strictly speaking, the fact that he had received the tonsure and minor orders constituted him a *clerc* both in the eyes of the Church and before the law.[18] We do not know when Jolliet notified Laval that he did not feel called to the priesthood, but an entry in the Journal of the Jesuits might be taken as an indication that it was sometime during the first months of 1667. In the philosophical disputation held on July 15, 1667, Amador Martin and not Jolliet is mentioned as Francheville's codefendant.[19]

As we have just noted, the account of October 1668 enables us to determine the date when Jolliet sailed for France. After leaving the seminary, he had to find some means of livelihood. "We do not know for what purpose or on whose advice a voyage to France was immediately (aussitôt) decided upon."[20]

---

[14] B. Sulte, *Histoire des Canadiens-Français* (8 vols., Montreal, 1882-1884), 4: 65, col. 1.

[15] Gosselin, "Jean Jolliet et ses enfants," *loc. cit.*, 69, note 3.

[16] *Infra*, p. 189, note 51.

[17] "Parce que présentement je me trouve fort indisposé, je remets encore au départ des autres vaisseaux qui sont en cette rade à vous envoyer Le Rolle des habitants que vous recevrez fort exact." Talon to Colbert, August 25, 1667, RAPQ, 1931, 75.

[18] In a legal document of the preceding year, in which mention is made of power of attorney given by his brother Adrien in 1665, he is designated as "Mr Louis Jolliet Ecclesiastique." AJQ, Greffe Becquet, minute, May 7, 1666.

[19] *Journal des Jésuites*, 355.

[20] Gosselin, "Jean Jolliet et ses enfants," *loc. cit.*, 69.

If his not taking part in the philosophical disputation of July 1667 means that he had already notified Laval of his intention to leave the seminary, then instead of "aussitôt" several months must have elapsed between his decision and his voyage to France. Gagnon speaks of "special studies" as the reason for the voyage, and he asks whether these studies had not been suggested by Tracy or Talon.[21] There is no evidence to support these conjectures, all that we know is that Bishop Laval made the voyage possible.

Even if Jolliet did not have to pay his fare, he had to find money somewhere for his other expenses, for he was penniless. The Bishop of Petraea who knew the young man well, and who appreciated his talents and his fine qualities, opened his purse and advanced the necessary funds. This we learn from Jolliet himself in the document which we shall quote *in extenso*.[22]

Below is the translation of that part of the itemized account of the money borrowed directly or indirectly from Laval by Jolliet. The document is in the archives of the Séminaire of Quebec (Laval University) and is reproduced photographically in the fourth reprint of Gagnon's life of Jolliet.[23]

Itemized account of what was furnished to me from the month of October 1667 to the month of November 1668 by my Lord of Petraea in my necessity.

	L.	s.	d.
For the passage[24] [and for] the suit of clothes when I left for France, ninety livres	90.	0.	0.
Received from Monsieur Poitevin, by order of my Lord [Laval], for wearing apparel as well as for my board and lodging at St. Josse, one hundred and sixty-one French livres	161	0.	0.
Received from Monsieur de Lauson by the same order of my Lord of Petraea:			
For the voyage from Paris to La Rochelle, twenty-eight French livres	28.	0.	0.
For the extra fare on the ship for the [return] journey, sixty French livres	60.	0.	0.

---

21 Gagnon, *Louis Jolliet*, 41–42.
22 Gosselin, "Jean Jolliet et ses enfants," *loc. cit.*, 69.
23 Gagnon, *Louis Jolliet*, between pages 80 and 81; transcribed in Appendix B, 289–294.
24 Sixty livres was the usual fare. Cf. Observations faites par Talon ..., RAPQ, 1931, 103.

For my expenses during my stay at La Rochelle, one
hundred French livres 10 sols ....100.   10.   0.
All of which together adds up to four hundred and
thirty-nine livres ten sols in French money, and five
hundred and eighty-seven livres in Canadian money....587.   0.   0.

The "Monsieur de Lauson" spoken of in the third item
was Charles de Lauzon-Charny, the youngest son of the fourth
governor general of Canada.   M. de Charny, as he was known
in New France, had left Quebec on October 17, 1666, for the
mother country,[25] where his presence was required to attend
to family affairs after his father's death, which had occurred
in Paris in the preceding February.   M. de Charny was a great
friend of Bishop Laval, and it was only natural that Jolliet, the
bishop's protégé, should visit him.   In Paris, he lodged at the
house of the parish priest of St. Josse, the "Monsieur Poitevin"
mentioned in the second item of the list, to whom Laval wrote
in 1668, shortly after the return of Jolliet to Canada.[26]

From the last entry, it appears that Jolliet did not spend all
his time in Paris,[27] but remained quite a while at La Rochelle.
In fact, according to the itemized list, he seems to have divided
his time equally between the capital and the port.   Whether

---

[25] *Journal des Jésuites*, 351.
[26] JR, 52: 42–50.
[27] I have discussed at length (*Frontenac and the Jesuits* [Chicago, 1939], 215–245) a document dubbed by Parkman a "remarkable memoir" of "unquestionable historical value." Upon examination this "monument" of impudence proved to be utterly worthless and containing little else than the wanderings of an unbalanced mind. In it Jolliet is said to be a Jesuit *donné*, and that he was sent to France by the Jesuits in 1677. On this occasion he supposedly brought to Paris a map "drawn from hearsay," and claimed the honor of having discovered the Mississippi. According to M. de Galinée—who allegedly gave this information to the author of the memoir—M. de la Salle was the only man in Canada capable of making such a discovery.
Every statement in this passage of the "remarkable memoir" is false. Jolliet went to France in 1667, long before the discovery of the Mississippi; he never was a *donné*; neither in 1667 nor at the time of his second voyage, thirty years later, did Jolliet bring a map of the Mississippi to France, the map which he made in 1674 was not from hearsay, for he had actually descended the Mississippi nearly one thousand miles, and this took place more than seven years before La Salle even saw the river. M. de Galinée who was dead when this memoir was written could be quoted without fear of contradiction; unfortunately for the memorialist, he had left on record what he thought of La Salle's ability as an explorer.

he also went to Sézanne-en-Brie,[28] the birthplace of his father,[29] we do not know; and as for the "special studies," it is
difficult to see what they could have been and how he could
have profitably engaged in studies of any kind during such a
brief stay in Paris or in La Rochelle. He can hardly have
reached Paris before January 1668, and he sailed for Canada,
at the latest, in the beginning of August of the same year.

The length of time which he spent in France is deduced
from the second part of the itemized account. Although we
do not know the date of his return to Quebec, he had already
been there for some time by October 9, 1668; on this day he
bought from Charles Aubert de la Chesnaye twelve ells of
cloth, a hat, and two pairs of shoes. From the same merchant
he also bought goods which give some indication of his future
activities: "Trade goods, namely, two guns, two pistols, six
packages of wampum; twenty-four hatchets; a gross of small
bells; twelve ells of coarse cloth; ten ells of canvas; forty
pounds of tobacco. Cost: three hundred and fifty-four livres
six sols."

This itemized account is dated October 14, 1668. In the
last paragraph Jolliet acknowledges that the money was advanced by Bishop Laval, whom he promised to repay; his mother and his elder brother helped him to meet his obligations in
the following manner. A week earlier, on October 8, 1668,
the bishop had bought a piece of land from the Jolliet's estate
for 2,400 livres; half of this sum was to be paid to Jolliet's
mother, and 300 livres to each of the four children of Jean
Jolliet: Adrien, Louis, Marie, and Zacharie. When the deed
was drawn, Marie d'Abancourt had consented that, in order
to reimburse himself, Laval could retain 180 livres from the
installment payments of her share.[30] On November 9, 1668,
Adrien Jolliet sent the following note to Laval:

I agree that my Lord the Bishop of Petraea may hand over to my
brother Louis Jolliet the 300 livres due to me as my share of the price
of the land which was sold to him. In testimony thereof, I have

---

28 Gagnon, *Louis Jolliet*, 41.
29 J. B. Ferland, *Notes sur les registres de Notre–Dame de Québec* (2d ed., Quebec, 1863), 27.
30 AJQ, Greffe Rageot, no. 339, October 8, 1668. The deed is
printed in Gagnon, *Louis Jolliet*, 294–299.

signed the present note to serve him as receipt. Done at Cap-de-la-Madeleine, November 9, 1668. [Signed] Adrian Jolliet.[31]

All the above financial help, writes Gosselin, was "to enable Jolliet to pay his debts, or to enable him to make the voyage to the Great Lakes which he was about to undertake." From the dates of these various documents, however, and from other evidence to be quoted presently, it is practically certain that Jolliet did not make his first western journey in 1668. The above mentioned note was written by Louis Jolliet and signed by his brother Adrien. This means that Louis Jolliet was at Cap-de-la-Madeleine on November 9, 1668, but the season was too far advanced for him to leave for the West; in 1668, he had not yet begun the strenuous apprenticeship of a voyageur. Moreover, it is difficult to believe that he would have made his first voyage to the West without his brother, who had gone to the Ottawa country at least twice before, and it is certain that Adrien and Louis were in Quebec on April 13, 1669.[32] Now the journey by canoe from Montreal to Sault Ste Marie took ordinarily six weeks, and would have taken much longer in winter. Hence if Louis Jolliet actually went with his brother to the West in November 1668, he would have had just enough time to reach Sault Ste Marie by January 1669, and would have had to return immediately in order to be in Quebec before the middle of April. It should also be remembered that journeys from the West to Lower Canada in winter were very rare occurrences and were only undertaken in case of the most urgent emergency.[33]

We do not know what Louis Jolliet did or where he went during the latter part of 1669 and the first half of 1670. A Jolliet is mentioned in a document of 1670 referring to events

---

[31] Archives of the Séminaire of Québec (Laval University); printed in Gagnon, *Louis Jolliet,* 299.

[32] Gosselin, "Jean Jolliet et ses enfants," *loc. cit.,* 75; see also AJQ, Greffe Rageot, no. 339, printed in Gagnon, *Louis Jolliet,* 298.

[33] Cf. "Narrative of the most remarkable occurrences in Canada, 1689, 1690," NYCD, 9: 463; C. C. Le Roy de Bacqueville de La Potherie, *Voyage de l'Amerique, cotnenant Ce qui s'est passé de plus remarquable dans l'Amerique Septentrionale depuis 1534. jusqu'a present,* (4 vols., Amsterdam, 1723), 3: 60f; P. F. X. de Charlevoix, *Histoire et description generale de la Nouvelle-France, avec le Journal historique d'un Voyage fait par ordre du Roi dans l'Amérique Septentrionalle* (3 vols., Paris, 1744), 1: 568.

which took place in 1669, and it has been taken for granted that he was Louis; but, as we shall see, all the evidence shows that this Jolliet was Adrien, Louis' elder brother.

On September 24, 1669, this Jolliet was met by MM. Dollier and Galinée at Tinawatawa, an Indian village situated at the western end of Lake Ontario. He was returning from Lake Superior where he had been sent by Talon to locate a copper mine. "After finding this mine, he was to find an easier route than the ordinary one to transport the ore to Montreal. M. Jolliet had not been able to see this mine because time pressed for his return."[34]

He had found Iroquois prisoners among the Ottawa and was bringing one of them back home to his own country as a token of the peace which the Ottawa wished to have with the Iroquois. "This Iroquois showed M. Jolliet a new route, heretofore unknown to the French, from the Ottawa country to that of the Iroquois." Had it not been for the Indian's fear of falling into the hands of the Conestoga, the party could have traveled by water as far as Lake Ontario; the only portage would have been at Niagara Falls. As it was, the fear of the Iroquois prisoner forced Jolliet "to travel fifty leagues overland and to abandon his canoe on the shore of Lake Erie." Besides informing MM. Dollier and Galinée of this new route, *i.e.*, by way of Lakes Huron, St. Clair, and Erie,[35] Jolliet also told them "that he had sent some men of his party in search of a very numerous nation of Ottawa called the Potawatomi, amongst whom there had never been any missionaries, and that this tribe bordered on the Iskoutegas and the great river that leads to the Shawnee." The Sulpician missionaries determined to take this route, especially since "M. Jolliet offered us a description he had made of his route from the Ottawa country. I

---

34 "Ce qui s'est passé de plus remarquable dans le voyage de M[essieu]rs D'Olier et Galinée," BN, Mss. fr., n.a., 7485: 16. The document—a copy—is printed in Margry, 1: 112–116; the French text and its English translation on opposite pages in J. H. Coyne, *Papers and Records*, Ontario Historical Society, vol. 4, part 1 (Toronto, 1913); this English version was reissued by L. P. Kellogg, *Early Narratives of the Northwest 1634–1699* (New York, 1917), 167–209.

35 Cf. "Description du Canada et de ce qui sy trouve d'advantageux tant pour les interests de Sa Majesté que pour ceux des colonies françoises qui y sont etablie [*sic*]. 1671." AC, C 11A, 3: 193.

[Galinée] immediately translated his description into a *carte marine*,[36] the information which he gave greatly helped us in our journey . . ."

When La Salle, who was with the Sulpicians at this time, saw that they were determined to follow the route indicated by Jolliet, he "begged to be excused for leaving them so as to return to Montreal." La Salle parted from MM. Dollier and Galinée at Tinawatawa on September 30; we have no record of his movements until the summer of the following year, 1670, when Nicolas Perrot met him hunting with some Frenchmen and Iroquois on the Ottawa River.[37] As for Jolliet, we do not know when he left for the Iroquois country, *i.e.*, we do not know whether he was still at Tinawatawa on September 30 or whether he left with La Salle on that date.

The immediate reason for sending this Jolliet to investigate the Lake Superior copper mine was because in August 1667, Father Allouez had brought to Talon samples of copper ore[38] "extracted, so he assures me, from a rock which he saw several times in Lake Huron [*i.e.*, Superior]; but the distance from here to there is so great that one does not dare to expect great advantages therefrom. The copper, he says, is very pure and very abundant. A piece is being brought to you that you may judge of its purity."[39]

The existence of a rich copper mine in "Lake Huron," in spite of its distance from Quebec, was good news to Talon, who had been ineffectually searching for mines around Quebec and along the banks of the St. Lawrence ever since his arrival in Canada in 1665.[40] In his answer to Talon's letter saying that the ore brought by Allouez was being sent to Paris, Colbert replied that if there really was copper in Lake Huron, and if it could be easily mined, it would be something well worth

---

36 From Galinée's description of this map, it appears that by *carte marine* he means one of the cylindrical projections, very probably the equal-spaced or plate-carrée projection.

37 J. Tailhan, ed., *Memoire sur les, Moeurs, Coustumes et Relligion des Sauvages de l'Amerique Septentrionale par Nicolas Perrot* (Leipzig and Paris, 1864), 120.

38 JR, 54: 162, and cf. JR, 50: 264–266.

39 Talon to Colbert, October 27, 1667, RAPQ, 1931, 80.

40 Talon to Colbert, October 4, 1665, *ibid.*, 33; Colbert to Talon, April 6, 1666, *ibid.*, 43; Talon to Colbert, November 13, *ibid.*, 55; Colbert to Talon, April 4, 1667, *ibid.*, 68.

following up; but, said the minister, the means of bringing the ore to Quebec should be carefully considered.[41]

Talon received this letter of Colbert in the summer of 1668. Before leaving New France in November, the intendant appointed two men to "make sure whether there was copper in Lake Huron," and gave them a substantial subsidy.[42]

Now we know that Louis Jolliet returned from Europe in the summer of 1668, and as we have seen, he was in Quebec on October 14 of that year. It is difficult to believe that the intendant would have selected for the expedition a young man only twenty-three years old who had left the seminary the year before and who had been out of the country ever since. He would more likely have chosen Adrien Jolliet, Louis' brother, who was a veteran voyageur. Furthermore, as we shall see presently, the Jolliet who was sent to investigate the copper mine was paid 400 livres; and at this very time Louis Jolliet acknowledges having been advanced 450 livres by Bishop Laval to equip himself and to buy trade goods.[43]

On November 11, 1669, Jean-Baptiste Patoulet, acting for Talon, wrote to Colbert as follows:

Sieurs Jolliet and Péré,[44] to whom M. Talon paid 400 and 1,000 livres, respectively, in order that they might go and find out whether the copper mine, which is beyond Lake Ontario and of which you have seen some samples, is rich and easy to exploit, and whether the ore can easily be brought here, have not yet returned. The former should have been back here any day during the whole of last September, and yet, even now, we have no news whatever of him, so that it is necessary to wait until next year before giving you definite information as to how productive the said mine can be expected to be.[45]

The Péré mentioned by Patoulet was Jean Péré who, like Adrien Jolliet, was a veteran western trader;[46] and it is clear

---

[41] Colbert to Talon, February 20, 1668, ibid., 97.

[42] This sum of money is not mentioned in the itemized account of expenses for 1668, because it was taken from the funds set aside for "despenses extraordinaires." See Talon's memoir of 1669, RAPQ, 1931, 107.

[43] Gagnon, Louis Jolliet, 292.

[44] See what Talon says about Péré in his letter to Colbert of February 24, 1669, to Colbert, AC, C 11A, 9: 269–269v, printed in Margry, 6: 19, note, translated in NYCD, 9: 787.

[45] Patoulet to Colbert, November 11, 1669, Margry, 1: 81.

[46] Cf. P[ierre]-G[eorges] R[oy], "Jean Péré et Pierre Moreau dit la Taupine." BRH, 10 (1905): 213–221; Jugements et délibérations du Conseil Souverain, 1: 634 f.

that the Jolliet he speaks of is the same man referred to by
Galinée. This Jolliet, says the Sulpician, had left Montreal,
"shortly before us,"[47] *i.e.*, shortly before July 6, 1669. Since
Patoulet had been expecting him in Quebec "any day during
the whole of the month of September," and since the journey
to Sault Ste Marie took from four to six weeks, this Jolliet
must have left Montreal sometime in June.

The Jolliet who was expected in Quebec in September was
still at the western end of Lake Ontario at the end of that
month. In view of the fact that he was bringing back an Iroquois prisoner, he can hardly have failed to pass through the
Iroquois country. To go from Hamilton, Ontario, to Quebec,
even by way of the Iroquois country, certainly did not require
six weeks; and as we know from Galinée, the Jolliet whom he
met was especially anxious to return to Quebec as soon as possible. But on November 11 he had not as yet arrived in Quebec, and Talon makes no mention of him in his letter of November 10, 1670, in which he inveighs against Péré's failure to
report. There is no doubt that the Jolliet who was sent to the
West in 1669 would have reported to the authorities as soon
as he reached Quebec, for he was returning from an official
mission, and had found a new route which avoided the rapids
of the Ottawa River,—a matter of such importance that as
soon as Talon heard of this route he reported it to Colbert.[48]

The silence of Talon in his letter of November 10, 1670,
and the absence of any record of Jolliet's return to Quebec
later on, can only be explained by the fact that he was dead
at that time. Hence this Jolliet must have been Adrien and
not Louis.

As long as the earliest positive evidence for the death of
Adrien Jolliet was a statement made by Louis on September 12,
1671, in which the latter refers to his brother as "deffunct,"[49]
the above reasoning was not conclusive. But two notarial documents which recently came to light show that Adrien Jolliet

47 In the printed account of his narrative (*supra*, p. 8, note
34) Galinée is made to say: "qui etoit parti avant nous de Montreal,"; the manuscript has "qui etoit parti *un peu* avant nous de
Montreal."
48 Talon to Colbert, August 29, 1670, RAPQ, 1931, 117.
49 Gagnon, *Louis Jolliet*, 296.

died much earlier: one of these documents proves that he was dead twelve months by September 12, 1671; the other that he died at least eighteen months previous to this date.

In the first of these two documents dated Quebec September 20, 1670, Jeanne Dodier is called "veufue Adrien Jolliet."[50] In the second document dated Cap-de-la-Madeleine March 22, 1670, Jeanne Dodier is said to be "Veufue de deffunt le Sr Adrien Jolliet."[51] Hence in March 1670, Jeanne Dodier, the wife of Adrien Jolliet, was already a widow. How much time had elapsed since the death of her husband has not been ascertained; but considering that Adrien Jolliet's name does not appear in the burial registers of Quebec nor in those of Three Rivers, the presumption is that he may have died en route from the West.[52]

Another argument pointing to Adrien as being the Jolliet who went to the West with Péré is the following. It was the custom in New France for those about to leave for the long and perilous journey to the West to donate their belongings and property to their relatives, a donation which would take

[50] AJQ, Greffe Becquet, cahier 5, September 20, 1670. Jeanne Dodier went to Quebec in September 1670; she had returned to Cap-de-la-Madeleine by October 20, on which day she appeared before the notary of the place to have a contract legalized. Archives Judiciaires, Three Rivers. Greffe Jean Cusson, minute.

[51] Archives Judiciaires, Three Rivers, Greffe Jean Cusson, March 22, 1670, minute.

[52] With regard to the place where Adrien died, Gosselin ("Jean Jolliet et ses enfants," loc. cit., 75) quotes from a memoir analyzed elsewhere (Frontenac and the Jesuits, 176 ff). The passage reads as follows: "The burial of the brother of Jolliet [this can only be Adrien] who died while in the service of Sieur de la Salle and who was buried during the latter's absence cost him 53 livres." BN, Clairambault, 1016: 44.—We must note that this memoir was written at least five years after the event, and that it contains too many inaccuracies—not to use a harsher word—to take for granted such assertions as are not supported by independent evidence. Thus it is difficult to believe that in October 1669, La Salle hired Adrien Jolliet who was on his way to Quebec, while La Salle himself was wandering in the Lake Ontario region until the following summer. Moreover, in October 1669, Adrien Jolliet was in the service of the government, not of Sieur de la Salle. Although Bernou, the author of the memoir, does not specify the place where Adrien Jolliet died, he is speaking of Quebec in this passage, and is contrasting the cost of burial in the church with the cost of burial in the cemetery. As for Adrien Jolliet being buried in Montreal, Gosselin's arguments are invalid; they are based on gratuitous suppositions or are contradicted by positive evidence.

effect should the donor die during the voyage; more often those who were about to leave gave power of attorney to relatives or friends who took care of their interests while they were away. Now on April 13, 1669—that is, a little more than a month before the departure from Quebec of Péré and the Jolliet who went with him—Adrien Jolliet gave such a power of attorney to his brother Louis.[53]   This may be taken as another indication that the Jolliet who was sent to the West to investigate the copper mine was Adrien and not Louis.

Finally, if the Jolliet mentioned by Patoulet were really Louis, his failure to report to Quebec on this occasion would hardly have inspired Talon to commission him in 1672 to find out where the great river of the West emptied its waters.

The earliest positive evidence of Louis Jolliet's presence in the West is dated June 1671, when his name appeared in a document drawn at Sault Ste Marie.   As will be seen from the chronology of events, Louis Jolliet began his career of explorer in 1670.

In the instructions given to Talon before leaving France for his second term as intendant of Canada, the king urged him to continue the search for iron, lead, copper, and tin mines, telling him "to consider this work as most important for the prosperity of Canada."[54]   In a marginal note of November 1670, Talon says that he has sent men to discover copper mines, and less than two weeks after his arrival in 1670, he had already notified Colbert that "the iron-master swears that the iron mine which I showed him is excellent."   In the same letter he notes that a Sulpician [M. de Galinée] had made a journey "far to the West."   One of the immediate results of this voyage was the knowledge of "a river [the Detroit River, Lake St. Clair and the St. Clair River] I was looking for, which joins Lake Ontario [i.e., Erie] to Lake Huron, where the copper mine is said to be."[55]

In a long memoir added to his letter of November 10, 1670, Talon informs Colbert that he has sent St. Lusson to the West,

---

53 AJQ, Greffe Rageot, no. 339, addition of September 12, 1671, on the document of October 8, 1668.
54 Mémoire succinct..., May 18, 1669, RAPQ, 1931, 112.
55 Talon to Colbert, August 29, 1670, ibid., 117.

instructing him to go as far as he could toward the setting sun, and ordering him to look for some waterway which would lead to the "Sea of the South which separates this continent from China; but only after he has given his first attention to the copper mine which is the main object of the expedition, and after having ascertained the accuracy of the memoirs which have been given him to that effect."[56]

From the above it is clear that the discovery of a water route to the Sea of the South was only a secondary consideration in Talon's mind. St. Lusson states in the procès-verbal that he was sent by Talon "to seek and find mines of all sorts, but especially the copper mine." The "memoirs" given to St. Lusson by Talon were very probably a copy of the chapter on copper mines of Lake Superior in the Relation of 1669–1670, the manuscript of which had certainly reached Quebec when Talon arrived in August 1670.[57]

In the same memoir to Colbert, Talon refers to the previous Péré-Jolliet expedition, but makes no mention of the latter:

I have been unable to figure out why and by what machinations I failed to find here on my arrival the information which I expected from Sieur Péré who was sent [to the West] last year [1669] with a gratuity of more than one hundred *pistoles*. This fellow Péré did not come back, but remained with the [Jesuit] Fathers, who have a mission in the Ottawa country, whence he writes very obscurely. This gives rise to the suspicion that his investigations may have been interfered with, and that he has been prevented from sending an unalloyed report.[58]

The French wording of this passage makes clear Talon's implications, which, incidentally, are quite unfounded: "Ce qui donne lieu de douter qu'*on* n'ait retardé les connoissances qu'il devoit prendre de cette mine, et empesché qu'il ne communiquast ses lumieres dans leur pureté." "*On*" in this case

---

56 Talon to Colbert, November 10, 1670, *ibid.*, 136.
57 Dollier and Galinée reached Montreal on June 18, 1670 (Kellogg, *Early Narratives of the Northwest*, 208); and Galinée says that "a Jesuit brother who descended after us" wrecked his canoe in the rapids of the Ottawa River. This "Jesuit brother" was probably one of the *donnés* who generally acted as couriers for the missionaries. Cf. *Lettres de la Venerable Mere Marie de l'Incarnation premiere Superieure des Ursulines de la Nouvelle France* (Paris, 1681), 640.
58 Talon to Colbert, November 10, 1670, RAPQ, 1931, 136 f.

can only mean the Jesuits, who had made known to Talon himself, three years earlier, the existence of copper mines in Lake Superior. There is no reason whatever to suppose that they would interfere with Péré's investigations, or prevent him from sending an "unalloyed" report. As M. Roy observes, the reason why Péré remained at Sault Ste Marie was very likely because he considered "trade more profitable than scientific investigations" of mines.[59] Furthermore, when St. Lusson returned to Quebec late in the summer of 1671[60] and brought back an "unalloyed" report without having been impeded by the machinations of "*on*," there was nothing in his report[61] that had not already been recorded in greater detail in the Relation of 1669–1670.

St. Lusson left Montreal so late in 1670, that he was unable to reach Sault Ste Marie that year. Forced to spend the winter on Lake Huron,[62] he arrived at the Sault at the beginning of May 1671, and there, on June 4, he took solemn possession of the West in the name of the King of France.[63] Among the witness of the ceremony was "le sieur Jolliet."

---

[59] Roy, "Jean Péré et Pierre Moreau dit La Taupine," BRH, 10 (1905): 215.

[60] He arrived at Quebec before August 26, 1671. "Saisie d'une chaloupe et pelleterie a la Req. de François Daumont Sr de St Lusson contre Nicolas Perrot et ses associés venant du Outaouak," September 3, 1671. Archives de la Province, Quebec. The bundle, dated October 1672, in which this document is found is listed in P.-G. Roy, *Inventaire d'une collection de pièces ... conservées aux Archives judiciaires de Québec* (2 vols., Beauceville, 1917), 1: 13, no. 96.

[61] Cf. Talon's memoir to Louis XIV, November 2, 1671, RAPQ, 1931, 158 f.

[62] "Je party donc avec le Sr. de Saint Lusson son [Talon's] subdélégué, et nous arrivâmes à Montréal, où nous restâmes jusqu'au commencement du mois d'octobre [1670]. Nous fumes contraints, dans le voyage, d'hyverner chez les Amikoüets." *Memoire sur les Moeurs ... par Nicolas Perrot*, 126. Cf. JR, 55: 106.

[63] The procès-verbal in AC, C 11A, 9: 292–293v is a copy added to a "Memoire sur la domination des françois en Canada jusqu'en 1687" ff. 260–291) ; a few lines at the end of the memoir are of 1706. The whole document printed in NYCD, 9: 781–804, is entitled "Memoir on the French Dominion in Canada 1507–1706," the procès-verbal is on pp. 803–804. The original procès-verbal, says the editor of the *Collections* of the State Historical Society of Wisconsin (9: 26), "is in Margry, 1: 96–99," adding that the translation which he reprints "is from NYCD, 9: 803–804 with some errors of nomenclature corrected." Margry printed the copy in the Archives des Colonies and Gagnon reprinted Margry's text in *Louis Jolliet*, 49–52. A copy made by Father Tailhan on the copy in the "Archives de la Marine"

Without giving any proof for his statement, Sulte asserts that this Jolliet was Adrien,[64] which is quite impossible, for, as we have seen, Adrien Jolliet was dead by March 22, 1670, that is, fourteen months before the date of the procès-verbal. The proof that the Jolliet who witnessed the ceremony at Sault Ste Marie was Louis is based on solid evidence.

After the death of her first husband, Adrien Jolliet, Jeanne Dodier married before October 11 1671, one Antoine Baillargé,[65] and after the death of the latter on December 19, 1672,[66] she married, at a date which has not been ascertained,[67] Mathurin Normandin *dit* Beausoleil. At the end of June or the beginning of July 1674, as soon as he heard of Louis Jolliet's

---

(today Archives des Colonies), is in the Jesuit Archives of the Province of France, Fonds Brotier 155, Canada–1. Tailhan printed the procès-verbal in his edition of Perrot's *Memoire sur les Moeurs*, 292–294, but left out the names of the witnesses. He has "July 3 last [1670]" as the date of Talon's order to St. Lusson, instead of September 3. Talon arrived in Quebec on August 18. The procès-verbal is dated June 14; Dablon, however, wrote out the date when the ceremony took place: "le quatrième de Juin."—JR, 55: 106.

There is an earlier, much shorter copy of the procès-verbal in the Archives des Affaires Étrangères, Mémoires et Documents, Amérique, 5: 283, and a transcription of it by a professional copyist, *ibid.*, 282–282v. These copies are dated May 16, 1671, on the day following the assembly of the Indians at Sault Ste Marie; St. Lusson signed the original, and there is no question of witnesses. According to the *Memoire sur les Moeurs*, 127, Perrot arrived at the Sault on May 5; Dablon wrote that St. Lusson reached the mission "at the beginning of May."—JR, 55: 106.

64 B. Sulte, "Les français dans l'Ouest en 1671," *Proceedings and Transactions* of the Royal Society of Canada, 3rd series, 12 (1918), section 1, 19.

65 On October 11, 1671, "Le Sr Anthoine baillargée et damme Jeanne dodier sa famme" were witnesses of the marriage contract between Charles Lesieur, Sieur de la Pierre and Françoise Lafonds. Archives Judiciaires, Three Rivers, Greffe Jean Cusson.—See "Louis Jolliet. Early Years," MA, 27 (1945) : 19, note 74. This article was written before I had an opportunity of examining the documents in the Greffe Jean Cusson.

66 On December 18, 1672, Antoine Baillargée appeared before Jean Cusson, the notary of Cap-de-la-Madeleine, to legalize the leasing of his house to Sébastien Provencher. The same document has an addition dated December 20, 1672, which says that on this day Jeanne Dodier "vefve de deffunt led. baillargé" appeared before the same notary and declared that she wished to ratify the lease made two days earlier by her late husband. Archives Judiciaires, Three Rivers, Greffe Jean Cusson.

67 The first entry in the church register (baptisms, marriages, burials) of Cap-de-la-Madeleine is dated November 9, 1673. A copy of this register (Ms. 34) is in the Archives of the Séminaire de Québec (Laval University).

arrival in Montreal from Sault Ste Marie, Normandin had papers served on the explorer.

In these papers, there is a clear reference to two voyages to the West. Louis Jolliet is said to have returned from the West the *first time* in 1671, and that he had "obtained his trade permit (congé) the *second time* he went to the Ottawa country" solely in order to bring back pelts which he had failed to bring back from the West in 1671.[68]

One of these two documents mentioning these facts is undated, but it is clearly anterior to July 7, 1674, the date of the second document.[69] It is evident that the *second time* Jolliet went to the West can only have been in 1672, when he left Quebec with the commission to find out into what sea the Mississippi discharged its waters. There is no difficulty with regard to the date of his *first voyage* to the West, for the document specifies that he returned from the Ottawa country in 1671 [gbjᶜ soixante & Unze], and we know that Louis Jolliet was in Quebec on September 12 of that year.

In a previous discussion of these two documents I stressed the year when Jolliet went to the West the *second* time, but failed to emphasize that the year of Jolliet's return from his *first voyage* to the Ottawa country is explicitly stated as 1671. This may have been the reason why M. Georges-Henri Dagneau asked in the Quebec *Action Catholique* for August 17, 1945, whether the argument based on the permit to go to the Ottawa country the *second time* is apodictic, and whether this argument excludes a voyage prior to 1670. By themselves, even the two dates do not exclude a western voyage prior to 1670, but we know that Louis Jolliet certainly did not go to the West in 1668, nor, as we have seen, was it he who went with Péré in 1669, hence he did not make a voyage to the Ottawa country prior to 1670.[70]

---

[68] In 1672, Jolliet was not given a *congé* "solely" in order to bring back the pelts which had been left in the West; Talon gave him a trade permit to defray the expenses of the journey.

[69] The two documents are published in "Louis Jolliet. Early Years," *loc. cit.*, 26–29.

[70] I have examined elsewhere the texts produced by M. Dagneau which seem to imply that Jolliet made several voyages to the West prior to that of 1672.—"The 'Récit des voyages ... du Père Jacques Marquette'," MA, 28 (1946): 217–219.

It now remains to inquire in what year Louis Jolliet left Quebec for his first voyage to the West. Since he was at Sault Ste Marie in May–June 1671, he must have left Lower Canada in 1670, before the departure of the St. Lusson party in October, and he very likely spent the winter of 1670–1671 at the Sault. This seems to be confirmed by a passage in the memoir of Nicolas Perrot, in which the latter says that the procès-verbal of June 1671 was signed by "Frenchmen who were trading in those parts."[71]

We have seen that Louis Jolliet was in Quebec on September 12, 1671, but we do not know what he did or where he went between this date and the following summer, when Talon commissioned him to search for a water route to the Sea of the South. Although Jolliet was officially sent on this exploratory voyage, the expedition was not financed by the government any more than St. Lusson's expedition had been.[72] Talon had not forgotten what had happened in 1669, when he subsidized in advance Péré and Adrien Jolliet. Henceforth explorers would receive trade permits and would have to defray the expenses of the journey with the profits of their trade.

---

[71] Tailhan, Memoire sur les Moeurs ... par Nicolas Perrot, 128.
[72] Talon to Louis XIV, November 2, 1671, RAPQ, 1931, 158. In the preceding year the intendant had written to the minister: "En cet endroit je puis dire que sy en distribuant quelques medailles du Roy a ceux qui se porteront aux grandes entreprises ou aux decouvertes utiles, ou de pays nouveaux, ou de mines, ou de forests, on ne rendoit pas cette marque d'honneur trop familiere, Je vous en demanderois une douzaine pour servir d'esguillon et faire agir aux choses plus difficiles des personnes que L'argent ne contenteroit pas si fortement." Talon to Colbert, November 19, 1670, ibid., 129.— This recommendation fell on deaf ears; there is no record of Frenchmen or Canadians having been decorated for discoveries during this period.

CHAPTER II

KNOWLEDGE OF THE MISSISSIPPI
BEFORE 1673

In this chapter we shall ascertain what were the geographical concepts of men in New France who were interested in the geography of North America, and in particular, what was known in Canada by 1673 about the objectives of Jolliet's voyage to the Mississippi.

The earliest mention of a great river in the West occurs in the Relation of 1659–1660. In 1659, on returning to Quebec, a Jesuit met there two Frenchmen who had just arrived from the West. These two men had spent the preceding winter exploring the shores of Lake Superior. In one of their excursions, they went six days' journey southwest of Lake Superior, where they saw remnants of the Huron nation who had been driven to those parts by the Iroquois. In their flight from their enemies, the Hurons had "fortunately encountered a beautiful river, large, wide, deep, and worthy of comparison, they said, with our great river St. Lawrence. On its banks they found the great nation of the Alimi8ec who received the Hurons very kindly."[1]

The annotator of this passage in the *Jesuit Relations* identifies the two Frenchmen as Médard Chouart *dit* des Groseilliers and Pierre-Esprit Radisson, "who had just returned from their second western voyage after an absence of two years."[2] Recent research has established beyond doubt that Radisson made no voyage to the West in 1654–1656,[3] the date of the earlier voyage referred to by the annotator. Hence this latter one cannot have been his "second western voyage."

It is impossible to identify the river spoken of by the Indians. Moreover, it appears from the text of the Relation that

---

[1] JR, 45: 234.
[2] *Ibid.*, 272.
[3] G. L. Nute, *Caesars of the Wilderness* (New York, 1943), 29–31, and 43, note 10. It is practically certain that one of the two Frenchmen was Chouart, but "we may never know the name" of his companion. *Ibid.*, 23 f.

the Hurons had come upon this river before reaching the place where the two Frenchmen met them, that is, less than six days' journey southwest of Lake Superior. Again, from what is said of its size this river cannot be the Mississippi, for its upper reaches are certainly not comparable with the width of the St. Lawrence at any place of the latter's course which the Hurons may have seen.

Another mention of a great river in the West is found in Radisson's narrative of his supposed voyage. The third chapter of this narrative "*appears* to be an account of the expedition of 1654–1656," in which "Radisson tells the story in such a way that he becomes Des Groseilliers' partner on this trip." Miss Nute suggests that Radisson having heard his brother-in-law recount his experiences of 1654–1656, narrates them as though they were his own, or else that he is manufacturing a tale; she concludes that "all things considered, it seems plausible that his [Radisson's] narrative of the trip is what he had heard his brother-in-law describe."[4] We should add that Radisson may well have inserted fictitious elements in Chouart's description, for he was not averse to exaggerations and inventions. Thus on another occasion, he claimed to have gone to "the Lake of the Buffaloes which is larger than Lake Superior and is situated one hundred leagues farther west."[5]

In the narrative of his "voyage" of 1654–1656, Radisson says that "by the persuasion of some of them [Indians who they met on the way] we [himself and some companions] went into the great river that divides itself in 2, where the hurrons and some Ottanake [Ottawa] and the wild men that had warrs with them had retired." This is apparently the same river as that mentioned in the Relation of 1659–1660, with the difference that instead of Hurons and Illinois, the Indians dwelling on its banks are said to be Hurons and Ottawa. Radisson then goes on to say that "this nation have warrs against those of

---

4 Nute, *op. cit.*, 30 f.
5 "Le lac des Bufles dans la nouuelle France qui est *une fois* [these two words are deleted] plus grand que le Lac Superieur et a cent lieues d'iceluy vers l'occident, selong Mr. Radisson qui a esté jusques sur son riuage, mais il y a lieu de douter de ce lac."—Remarques géographiques et historiques, by Michel-Antoine Baudrand. BN, Mss. fr., 15541: 23.

[the] forked river. It is so called because it has 2 branches, the one towards the west, the other towards the South, which we believe runns toward Mexico, by the tokens they gave us."[6]

The additional data describing the "forked river" are clearly insufficient to identify it with the Mississippi; for these data could apply to many rivers of the Northwest. Radisson's belief that the south branch "runns toward Mexico" is no proof at all that he is speaking of the Mississippi. In 1669, when he wrote this narrative, he had seen maps of North America and any river flowing south in the Great Lakes region would, of course, flow "toward Mexico." Moreover, Radisson explicitly states in his narrative that in 1654–1656 Chouart did not make the journey to the "forked river";[7] hence it must have been made by his brother-in-law's companion, and we know that whoever the latter may have been, he was not Radisson. Finally, as Miss Nute pertinently observes, "in the early eighties [of the seventeenth century], Radisson . . . laid no claim at all to any knowledge of the Mississippi River. Is it likely that he would have let pass an occasion for saying that he had known of this river and its course since 1656?"[8]

In the Relation of 1661–1662, a great river is mentioned which has also been identified as the Mississippi.[9] In the first chapter of this Relation, Father Lalemant speaks of the incursions of the Iroquois who were roaming far and wide, spreading terror, ruin and devastation wherever they went. A band of Iroquois braves had gone

toward the south . . . proceeding more than two hundred leagues through the forests, without compass, yet unerringly, they finally reached the sea near the Virginia coast, as we suppose. Proceeding a little more toward the west than toward the south, another band of Iroquois went four hundred leagues from here [Quebec] in pursuit of a nation whose only crime consists in its not being Iroquois. It is called Ontôagannha,[10] as if to say 'the place where they can't speak,' because of the corrupt Algonquian in use there.[11]

---

[6] Kellogg, *Early Narratives of the Northwest*, 61.
[7] *Ibid.*, 53, 62.
[8] *Caesars of the Wilderness*, 35.
[9] JR, index, 73: 286.
[10] F. W. Hodge, *Handbook of American Indians North of Mexico* (4th impression, 2 vols., Washington, D. C., 1912), *s.v.* Ontwaganha.
[11] Kellogg, *Early Narratives of the Northwest*, 170, note 2, 183 f.

We must note that in all these reports obtained from Indians, the distances and directions so necessary to identify geographical features, are often so vague as to be practically useless. Lalemant then goes on to describe the country of the Ontôagannha according to the reports of "our Iroquois who have returned as well as according to the reports of the slaves whom they have brought thence." Their villages, he writes,

are situated along a beautiful river which serves to carry the people down to the great lake—for thus they call the sea—where they trade with Europeans who pray God as we do, who use rosary beads and bells for calling the people to prayer. From their description we judge them to be Spaniards. That sea must be the Bay of the Holy Ghost in the Gulf of Mexico on the coast of Florida, or else, the Vermilion Sea on the coast of New Granada in the great Sea of the South.[12]

Two points should be noted in connection with this report. In the first place, most of the Jesuit missionaries in New France knew Iroquois, and the slaves brought by the Iroquois spoke a dialect "very closely related to Sauk-Fox," which could be understood by Algonquian-speaking missionaries. They could therefore understand what both Iroquois and Shawnee said about the country. In the second place, we must distinguish between what these Indians said and Lalemant's speculation. In the sixties of the seventeenth century, the Shawnee were divided into two bodies, one living on the Cumberland River, the other in Tennessee and in South Carolina. According to ethnologists, the Shawnee of the second group are the same as the Savannah who dwelt on the river of that name, not far from the Spanish settlements on the Atlantic coast.[13] Father Lalemant was led to surmise that the sea into which the river emptied was the "Baye du S. Esprit or the Mer Vermeille [Gulf of California]," after comparing the data furnished by the Indians with a map of the period, very probably that of North America which had been published in Paris in 1650.

The next mention of a great river in the West occurs in the Relation of 1666–1667 which contains the journal of Father Allouez. This missionary, who had left for the West in 1665,

---

12 JR, 47: 142–146.
13 Hodge, *Handbook of American Indians*, s.v. Shawnee.

brought back to Quebec in 1667 definite information on western ethnography and geography. In his journal he twice speaks of a great river: "They [the Illinois] do not live in these parts [Chequamegon Bay], their country being more than sixty leagues from here toward the south, beyond a great river, which, as far as I can judge, empties into the sea toward Virginia." In a later passage, where he speaks of the Sioux, he says: "These are people dwelling to the west of this place [Chequamegon Bay], toward the great river, named Messipi. They are forty or fifty leagues from here in a country of prairies, abounding in all sorts of game."[14]

We are certain that Allouez is speaking of the Mississippi in both cases because we know that the Illinois were then dwelling on its banks, and also because of what Marquette wrote about the Mississippi in his letter of April 1670, namely, "it is hard to believe that the great river discharges its waters in Virginia, we think rather that it has its mouth in California."[15]

Allouez' conjecture as well as Marquette's arose from the fact that on the maps of the period, a huge mountain range surrounds the southeast of the United States. This range would of course be considered a barrier which would deflect the great river to the east or to the west.

In 1669, on returning to Quebec from his second western voyage, Allouez asked the Jesuit superior for additional missionaries. The editor of the Relation of 1668–1669 wrote as follows: "The lot happily fell on Father Claude Dablon. He has been sent to be Superior of the missions of the Upper Country, notwithstanding the abundant fruits of his ministry and the pressing necessity of his presence here."[16]

Of all the Jesuits in seventeenth century New France, none was more interested than Dablon in the geography of North America, especially in the geography of the country west of the Great Lakes and of the Hudson Bay region. Until the late fifties of the seventeenth century, there is little in the Jesuit Relations about these two sections of the continent, but in the

---

14 JR, 51: 46, 52.
15 JR, 54: 188.
16 JR, 52: 198. Cf. "Claude Dablon, S.J. (1619–1697)," MA, 26 (1944) : 99.

third chapter of the Relation of 1659-1660 there is a detailed account of the country west of Lake Superior given to a Jesuit by an Indian who had spent two years wandering in the West and who said he had gone to the shores of Hudson Bay. As will be seen, the author of this description combined what was learned from this Indian with the geography of North America as represented on maps then available in Canada.

> The Indians dwelling at the farthest end of this Lake [Superior] have given some altogether new and enlightening information which will gratify those interested in the route to Japan and China, for which so much search has already been made. For we learned from these peoples that they have the sea on three sides, toward the south, toward the west and toward the north. Hence, if this be so, we have here a strong argument and a very certain indication that these three seas, being contiguous, form in reality but one sea, that of China. For that of the south, which is the Pacific Ocean, is well known, and is connected with the Sea of the North, also well known, by a third one, the sea about which we are concerned. All that is needed, therefore, is to find a passage into this third sea, which is at once a western sea [insofar as it is located to the west of New France] and an eastern sea [insofar as it is the China sea].
>
> Now we know that by proceeding southward for about three hundred leagues from the end of Lake Superior of which I have just spoken, one comes to the *Baye du St. Esprit*, which lies in latitude 30° and in longitude 280°, in the Gulf of Mexico, on the coast of Florida; and from the same western end of Lake Superior, in a southwesterly direction, a journey of about two hundred leagues leads to another lake emptying, on the coast of New Granada, into the Vermilion Sea [Gulf of California], [which communicates with] the great Sea of the South [Pacific Ocean]. And it is from one of these two coasts [Gulf of Mexico and Gulf of California] that the Indians who live some sixty leagues to the west of our Lake Superior obtain European goods, and they even say that they have seen Europeans there.[17]

The author of the above passage evidently combined the information learned from Indians with the representation of North America on Sanson's map of 1650. On this map the 280th meridian intersects the thirtieth parallel in the "B. de Spiritu S*o." On the same map "another lake" lying in the southwest of Lake Superior is shown emptying into the "Mar Vermejo" through the "Rio de Norte," and the distance between this lake and the western end of Lake Superior is about

---

17 JR, 45: 220-222.

two thirds of the distance between Lake Superior and the "B. de Spiritu S^to." Again, the "Mar Vermejo" is bordered by the shores of "Nouvelle Grenade" and opens on the "Mer du Sud."

The remainder of the passage removes all doubt that its author had the 1650 Sanson map before him.

Moreover, from this same Lake Superior, if one were to follow a river which flows toward the north, one would arrive after eight days' journey at Hudson Bay, which is at latitude 55°. From this place, in a northwesterly direction, it is about forty leagues by land to Button Bay, where Port Nelson is, at latitude 57° and longitude 270°. The distance from there to Japan is only 1,420 leagues, for [the longitudinal difference between Port Nelson and Japan] is only seventy-one degrees along the great circle. Since these two seas are known, namely, that of the South and that of the North, there remains only the Sea of the West, which by joining both would make all three into one sea. Now this is the fresh knowledge which we have gained from an [Indian] nation situated at about latitude 47° and longitude 273°. These people assure us that ten days' journey westward lies a sea which can be no other than the one we are looking for. This makes us believe that the whole of North America, being thus surrounded by the sea, on the east, the south, the west and the north, must be separated from Greenland by some strait, of which a good part has already been explored, that it only remains to push on some degrees farther to enter into the Sea of Japan. The attempt [to reach the Sea of Japan] by way of Hudson strait should not be made except during the months of August and September, for only during these months is the strait less blocked with ice.

On Sanson's map "Cap Henriette Marie" lies in latitude 55°, and two embryonic rivers coming from the southwest are shown emptying on each side of the cape. Button Bay is represented as connecting Hudson Bay with the "Mer Glaciale," and Port Nelson is located at latitude 57° and longitude 270°, the position mentioned in the Relation. The distance along the great circle, 71 degrees, is only six degrees less than the actual distance between Port Nelson and Tokyo, and the difference would be much less if by "Japan" the writer means the northeastern islands of the Nipponese archipelago.

By combining the information supplied by the Sanson map and by the Indians, the author of this geographical digression "discovered" the Northwest passage. According to him, a ship sailing up Hudson Strait in August or September, would then proceed due west through the northern part of Hudson Bay to

longitude 270°, where it would turn south, pass through Button Bay to the "Mer Glaciale," and reach the "great sea which
is at once a western and an eastern sea."

The Jesuit missionary to whom the Indian traveler spoke on
the banks of the Saguenay is probably Father Druillettes, but
I am inclined to think that the author of the above geographical
speculation is Father Dablon, because there are many instances
of such speculations in passages of the Relations which he either wrote or edited, whereas those in which he had no share
contain little descriptive or theoretical geography.

Dablon's contributions can be clearly detected in the Relation of 1660–1661. The third chapter of this Relation includes
the narrative of his voyage to Nikabau in company of Father
Druillettes.[18] This chapter is divided into three parts: first,
an introduction; then a letter addressed to Father Lalemant and
dated "Nekouba, one hundred leagues from Tadoussac, in the
forest, one the way to the Sea of the North, this second of July
1661"; and finally, the journal of the two missionaries. Although this Relation was edited in Quebec and further edited
in France, Dablon's style, his use of words, his expressions and
sentence structures are so characteristic that his personal contributions can easily be recognized in all three parts of the
chapter. Although the last two are supposed to be the collec-
tive work of the two missionaries, there is little doubt that they
were actually written by Dablon himself.

The length and width of Hudson Bay mentioned in the
introduction are taken from Sanson's map of 1650; the meridian of Tadoussac on this map was used as a basis to compute
the longiture of Nikabau. In the Relation of 1659–1660 we
are told that the Sea of the North is contiguous to that of
China; while in the journal of 1661 we are reminded that "our
North Sea is near the Sea of Japan" which, according to the
Relation of 1659–1660, is the same as the Sea of China. In
the journal there is a two page dissertation on the tides in the
St. Lawrence and the Saguenay, a phenomenon in which
Dablon was very much interested.

Dablon was as greatly interested in the geography of the

---

18 JR, 46: 246–294.

West as in that of the North.   On August 5, 1663, news of the death of Father Ménard reached Quebec.[19] Father Lalemant commented as follows on the place where he died: "He had the consolation of dying in search of new sheep having traversed five hundred leagues of rapids and precipices in that work; of all our missionaries he approached nearest to the China Sea."[20]   And on September 1, 1663, Dablon wrote to the Father General in Rome:

He [Ménard] was another St. Francis Xavier whom he imitated both in life and in death, not only because of the magnitude of his zeal, but also because of the nearness of the place where he died. Of all our Fathers he went nearest to the mission of the Apostle of the Indies, for he went more than 500 leagues from Quebec, towards those parts contiguous to the Sea of Japan, there devoting himself to the salvation of the barbarians and even sacrificing his life for their sake.[21]

Dablon does not seem to have collaborated in editing the Relation of 1666–1667 which contains the journal of Allouez' first western voyage; but in subsequent Relations he discussed various points mentioned by Allouez.   Besides the name of the great river of the West, the latter's journal also contains the first mention of Lake Michigan, "a large lake previously unknown to us"; and Allouez made conjectures concerning the situation of the "Sea of the North."[22]

As we have seen, Dablon left Quebec with Allouez for the West in the summer of 1669.   It was to be expected that he would gather detailed information about the country while working in that region, and the third part of the Relation of 1669–1670 shows that, as superior of the Western missions, he urged his subordinates to embody in their reports whatever they might learn from the Indians about the geography of the continent.   The third part of this Relation extends over three chapters, dealing with Sault Ste Marie, Chequamegon Bay and Green Bay, respectively.   These are chapters ten to twelve of the Relation as a whole.

The tenth chapter has the following sub-title: "The Super-

---

19 *Le Journal des Jésuites*, 330.
20 JR, 48: 142.
21 Dablon to Oliva, September 1, 1663. Jesuit Archives, Rome, *Gallia*, 110, I, 30.
22 JR, 51: 26, 46, 52.

ior of these [Ottawa] missions is Father Dablon, who sent
this Relation to Quebec to Reverend Father François Le Mercier, Superior General."[23]   It opens with an explanation of the
generic term "Outaoüaks," which comprises more than thirty
different tribes.   Dablon then mentions six other nations of
which he says: "some such as the Guilistinous [Cree] and the
Ovenibigons [Winnebago] dwell on the shores of the North
Sea, other are tribes wandering in the regions near the same
sea; most of them have been driven out of their country by
famine and have repaired hither [Sault Ste Marie] from time
to time on account of the abundance of fish."[24]

Nine years earlier Dablon and Druillettes had vainly tried
to reach the Sea of the North from Tadoussac.   Now, he
thought, the time had come for another attempt from Sault
Ste Marie.   "Two reasons, among others, have determined us
to make a journey to that Sea of the North."   The first reason
was to investigate means and methods best adapted to evange-
lize the nomadic tribes of that region.   "The second reason for
making this journey is to discover at last that Sea of the North,
of which so much has already been said, and which has not
yet been found by land."

Dablon then lists special motives for this discovery.   First,
to find out whether this Sea of the North is the same as Hudson Bay.   This, he says, can be determined by comparing the
longitudes and latitudes computed on the spot with the coordinates of Hudson Bay on available maps.   Another motive is,
to find out whether

communication can be had from Quebec all the way to that sea by
following the northern coasts [i.e., the Labrador coast], as was attempted some years ago.[25]   This will depend on the position of that
bay, which lies north of here [Sault Ste Marie], for if it should turn
out to be Hudson Bay, or another one farther west, an easy communication between Quebec and that northern sea cannot be hoped for,
since [to reach it] we should have to round a point situated above
latitude 63°.

We have here another bit of evidence that Dablon based

---

23 JR, 54: 126.
24 Ibid., 134.
25 This is a reference to the voyage of Jean Bourdon in 1657.
See infra, 154.

his theorizing on Sanson's map of 1650, for on this map "Cap Weston holme" [Cape Wolstenholme] lies above latitude 63°.

[The third motive for making the journey to the Sea of the North] is to verify the quite probable and long standing conjectures that the Sea of Japan can be reached *via* the Sea of the North; for what has been noted in some of the Relations of the preceding years concerning this matter has been more and more confirmed by reports from Indians and by the information we have elicited from them. This information is as follows. A few days' journey from the St. Francis Xavier mission [situated at the end of] Green Bay, there is a great river, more than a league in width. It comes from the north and flows toward the south, and so far that the Indians who have descended it in search of enemies, after many days' journey have not found its mouth, which can only be toward the Sea of Florida [Gulf of Mexico] or that of California. Mention will be made hereafter of a very large nation living in the direction of that river, and of the journey we hope to make thither in order to bring the Faith to these people and at the same time to gain a knowledge of these new countries.

Dablon, it may be observed, makes no mention of the *Baye du St. Esprit,* but only of the Gulf of Mexico in general, because on the maps of that time, as we have already remarked, "Florida," as the southeast of the United States was then called, was surrounded by a mountain range at which the great river would have to turn, and so would reach the Gulf at a lower latitude than that of the *Baye du St. Esprit;* or else the river would flow westward north of the mountain range and would have its mouth in the Gulf of California. From the direction of its course and from the mention of a very large nation [the Illinois] living on its banks, we know that this river was in fact the Mississippi. It should also be observed that the journey to this river which Dablon says "we plan to make this year," 1670, was supposed to be made by Marquette, as the latter tells us in the same Relation.

Although Dablon surmised that the great river of the West might possibly have its mouth in the Gulf of California, he did not discard the other route to the Sea of the West which had been described in the Relation of 1659–1660; in fact, he even seems to consider the earlier information more reliable.

Besides, we are also assured by the report of many other Indians whose accounts are quite in agreement with one another, that two hundred leagues from the St. Esprit mission among the Ottawa [La Pointe],

toward the setting sun, is the Sea of the West, to which one descends
by another great river, reached at a point eight days' journey from the
said mission, and this river comes and goes far inland, for thus the
Indians speak of the ebb and flow of the sea, and one of them declares that he has seen four sailing vessels there.

Considering that the Sea of the South and that of the West are
in these directions, all that is needed to make us surrounded by water
on all sides is a sea of the north. Once the latter is discovered, the
following advantages will be derived: first, it will not be impossible
to pass from the Sea of the North to that of the South or to that of
the West; second, since this Sea of the West can only be the Sea of
Japan, it would be easy to pass [from one to the other] and thus facilitate trade [with the East].[26]

In the eleventh chapter of the Relation of 1669–1670, before speaking of the activities of the St. Esprit mission at La
Pointe, Dablon gives a detailed description of Lake Superior
and has a long account of the copper mines on its shores, two
topics which had been mentioned by Allouez in the journal of
his first western voyage. In the third section of this chapter
are listed the tribes which depend on the St. Esprit mission.
Among these are the Illinois who dwell to the southward and
who occasionally come to La Pointe. "Hereafter, fuller mention will be made of these [Illinois] Indians, and of the desire
they manifested to have one of our Fathers to instruct them;
and also of the plan formed by Father Marquette to go thither
this coming autumn [1670]."

The "fuller mention" is found in Marquette's letter, which
forms the fourth section of Chapter Eleven. Although undated, this letter was written after April 6, 1670. Marquette,
who had left Lower Canada in 1668, was sent in the following
year to take the place of Allouez as missionary at La Pointe,
where he arrived on September 13, 1669. Early in the spring
of 1670, Dablon had reminded him to send in his report on
the state of the La Pointe mission and had ordered him to go
to the country of the Illinois in the autumn of 1670.[27]

In his letter of April 1670, Marquette tells what he has
learned about the Illinois Indians. They live, he wrote, toward
the south-southwest, thirty days' journey from La Pointe, and

---

[26] JR, 54: 136–138.
[27] JR, 54: 168, 184.

the route to their country is very difficult.   To reach it one must pass through the village of the Kitchigami and that of the Miami.   Some Illinois who came to La Pointe had promised Marquette "to embrace Christianity and to do all that I shall tell them [when I am] in their country." To enable him to teach the Illinois the truths of Christianity.

the Ottawa gave me a young man who had lately come from the country of the Illinois, and who taught me the rudiments of their language during the leisure allowed me by the Indians of La Pointe in the course of the winter.   One can scarcely understand it, although it is somewhat like Algonquian; still I hope, by the grace of God, to understand it and be understood if God in his goodness leads me to that country.[28]

We do not know to what tribe this Indian belonged; all that we know is that he himself was not an Illinois.   After speaking of the products of the soil of the country of the Illinois and of the abundance of game in that region, Marquette goes on to say:

When the Illinois come to La Pointe, they cross a great river which is about one league wide.   It flows from north to south, and to such a distance that the Illinois, who do not know what a canoe is, have not yet heard any mention of its mouth.   All they know is that there are some very large nations lower down its course; some, who live toward the east-southeast of their country, raise two crops of Indian corn a year.   A nation which they call Chaoüanon [Shawnee] came to visit them last summer, and the young man who is teaching me Illinois saw them.   They are laden with glass beads, which shows that they are in contact with Europeans.   They came overland, and it took them thirty days to reach the country of the Illinois.   It is hard to believe that the great river discharges its waters in Virginia; we think rather that it has its mouth in California.   If the Indians who are promising to make me a canoe keep their word, we shall go down this river as far as we can, with a Frenchman and this young man who has been given me, who knows some of those languages and has a facility for learning the others.   We shall visit the nations dwelling there, in order to open the way to a great many of our Fathers who have been awaiting this good fortune for so long.   This discovery will give us a full knowledge either of the Sea of the South or of that of the West.

Six or seven days' journey below the country of the Illinois, there is another great river on which live some very large nations who use

---

[28] JR, 54: 186.

wooden canoes. This is all we can write about them until next year, if God grant us the grace of conducting us thither.[29]

A few remarks on the above-quoted passage are in place here. Firstly, although Marquette does not give its name, the river which the Illinois had to cross when they came to La Pointe, is the Mississippi. Its width—about one league—is exaggerated, for nowhere in its upper course is the Mississippi 2.5 miles wide. Secondly, there is nothing in the text to the effect that Marquette saw the Shawnee at La Pointe. Instead he plainly states that his Indian teacher saw them in the country of the Illinois during the summer of 1669. Thirdly, we learn from this letter that in April 1670, Marquette fully intended to descend the river as far as he could; so that Dablon was telling the truth when he wrote in 1678 that Marquette had long had the intention of discovering the Mississippi and of finding where it led. Fourthly, the last words of the first paragraph—"or of that of the West"—seem to be an interpolation by Dablon; for there is nothing in the whole paragraph about the Sea of the West, but merely about California, whose shores, Marquette knew, bordered on the Sea of the South. It is true that a few pages farther down, Marquette speaks of a "great river leading to the Sea of the West," but this river was in the country of the Assiniboin, who lived some fifteen or twenty days' journey west of La Pointe. This latter river was different from the one passing through the country of the Illinois as is clear from the general direction of the course ascribed to each.

Some writers have offered the opinion that Marquette is referring to the Missouri when he says that six or seven days' journey below the Illinois villages there is another great river on which live very large nations who use wooden canoe. Such vague data are evidently insufficient to identify this river as the Missouri; as a matter of fact, in 1673, Jolliet and Marquette found wooden canoes among the Peoria who lived on the banks of the Iowa River.

Nearly all of Chapter Twelve of the Relation of 1669–1670 consists of the journal of Allouez from November 3, 1669, to

---

[29] JR, 54: 188.

May 20, 1670. This journal contains the second reference to the Mississippi by name. On April 29, 1670, Allouez entered a river which passed by the Mascoutens village. This river, he says, is "very beautiful, without rapids or portages, and flows toward the southwest." Since this is in fact the Fox River, there is clearly an error in the text. The reading should be "elle *vient du* Sur-Oüest" instead of "elle *va au* Sur-Oüest." In a later passage he writes that this river "leads to the great river called Messi-Sipi, and it takes only six days to reach it."[30] Allouez here seems to have misunderstood what the Indians told him, for the river which leads to the Mississippi is not the Fox but the Wisconsin.[31]

The manuscript of the Relation of 1669–1670, or at least that part of it which deals with the West, reached Quebec before the arrival of Talon in August 1670.[32] Three months later, in a memoir to Colbert, the intendant speaks of the hydrography of New France as follows:

[The geography of] this country is such that by the [St. Lawrence] River one can go everywhere. By means of the lakes we can reach its headwaters [located] to the westward, and the rivers which empty into it open the route to the north and to the south; thus by means of the [St. Lawrence] River we may hope to find some day a door to Mexico. It is to make the first of these discoveries that M. de Courcelle and I have sent Sieur de la Salle, who is all afire for undertakings of this kind;[33] whereas I have sent Sieur de St. Lusson in another direction, ordering him to push on toward the west as far as he can go while managing to find means of subsistence. His orders are to investigate carefully whether there is some means of communication by lakes or rivers [between the St. Lawrence] and the Sea of the South which separates this continent from China.[34]

---

30 JR, 54: 228, 232.

31 In his *Notes pour servir à l'histoire, à la bibliographie et à* la *cartographie de la Nouvelle-France et des pays adjacents 1540–1700* (Paris, 1872), 135, Harrisse makes the following comment on this passage: "Le P. Allouez à son tour, donnait, de sa mission de la Baye des Puants, des détails dans un style qui laisse supposer que c'est de visu qu'il décrivait le grand fleuve." It is clear from the Relation that Allouez speaks of the Mississippi *de auditu*, not *de visu*. For if he had seen the Mississippi he would have said so, and would not have written that the river leading to it was the Fox.

32 *Supra*, pp. 27 and 30.

33 On this journey, cf. "A Calendar of La Salle's Travels, 1643–1683," MA, 22 (1940): 284 f.

34 Talon to Colbert, November 10, 1670, RAPQ, 1931, 136.

We have already called attention to the fact that the discovery of the Sea of the South was secondary to the main purpose of St. Lusson's expedition which was to find the copper
mine;[35] and we have seen that on June 4, 1671, at Sault Ste
Marie, St. Lusson took formal possession of

Lakes Huron and Superior, of the island of Caeintoton [Manitoulin]
and of the other countries, rivers [fleuves], lakes and tributaries
[rivières] contiguous and adjacent thereto, of the length and breadth
of all that has thus far been discovered as well as of all that is to be
discovered which is bounded on the one side by the Sea of the North
and that of the West, and on the other side by the Sea of the South.[36]

It is not surprising that the wording of St. Lusson's procès-
verbal and also the above passage of Talon's letter express
Dablon's concept of the geography of North America as we
find it in the Relation of 1669-1670. For Dablon was present
when St. Lusson took formal possession of the West, and this
similarity may perhaps be taken as an indication that he helped
Talon's delegate in drawing the formal procès-verbal.

Shortly after the ceremony at Sault Ste Marie, Dablon returned to Quebec; on July 12, 1671, he was installed as rector
of the Jesuit college there, and superior general of the Jesuit
missions in New France. In the latter capacity it was his duty
to edit the Relations. In the letter of transmittal of the first
Relation for which he is responsible, that of 1670–1671, he
begins by saying that last summer (1670), he went with another missionary, Allouez, to the Mascoutens village, while
another missionary, Marquette, preached the name of Jesus
Christ at the farthest end of Lake Superior, and Father André
did the same on the north shore of Lake Huron.

Dablon also speaks of the work of Jesuit missionaries
among the Iroquois and the departure of Father Albanel for
Hudson Bay, so that it can be said "that the torch of Faith now
shines in the four quarters of this New World." But however
bright the prospects, "the Iroquois are still Iroquois, and the
Ottawa still barbarians." To strike terror into the hearts of

---

[35] *Supra*, p. 14.—In the following year, Talon put the expedition
"pour la découverte de la mer du Sud" on a par with the discovery
of the copper mine.—Talon to Louis XIV, November 2, 1671, RAPQ,
1931, 158. This, however, was an afterthought.
[36] Margry, 1: 197.

the Iroquois, M. de Courcelle with a body of Frenchmen went on an excursion to the country of these Indians, and M. Talon inspired the Ottawa with the respect they ought to have for His Majesty by the ceremony at Sault Ste Marie.

In the last paragraph of his letter of transmittal, Dablon calls attention to the fact that at the beginning of the third part of the Relation, which treats of the Ottawa missions, "will be found a map showing the region, with their lakes and rivers on which the missions are situated." This is the well-known map of Lake Superior "drawn by two Fathers, rather intelligent, much given to research and very painstaking, and who did not wish to set down anything they have not seen with their own eyes."[37] I have elsewhere presented evidence of the identity of these "two Fathers," indicating that they were Allouez and Dablon himself rather than Allouez and Marquette.[38]

The third part opens with a description of Lake Superior and a commentary on the map of this lake. Speaking of the St. Esprit mission, Dablon notes that it will be easy to find out what rivers and routes lead from this mission to the various Indian tribes which have trade relations with the Ottawa and the Hurons settled on Chequamegon Bay, for

the great river which the Indians call Mississippi flows toward the south and can only empty somewhere into the Sea of Florida [Gulf of Mexico], more than four hundred leagues away. Fuller mention of it will be made hereafter. Beyond that great river are located the eight villages of the Illinois, one hundred leagues from La Pointe; and forty or fifty leagues from the latter place, to the westward, is found the nation of the Nadoüessi [Sioux], very large and warlike . . . Still farther away is another nation speaking an unknown tongue, beyond which, it is said, lies the Sea of the West. Again, proceeding toward the west-northwest one sees [on the map] the tribe called Assinnipoüalac [Assiniboin] constituting one large village, or, as others say, [a group] of thirty small villages, not far from the Sea of the North and fifteen days' journey from the same St. Esprit mission.[39]

The distance from Lake Superior to the Gulf of Mexico was computed as follows. On the map of Lake Superior the 46th parallel runs along the south shore of the lake, and on the

[37] JR, 54: 250–254.
[38] "Marquette's Autograph Map of the Mississippi River," MA, 27 (1945): 32.
[39] JR, 55: 96–98.

Sanson map of 1650 the north shore of the Gulf of Mexico lies in latitude 30°. Since Dablon, like most landsmen, counted twenty-five leagues to the degree of latitude, he computed the distance from Lake Superior to the Gulf of Mexico as 400 leagues.

Following the description of Lake Superior, Dablon gives a few particulars about Lake Huron and the mission of Saint Simon, situated on the north shore of this lake. If peace between Algonquians and Iroquois is firmly established, he says, those Indians who are now dwelling at the west end of Lake Superior intend to return to Michilimackinac Island, for the waters of Lake Huron near this island are noted for their abundance of fish. "It is for this reason that we [i.e., Dablon] have already laid the foundation of the mission of St. Ignace [on the island] where we spent last winter [1670–1671]." This island is at the entrance of the lake called Mitchiganons [Michigan], which is also known as Lake of the Illinois. The latter formerly lived near the Sea of the West, but they were driven thence by their enemies and took refuge on the shores of Lake Michigan. Afterwards, when the Iroquois chased them away from the shores of this lake, they removed their villages seven days' journey west of the great Mississippi River.

Dablon ends his commentary on the map of Lake Superior by saying that Indians dwelling toward the south and the southwest are beginning to draw nearer to the western missions; some Illinois and Miami are already near Green Bay, while other Indians are waiting for missionaries to go to them.

The next section of the introduction to the third part of the Relation of 1670–1671 deals with St. Lusson's arrival at Sault Ste Marie and with the ceremony which took place there on June 4, 1671. Dablon gives the following reasons for sending St. Lusson to the West:

Monsieur Talon had no sooner landed than he considered means for insuring the success of these plans, choosing for that purpose Sieur de Saint-Lusson whom he commissioned to take possession in His Majesty's name of as much as possible of the territory lying west of Montreal and north of the Sea of the South.[40]

According to Dablon, these "plans" were orders to Talon

---

[40] JR, 55: 106.

from Louis XIV to "exert himself strenuously for the establishment of Christianity by aiding our missions, and for having the name of our invincible monarch known and his sovereignty acknowledged by the least known and most distant nations." As is clear from the correspondence of the intendant, Talon's motives for sending St. Lusson to the West were not quite so lofty—he simply wished to obtain information about a copper mine on the shore of Lake Superior.

The first three chapters of the third part of this Relation contain no pertinent geographical data. In Chapter Four we are told of the warlike spirit of the Sioux who "live on the banks of, or near, that great river called Mississippi, of which we shall speak later on"; their villages are situated "sixty leagues from the western end of Lake Superior, toward the setting sun, and, so to speak, in the center of the western tribes."

The Hurons and Ottawa of Chequamegon Bay had been at peace with the Sioux until the summer of 1670, when some Indians of the St. Esprit mission killed several Sioux, thus rousing the survivors to retaliate. Fearful of further vengeance, the offenders deemed it safer to put the whole length of Lake Superior between themselves and the provoked Sioux.[41] Some of the La Pointe Ottawa began moving eastward in 1670 and settled on Manitoulin Island. They were followed by the Hurons and the rest of the Ottawa in 1671, and both tribes settled on the mainland, near present-day St. Ignace, Michigan. Marquette, who came with them, arrived at Sault Ste Marie between June 5 and July 2, 1671.[42]

These events explain why Marquette did not go to the villages of the Illinois on the Mississippi in the autumn of 1670. As we have seen, this journey depended on the Indians building a canoe, but owing to the unsettled conditions this could not be managed. It is interesting to note that if there had not been a "state of war" between the La Pointe Indians and the Sioux at this precise time, Marquette and "another Frenchman,"

---

[41] See the account in the *Memoire sur les Moeurs...par Nicolas Perrot*, 101 f.

[42] Cf. "The 'Récit des voyages...du Père Jacques Marquette',"
MA, 28 (1946): 218 f.

guided by the missionary's teacher of Illinois, might have discovered the Mississippi in 1670.

In the fifth chapter of the third part of the Relation of 1670–1671, Dablon gives a full account of all that he had learned about the Mississippi during his sojourn in the West. This chapter, divided into five articles, treats *ex professo* of the St. Francis Xavier mission center at Green Bay. After listing the tribes dwelling on the shores of the bay and on the lower reaches of the Fox River, he tells of his journey in company with Allouez from Sault Ste Marie to the Mascoutens village where they arrived on September 15, 1670. In describing the Fox River Valley, Dablon takes occasion to set down what had been learned about the Mississippi.

It seems to form an enclosure, as it were, of all our lakes, rising in the northern regions and flowing southward to the sea, which we suppose to be either the Vermilion or the Florida Sea, because we do not know of any large rivers in that direction except those which empty into these two seas. Some Indians have assured us that this river is so great that, more than 300 leagues from its mouth, it is wider than the one flowing before Quebec, for, they say, it is one league wide.[43] All this vast stretch of country, they also state, consists of treeless prairies, so that its inhabitants are obliged to burn peat and animal dung dried in the sun. There are no forests within twenty leagues of the sea. Some warriors of this country [Fox River Valley], who tell us they have made their way thither, declare that they saw there men who resembled Frenchmen and who were splitting trees with long knives; and that some of them had their houses on the water, for this is their way of describing sawed boards and ships. They further state that all along the great river there are various tribes, speaking different languages and having different customs, and all are at war with one another. Some dwell on the banks of the great river, but many more are in the interior as far as the nation of the Nadoüessi, who are scattered over more than one hundred leagues of territory.

Now the Illinois of whom we are speaking have their villages on the other [west] side of this great river. Those Illinois who are living with the Fire Nation [Mascoutens] have come here for the purpose of forming some kind of transplanted colony. We hope that they will soon be followed by others whom the Holy Ghost will lead hither that they may be instructed [in the Christian religion]. For it is almost impossible for us to make the long journey to their coun-

---

43 The width of the St. Lawrence between the Quebec and the Lévis' ferry landings is actually 3,150 feet, that is, about one fourth of a *lieue moyenne*.

try, and indeed many Illinois have already joined their compatriots here; they offer a fine field for apostolic laborers, as no tribe is better prepared for Christianity.[44]

The above is the most detailed and most accurate description of the Mississippi before its discovery; and except for the location of its mouth every detail was supplied by the Indians.[45]

What report St. Lusson gave Talon after his return from the West in August 1671, may be gathered from the intendant's letter to Louis XIV.

According to the Jesuit Fathers who assisted at the ceremony [the taking possession of the West at Sault Ste Marie], this affair was conducted with all the pompe and éclat which the country could afford ... It is believed that from the place reached by the said Sieur St. Lusson, there are no more than 300 leagues to the shores of the Vermilion or South Sea, and from the calculations based on the reports of the Indians, it does not seem that the distance from the country discovered by the French to the country bordering on the Sea of the West is greater than 300 leagues. Judging from the maps, it does not seem that the distance to Tartary, China and Japan, is more than 1,500 leagues.[46]

The above passage clearly shows that Talon is simply echoing the geographical theories elaborated by Dablon in the Relations.

During the latter part of 1671, MM. Dollier and Galinée also wrote about the great river which the Ottawa called Mississippi. As we have seen, Dablon mentions Courcelle's expedition to Lake Ontario in the letter of transmittal of the Relation of 1670–1671, and M. Dollier, who accompanied Courcelle as chaplain wrote an account of it.[47] Dollier's narrative written in the autumn of 1671 gives another version of what white men in Canada knew, or thought they knew, about the Mississippi.

After recounting the various motives which determined Courcelle to go to Lake Ontario, Dollier goes on to say:

---

44 JR, 55: 206–208.
45 This description of the Mississippi was expressed cartographically by Claude Delisle. Archives Nationales, JJ, 75–197.—On the sketches by this geographer based on the Jesuit Relations, see "The Sources of the Delisle Map of America, 1703," MA, 25 (1943): 283.
46 Talon to Louis XIV, November 2, 1671, RAPQ, 1931, 158.
47 BN, Mss. fr., 13516: 207–217v; printed in Margry, 1: 169–192, translation in NYCD, 9: 75–85.

I shall add here a not unimportant reason for this voyage. Two years ago, two ecclesiastics left here to visit several Indian nations, situated along a great river which is called Ohio by the Iroquois and Mississippi by the Ottawa. They were unsuccessful [with regard to the main object of their voyage] on account of some difficulties very usual in enterprises of this kind. They learned, however, in their journey toward this river, that it was larger than the St. Lawrence, that the tribes settled along its banks were very large, and that its general course was from east to west. After having closely examined the maps which we have of the coast of New Sweden, of the two Floridas, of Virginia and Mexico, I did not discover any river's mouth comparable to that of the St. Lawrence. This leads us to think that the river of which we speak disembogues into another sea; I leave it to the judgment of the more learned to determine which sea. Nevertheless, it is probable that it passes through the countries toward New Spain, which abound in gold and silver.

The shortest and easiest route to this river is by way of Lake Ontario...[48]

The river spoken of by Dollier is clearly the Ohio. By 1671, he had certainly heard of the great river of the West, and thought that it was the same as the Ohio because of its name and the way it was described by Algonquian Indians. The voyage of the two ecclesiastics to which he refers is that made by Dollier himself and Galinée of which mention is made in our preceding chapter. We learn from the narrative of this voyage written by the latter, that when Dollier went to Quebec in May 1669, to ask Bishop Laval's leave to go to "nations called Ottawa,"[49] he was persuaded by Courcelle to take La Salle with him on the voyage,

in order that they might together make the journey M. de la Salle had long been premeditating toward a great river, which he understood (by what he thought he had learned from the Indians) had its course toward the west, and at the end of which, after seven or eight months' traveling, these Indians said that the land was "cut," that is to say, according to their manner of speaking, the river fell into the sea. This river is called "Ohio" in Iroquois. On it are settled a multitude of tribes, from which as yet no one has been seen here, but so large are they that, according to the Indians' report, a single nation includes fifteen or twenty villages. The hope of beaver, but especially the hope of finding by this route the passage to the Vermilion Sea, into which

---

[48] Margry, 1: 181 f.
[49] E. Z. Massicotte, *Montréal sous le régime français* (Montreal, 1919), 7.

M. de la Salle believed the River Ohio emptied, induced him to undertake this expedition, so as not to leave to another the honor of discovering the passage to the Sea of the South, and thereby the way to China.[50]

Besides his narrative of the expedition of 1669, Galinée wrote geographical descriptions of Canada. Of these, only five pages of notes taken by Michel-Antoine Baudrand are extant.[51] After describing the St. Lawrence from Lake Superior to the Atlantic, and saying that the river "can pass for one of the longest in the world, for nearly one thousand leagues of its course are known," Galinée continues,

However, all the Indians of New France who have roamed over the country and who have been questioned agree that the St. Lawrence is not the greatest river of Canada. They know of another one which the Iroquois call "Ohio" and the Algonquian and Ottawa "Missi sipi," as if to say "all the rivers in one," and is called by them *the* great river, as though the St. Lawrence which they all know were but a small stream in comparison. On its banks, they say, dwell large Indian tribes; its width is double that of the St. Lawrence. Some say that its course is even; others, that there is a considerable fall, but all agree that its course is very long, and the Iroquois who often go to that river to take prisoners, usually made the journey in two and a half or three years. Some Iroquois even say that they went so far that they reached the place where the water is intelligent [ou l'eau auoit de l'esprit], for thus they call the ebb and flow. Others say that they went to where the land is cut, for thus they call the seashore, and that they saw there a small chapel inhabited by a Frenchman (they call "Frenchmen" all Europeans). They say that in those places the heat is excessive. The headwaters of this river, according to them, are between Lake Ontario and New York, about sixty leagues south of an Iroquois village called Sonontouan [Seneca]; its course parallels that of the St. Lawrence, but its waters flow toward the southwest, that is, in the direction opposite to those of the St. Lawrence; the shortest distance between the two rivers, thirty-five or forty leagues, is near the tip of the bay of the Puteotamites [Green Bay], in a very fertile country. It is difficult to say where this river empties. Apparently not into the Sea of the North [the Atlantic Ocean], where no river like the Ohio disembogues; nor does it empty into Hudson Bay, for the Indians say that it is warm at its mouth, so it seems that it can only discharge itself into the Vermilion Sea.

---

[50] Kellogg, *Early Narratives of the Northwest*, 168.
[51] The volume (BN, Mss. fr., 15451) is entitled: "Remarques géographiques et historiques." Baudrand's subtitle reads: "Extrait des memoires de Mr. l'Abbé de Galinée sur le Canada ou Nouuelle France," ff. 11–17.

Dollier and Galinée had learned Algonquian and knew that "Mississippi" meant "great river." Since both say that "Ohio" means the same thing, it would seem that in 1671 the affix *io* still retained its original meaning.[52] However that may be, Galinée's description combines some characteristics of the Mississippi with those of the Ohio. Barring patent exaggerations with regard to the size of the river and the length of time to make the voyage to the sea, the Iroquois seem to have been describing a journey down the Ohio and the Mississippi to the Gulf. If they ever made such a journey, they did not see a chapel on the seashore. This last detail seems to have been learned from Iroquois who had journeyed to the southeast, such as those whom Lalemant mentions in the Relation of 1661–1662.[53]

It stood to reason that since the Ohio-Mississippi flowed from east to west or from the northeast to the southwest, it would surely have its mouth somewhere on the west coast of the North American continent. As we have seen, Dollier thought that it flowed "toward New Spain"; La Salle believed that his Ohio emptied into the Vermilion Sea; and although the Jesuits who wrote the Relations mention the Gulf of Mexico as an alternative, they tended toward the idea that the Mississippi had its mouth in the Gulf of California. In this case the wish was father to the thought, for what the French in Canada mostly wanted and hoped to find was a continuous waterway to the Pacific Ocean. As we shall see, one of the main results of the expedition of 1673 was the conviction that the Mississippi emptied into the Gulf of Mexico, and as we shall also see, people in Canada and in France were disappointed on learning that the Mississippi was not the direct waterway to the Sea of the South.

There is no new information concerning the Mississippi in the Relation of 1671–1672. The most important news in this Relation was the certainty that "the sea to the north of us is the famous bay to which Hudson gave his name."[54] This was

---

[52] *Ohia*, river; *io*, great; hence *Ohiio* or *Ohiyo*, great river. Cf. H. E. Hale, *Iroquois Book of Rites* (Philadelphia, 1883), 176, note B.
[53] JR, 47: 142–146.
[54] JR, 56: 148.

the result of Albanel's overland journey to the mouth of the Rupert River.   During this journey, wrote Dablon in the letter transmitting the Relation of 1671–1672, the Jesuit missionary preached "the Faith in countries where it had never been proclaimed."[55]   He then mentions the sending of Jolliet to search for a water route to the Sea of the South by way of the Mississippi.

---

[55] JR, 56: 234.

CHAPTER III

THE DISCOVERY OF THE MISSISSIPPI

Primary Manuscript Evidence

The numerous accounts of the expedition of 1673 are based on a document which is itself compiled from contemporary authors sources. The authors of these accounts did not as a rule examine the sources themselves, or if they did, their examination was perfunctory, most of them being satisfied with re-writing what their predecessors had re-written; the "originality" of these successive accounts consists in the addition of literary frills, bits of fine writing, moral reflections, and silly theories supported by no evidence whatsoever. These authors seem to have been under the illusion that by employing such artifices they could dispense themselves from critically examining the evidence for the voyage of 1673 which has come down to us.

The sources for our knowledge of the voyage of 1673 consist of manuscript and cartographical evidence. The cartographical evidence comprises Marquette's map and five contemporary maps based on that which Jolliet drew from memory after his return to Quebec in 1674.

The manuscript evidence is twofold, primary and secondary. The first includes 1) Dablon's account of the discovery of the Mississippi dated Quebec, August 1, 1674; 2) Jolliet's letter to Bishop Laval, dated Quebec, October 10, 1674; 3) Jolliet's letter to Frontenac inscribed as a dedicatory epistle on the map which he drew from memory; 4) a passage in Frontenac's letter to Colbert of November 14, 1674, wherein the governor notifies the minister of the return of Jolliet. The secondary manuscript evidence consists of 1) an anonymous document entitled "Relation de la Nouvelle France, 1673"; 2) several questionnaires and a memoir of Abbé Claude Bernou; 3) the "Récit des voyages et des découvertes du Père Jacques Marquette," by Father Dablon.

All the above evidence has been analyzed at length in a

series of six articles published in *Mid-America.* Such a detailed
analysis was necessary because Marquette's and Jolliet's journals of the expedition are lost. Since there was no point in reproducing here this analysis in its entirety, we have restricted
ourselves to a description of its main stages and have set down
the main conclusions arrived at.

1) THE 1674 ACCOUNT OF THE DISCOVERY OF THE MISSISSIPPI

Shortly after his return to Quebec in the latter part of July
1674, Louis Jolliet was interviewed by Father Dablon, who, on
August 1, set down in writing what he had learned about the
voyage of 1673 from the explorer. The original of this document is lost, but several copies of it are extant. In 1944 we
printed one of these copies conserved in the Jesuit Archives of
the Province of France which until then had remained unpublished.[1]

The volume in which the document is found is made up of
six manuscripts of which the account of the discovery of the
Mississippi is the second. This account covers four full pages
and three lines of a fifth. The title of the whole manuscript
reads: Relation ‖ De ce qui s'est passé dans les Missions ‖ Des
Peres de la Compagnie de Jesus ‖ en la Nouuelle France ‖
L annee 1673 ‖ Enuoyée par le RP. Claude d'Ablon ‖ Superieur
des dites Missions ‖ Au R. P. Jean Pinette ‖ Prouincial de la
meme Compe. ‖ En la Prouince de France. ‖[2] We shall inquire into the reasons why a document dated August 1, 1674,
is found at the beginning of the Relation of 1672–1673.

The Relation of 1672–1673 had already been composed
by Dablon when he was notified, in the summer of 1673, that
the publication of the *Relations de la Nouvelle France* would
be discontinued. There are reasons for believing that this Relation was not sent to Paris in that same year. One thing is
certain: a copy was kept at Quebec and in the following year,
1674, Dablon sent to his Provincial, Jean Pinette, the revised
Relation of 1672–1673, shortened in some places, lengthened

---

[1] "The 1674 Account of the Discovery of the Mississippi," MA,
26 (1944): 317–324.
[2] Jesuit Archives of the Province of France, Fonds Brotier 155,
Canada–1, 1–5.

in others, and he prefaced it with the account of the discovery of the Mississippi as reported to him by Jolliet.

Speaking of the Relation of 1672–1673, Thwaites says that according to the title-page, it is "credited to Dablon then the Quebec Superior of his order. But the first draft was from the hand of Jean de Lamberville; Dablon edited it with much freedom, and sent a perfected copy to Europe, retaining the original MSS., which is now conserved in the Archives of St. Mary's College, Montreal."[3]

Thwaites published the entire manuscript of this Relation; namely, Lamberville's draft, and all of Dablon's corrections, additions, and excisions. He printed in Roman type the Lamberville text, as retained by Dablon, and also any matter substituted or added by Dablon himself. These corrections he enclosed in brackets, and printed in italics the matter stricken out by Dablon.

What led Thwaites to write that "the first draft was from the hand of Jean de Lamberville" is a note in the upper right-hand corner of the first page: "Écriture du P. Jean de Lamberville f[élix] M[artin]." This is an erroneous identification; the manuscript is in the hand of a copyist who cannot be identified as that of one of the Jesuit priests then in Quebec. It is certainly not in the handwriting of Lamberville, but probably in that of a Jesuit lay-brother.

To say that the Relation is "credited" to Dablon is rather misleading, for there can be no doubt that Dablon is actually its author. One of the duties of the superior of the Jesuit missions in New France was to write the annual relations. In 1673, that superior was Dablon, and no one who has any knowledge of his character will believe that he entrusted the composition of the annual reports to any of his subordinates.[4] Moreover, the "Lamberville draft" bears Dablon's editorial touch and all the marks of Dablon's style. Finally, we know that Jean de Lamberville was among the Onondaga in 1673,[5]

---

3 JR, 57: 307.
4 Cf. "Claude Dablon, S.J. (1619–1697)," MA, 26 (1944): 92 ff.
5 Frontenac to Colbert, February 16, 1674, RAPQ, 1927, 52.

and that he remains among these Indians until 1678, the year of his return to France.

Since there is no doubt that the corrections, additions, or excisions are in the hand of Dablon, whose handwriting is as individual as his style, we shall inquire why and when the changes were made.

We have already noted that in his publication of the Relation of 1672–1673, Thwaites made use of typographical devices which enable the reader to see at one glance what portions were written in 1673—the so-called "Lamberville draft" —and what corrections Dablon made. "This manner of presentation," says Thwaites, "(which we have not found possible with any other Relation) gives an interesting and unique example of the methods of editing employed by the Father superior and incidentally throws much light on the mental attitude of the missionaries."[6]

I must confess that I do not see the force of this last remark. The "methods of editing employed by the Father superior" can hardly be called "unique" for it is difficult to see how he could have used any other methods under the circumstances. In 1674, Dablon had at his disposal the Relation of 1672–1673, and since he also had information about events that had taken place in the missions during 1673–1674, he combined the two Relations into one. In doing so, he naturally had to recast what he had written in 1673, besides making verbal or stylistic changes. Of this revision, which is dated 1672–1673, he had at least two copies made, one of which was sent to Paris in 1674, and the other kept in Quebec. The latter copy differs from the copy sent to Paris because it contains further changes made by Dablon between 1674 and 1678.[7] Hence the "methods of editing" mentioned by Thwaites simply amount to a normal revision by the author of the Relation of 1672–1673 in view of fresh information received in 1674.

Thwaites then goes on to say: "There are known to exist three Mss. of this [1672–1673] Relation: (1) The original in the Archives of St. Mary's College, Montreal—which is Lam-

---

6 JR, 57: 308.
7 Cf. "The 1674 Account," loc. cit., 305, note 10.

berville's text with Dablon's emendations."[8] Rather, as we
have seen, this manuscript is a copy in an unknown hand of
the text of Dablon, the true author of the Relation of 1672–
1673, with his own corrections, most of which were added in
the following year. "... (2) 'detached duplicates' of the same
with slight variations ... which is Lamberville's text, not corrected by Dablon." This shows that several copies of this Relation were kept in Quebec.   "... (3) One [copy] in the do-
mestic archives of the Society formerly at the Gesù, in Rome.
Of this last Father Martin says, in his introduction to Douniol's
Relations inédites, that it accords with the one in Montreal,
'save some slight modifications which concern the style, and
some curtailments of little importance'."[9] What is here attributed to Father Martin was actually written by Father de
Montézon[10] who goes on to say: "We have made use of it
[the Roman copy] in more than one passage to correct the
Canadian [i.e., the so-called Lamberville draft] manuscript,
because the copy sent to Rome, which seems to have been made
last, is in general more carefully made and more concise, and
it has all the authority of the original manuscript."[11]

The "Roman copy" mentioned by Father de Montézon was
indeed in Rome until the middle of last century when it was
brought to Paris along with other manuscripts; it is now in
the archives of the Province of France, at present housed in
St. Helier, Jersey Island. As was said above, the last three
lines of the account of the discovery of the Mississippi appear
on the fifth page of the manuscript, and the rest of this page
contains the beginning of Dablon's revision of the Relation of

---

[8] In 1861, Shea published in his Cramoisy series, no. 13, the
Relation...les annés 1672 et 1673 Par le R. P. Claude Dablon. This
is what Thwaites calls the "Lamberville draft," scl., the original Relation written by Dablon. Shea modernized the spelling, punctuated
the text and unified the copyist's haphazard capitalization.
[9] JR, 57: 208.
[10] "On peut dire sans se tromper que toutes les notes [biblio-
graphical and footnotes] ajoutées aux deux volumes des *Relations
[inédites]* sont dues aux éditeurs de Paris." Martin to Vignon, cited
in P. Desjardins, *Le Collège Sainte-Marie de Montréal* (Montreal,
1940), 248. Cf. "The 1674 Account," *loc. cit.*, 303.
[11] *Relations inédites de la Nouvelle–France (1672–1679) pour
faire suite aux anciennes Relations (1615–1672)* (2 vols., Paris, 1861)
1: 2.

1672–1673. This explains why the account itself, dated August 1, 1674, is found prefaced to a Relation of the year before.

De Montézon's text of the Relation of 1672–1673 in the *Relations inédites* is a hodgepodge of Dablon's 1673 original and of the Roman manuscript, both recast by De Montézon with interpolations, explanations, and additions. Although De Montézon knew of Dablon's 1674 revision of his original draft, he apparently did not realize the close dependence of the Roman manuscript on that revision. This dependence will be obvious to anyone comparing the text of the Roman manuscript with Dablon's 1674 revision as published by Thwaites.

These bibliographical details were unknown to Thwaites; which is the reason why he wrote that "two widely different versions" of the Relation of 1672–1673 appeared in 1861.[12] The versions to which he refers are Shea's edition of the text as written by Dablon in 1673, and De Montézon's combination of that text and of the text of the "Roman manuscript."

Since in the first page of the Jersey manuscript, besides minor excisions, three paragraphs are omitted which appear in the revised 1674 text of the Relation of 1672–1673, the following question arises. Did Dablon himself omit these paragraphs from the Relation of 1672–1673 before sending it to France in 1674, or are the omissions attributable to the French editor? If Dablon himself omitted these paragraphs, then the French copyist merely transcribed his text and forwarded it to Rome. If on the other hand Dablon's text was "edited" in France before being given to the copyist, we are confronted with a further problem. Since the account of Jolliet's voyage is found in the same manuscript as Dablon's Relation, and was copied by the same copyist, how can we know whether the Paris "editor" of this text did not also alter the account of the discovery of the Mississippi which Dablon wrote after interviewing Jolliet? It is impossible to settle this question by comparing the pages of the Jersey manuscript which contain the account of this discovery with some Canadian counterpart, because neither the original of this account nor a copy thereof are extant in Canada.

---

[12] JR, 57: 309.

I have given elsewhere the reasons for believing that the text of the account of the discovery of the Mississippi in the Jersey manuscript is the same as that which Dablon sent to France in 1674.[13]

I know of five extant copies of the original of this document which may be divided into two groups. The first group comprises three manuscripts; the second group two, and these differ from the manuscripts of the first group in one important respect. At the beginning of the manuscripts of the second group, and again at the end by way of a clausula, we find in a somewhat recast form the first and second parts respectively, of a paragraph which occurs in the middle of the document in the first group of manuscripts.

The first of these five copies is in the Jesuit Archives of the Province of France and has been described above.

The second copy is in the Bibliothèque Nationale, Paris.[14] It is endorsed: "A Mon R. Pere de Moisne de la Comp [agnie] de Jesus. A Reims." The manuscript is in a bad condition, and the lower right-hand corner of the first page is torn off. The name of the addressee suggests that it was sent to Rheims by a fellow Jesuit in Paris. Textual criticism shows that, like the Jersey manuscript, it was made on the lost archetype sent to France by Dablon in 1674. Except for a few variants, it reproduces this archetype more faithfully than the next three manuscripts.

The third copy of Dablon's narrative is in the Archives of the Seminary of Saint-Sulpice, Paris, and is followed by a letter of Jolliet dated Quebec, October 10, 1674.[15] Speaking of this letter, Harrisse wrote: "This document, mentioned by Abbé Faillon, is all in the hand of Jolliet and follows on the same page the relation of the discovery of the 'Sea of the South,' sent by Father Dablon from Quebec on August 1. This relation is also in the handwriting of Jolliet."[16] The handwriting of the whole document, narrative and letter, is not Jolliet's, as anyone can see by comparing genuine specimens of Jolliet's

---

13 "The 1674 Account," *loc. cit.*, 308.
14 BN, Moreau, 842: 31–32v.
15 A photograph of the whole document is in the E. E. Ayer Collection of the Newberry Library, Chicago.
16 Harrisse, *Notes pour servir*, 323.

script with the handwriting of the document. The erroneous identification was originally made by Faillon, who very likely had not then at his disposal a sample of Jolliet's handwriting.

There are many indications that the whole document, the narrative and the letter, is merely a copy of the lost originals. The copyist's mark "./." for instance, is found at the end of every paragraph. Even if it were wrongly supposed that the handwriting throughout is that of Jolliet, and that consequently the letter is his own original work and the rest is his copy of the narrative, this mark would show that the letter too is a copy, for the mark appears after every paragraph of the letter. Moreover, the account contains several mistakes which Jolliet would almost certainly not have made. Finally, there is the important fact that Jolliet's name is spelled wrongly whenever it occurs in this manuscript. In the other three which I personally examined, his name is spelled in two different ways; in the Saint-Sulpice manuscript it is spelled the same throughout: "Joliet."[17]

Now in every known example of Jolliet's autograph, his name has always two "l's," and never just one as in the Saint-Sulpice manuscript. From the fact that the dedicatory letter to Frontenac on the anonymous copy of Jolliet's map is not in Jolliet's handwriting, and the fact that his signature to this letter contains only one "l," Father Steck concluded that "Jolliet did not inscribe the letter himself, but had some one do it for him."[18] It is precisely these facts, namely, the difference in handwriting and the single "l" in Jolliet's name, which justify our conclusion that the Saint-Sulpice document is not a Jolliet autograph. To defend it as an autograph by saying that "here and throughout the copy Jolliet spells his name as Dablon wrote it—with one *l*,"[19] is most unconvincing. A man seeing his name misspelled in a document which he copies will automatically correct the misspelling. Moreover, how can Father Steck, or anyone else, know how Dablon spelled Jolliet's name? The original as Dablon wrote it is no longer extant, nor, for

---

[17] See the table of variants in "The 1674 Account," *loc. cit.*, 311.
[18] F. B. Steck, *The Jolliet–Marquette Expedition, 1673* (Quincy, Ill., 1928), 173, note 98.
[19] *Id., ibid.*, 174, note 101.

that matter, is the archetype sent to France in existence; and the spelling of his name in the various copies of the 1674 account of the discovery of the Mississippi makes it clear that it is impossible to determine how Jolliet's name was written either by Dablon in the original or by the copyist of the archetype sent to France.

Furthermore, if the account of the discovery of the Mississippi in the Saint-Sulpice document is a Jolliet autograph, why did Jolliet leave out several lines, found in every manuscript, which describe the route to be followed by water from Niagara Falls to the Des Plaines River, where mention is also made of the canal to be built at Chicago connecting the St. Lawrence with the Mississippi basin? This was an original Jolliet idea, which was ridiculed by La Salle a few years later. Again, if this document is a Jolliet autograph, why is it that in the letter itself, which begins at the bottom of the twelfth page of the manuscript, no reference is made to the preceding account which Jolliet supposedly wrote and sent along with this letter?

Of course, the real proof that Jolliet did not write the Saint-Sulpice document is the handwriting, which is in no way similar to his. The other arguments are merely confirmatory. We can reconstruct to a certain extent what actually took place. Someone at the Seminary of Saint-Sulpice or connected with that institution, probably obtained a copy of Dablon's narrative—there were several copies of it in Paris at the time—and also secured a copy of Jolliet's letter to Laval, and then transcribed both.

The two manuscripts of the second group are in the Archives du Service Hydrographique[20] and in the Bibliothèque Nationale,[21] respectively. I have not examined the latter, but from what Leland says,[22] and from the variants noted by Father Steck,[23] the latter document is a copy of that in the Archives du Service Hydrographique. As was already noted, the arrangement of the text of both these manuscripts is different in

---

20 ASH, 5: no. 16.

21 BN, Mss. fr., n. a., 7491: 351–355.

22 W. G. Leland, ed., *Guide to Materials for American History in the Libraries and Archives of Paris,* 1: 98; *Libraries* (Washington, D. C., 1932).

23 Steck, *op. cit.,* 174, note 100 and ff.

two particulars from the arrangement of the text of the first group.

On the flyleaf of the ASH document there is a note which deserves a few words of comment. The note was written by some unidentified clerk of this archival depository—probably in the eighteenth century—and resembles similar notes found on the flyleaf of other documents in the same *carton*.[24]

This memoir, short as it is, is interesting because it gives in brief what is found in a detailed narrative of La Salle's voyage, *pièce* no. 5 of this portfolio.[25]

By comparing the dates of these two documents, one can see from this one, dated 1673, that Jolliet had traveled over the country, had already seen, examined, and discovered everything that La Salle also saw and recognized in 1679, 1680, 1681. To give a detailed account was impossible, because the journal of Jolliet was lost in a shipwreck; hence one may suspect that La Salle wanted to get the credit for having discovered that which he knew Jolliet had seen and taken possession of.

That in 1673, Jolliet had gone farther into the interior than La Salle did in 1681 is obvious; for the former went almost to the mouth of the Arkansas River, whereas the farthest point reached by La Salle by 1681 was the mouth of the Illinois River.[26] That La Salle wished to rob Jolliet of the priority of discovery is a quite unfounded suspicion; and there is no proof that Jolliet took possession of the Mississippi basin in 1673,[27]

---

[24] *Infra*, 198 f, 209.

[25] This narrative is the "Relation des descouvertes," printed in Margry, 1: 435–544. The manuscript, now in ASH, 64: no. 4, was at one time in the same portfolio as the narrative of the discovery of the Mississippi. On the drafts of the "Relation des descouvertes," see "A Calendar of La Salle's Travels, 1643–1683," MA, 22 (1940): 283 f; the document is discussed in *Hennepin's Description of Louisiana* (Chicago, 1941), 55–64.

[26] La Salle first saw the Mississippi at the mouth of the Illinois River on December 5, 1680; cf. "A Calendar of La Salle's Travels," *loc. cit.*, 296.

[27] The first mention of a "prise de possession" by Jolliet in 1673 occurs in a document of 1685. In the latter year, on the occasion of a controversy with regard to the extent of the jurisdiction of the Bishop of Quebec, Saint-Vallier claimed that Jolliet arbored the arms of the King of France "partout ou le Pere Marquette a planté la croix," BN, Clairambault, 1016; 629.—It is quite possible that Talon instructed Jolliet to take possession of the country he would discover, for we know that the intendant particularly insisted on such a formality (*infra*, p. 163); but we need more than this single assertion to conclude that Jolliet did arbor the arms of France, the outward sign of his having taken possession for his sovereign. This doc-

any more than there is proof that La Salle took possession of anything before March 13, and 14, 1682, at the Quapaw village, and on April 9, 1682, near the mouth of the Mississippi.

When Margry saw this note on the flyleaf of the ASH document he wrote immediately below it: "Whoever wrote this note had doubtless no knowledge of the memoirs of Talon and of the Count de Frontenac, or even of the map of Jolliet, all of which speak of the voyages of Cavelier de la Salle [as having taken place] before that of Jolliet." Although it is not specifically so stated here, from his reference to the map of Jolliet, Margry is claiming priority of the discovery of the Mississippi for La Salle. This claim is unsupported by the very evidence which he cites. The "memoirs of Talon" speak of some journey of La Salle to the Iroquois country.[28] The "memoirs of the Count de Frontenac" simply say that Jolliet "n'a voyagé qu'apres le Sr de la Salle,"[29] and these memoirs were not written by Frontenac but by Bernou who, at the time, was anxious to boost La Salle's ability as an explorer.[30] With regard to the map of Jolliet which mentions La Salle's voyage, the reference to these voyages is a clumsy, later interpolation on Franquelin's map of 1675 by some unknown hand.[31]

Of the five copies of Dablon's version of the voyage of 1673, that in the Archives du Service Hydrographique was published by Margry.[32] This text was reprinted by Thwaites[33] who preferred it to De Montézon's,[34] because Rochemonteix had written that the document was "not exactly reproduced" by De Montézon, whereas Margry "gives the text very nearly

---

ument contains other statements about Marquette which we know are altogether inaccurate. It says, for instance, that Marquette was sent on the expedition of 1673 by the Bishop of Quebec; that the missionary made two voyages to the Mississippi; that he died in a "mission establie vers le milieu du lac des Ilinois," etc. These statements were made in answer to the sophisms of Bernou who had designs on the rights of the Bishop of Quebec. The document is replaced in its context and analyzed in *Some La Salle Journeys* (Chicago, 1938), 51–57.

28 "A Calendar of La Salle's Travels," *loc. cit.*, 284 f.
29 BN, Clairambault, 1016: 48v.
30 *Frontenac and the Jesuits*, 176–178.
31 *Some La Salle Journeys*, 32 f; "The Jolliet Lost Map of the Mississippi," MA, 28 (1946): 90.
32 Margry, 1: 262–270.
33 JR, 58: 92–108.
34 *Relations inédites de la Nouvelle-France*, 1: 193–204.

as we read it in the Roman manuscript."[35]   We ourselves published an exact reproduction of the text of the so-called "Roman manuscript" along with the variant readings of the other copies.[36]

2) JOLLIET'S LETTER TO LAVAL

According to Faillon the addressee of the letter of October 10, 1674, was "probably" Frontenac,[37] while Harrissee declares positively that it was addressed to the governor.[38] Jolliet would hardly have written a letter to Frontenac on October 10, 1674, for he himself had been in Quebec since the end of July of that year, and there is positive evidence that the governor had been in the same small town since August 20.[39] Moreover, Jolliet had already reported to Frontenac in person, and his map with a dedicatory letter was almost certainly in Frontenac's hands by mid-October.

Gagnon is more correct when he says that the letter of October 10 was "probably addressed to Monseigneur de Laval who was then in France."[40]   The Bishop of Quebec had helped Jolliet materially at the beginning of his career as an explorer;[41] and Jolliet would naturally have sent his benefactor news of his discovery of the great river of the West.   Neither the opening title of "my Lord" nor the clausula at the end of the letter,[42] suffices to identify the addressee as a bishop.   But Jolliet's mention of the Blessed Virgin and his modified quotation of the first verse of Psalm 13, make it practically certain that the letter was addressed to Laval.

We have already noted that this letter is a copy appended to a copy of Dablon's account of the discovery of the Mis-

---

[35] C. de Rochemonteix, *Les Jésuites et la Nouvelle–France au XVII*e *siècle* (3 vols., Paris, 1895–1896), 3: 23, note 1.

[36] "The 1674 Account of the Discovery of the Mississippi," *loc. cit.*, 317–324.

[37] E.-M. Faillon, *Histoire de la colonie française en Canada* (3 vols., Villemarie, 1865–1866), 3: 214.

[38] Harrisse, *Notes pour servir*, 143; the letter is printed, *ibid.*, 322 f.

[39] *Jugements et délibérations du Conseil Souverain*, 1: 816.

[40] Gagnon, *Louis Jolliet*, 70.

[41] *Supra*, pp. 4–6.

[42] An identical clausula is found in an autograph letter of Jolliet dated November 10, 1685, addressed to Seignelay, who was then minister of the colonies. AC, C 11E, 13: 135 f.

sissippi, and when comparing Harrisse's publication of the text with the manuscript, we have called attention to the changes in capitalization, accentuation, spelling, paragraphing, and to the omission of a few words.[43]

Jolliet begins his letter by saying that it is not long since his return from his voyage to the Sea of the South. Considering that he reached Quebec in the second half of July, two and a half months had elapsed since his return. He then tells the bishop of the accident near Montreal and of the drowning of the young Indian whom he was bringing back from the Mississippi country. He speaks of his own miraculous rescue through the intercession of the Blessed Virgin. He decided to return, he says, after reaching latitude 33°, for fear of falling into the hands of Europeans. There are no portages or rapids on the river which he descended; it is as wide as the St. Lawrence at Sillery[44] and it empties into the Gulf of Mexico.

We have explained certain discrepancies between a passage of Dablon's narrative and its counterpart in Jolliet's letter to Laval.[45] We have also commented on the size of the buffalo herds which the explorers saw. Dablon wrote: "The Father [Marquette] counted as many as 400 in one herd"; and Jolliet said to Laval: "I saw and counted as many as 400 together in a prairie." We have observed that these two statements are not particularly disturbing nor contradictory. Jolliet may well have told Dablon that Marquette counted 400 buffaloes and that he too counted 400 in one herd; when he wrote to Laval, it was only natural that he should speak of counting them himself. If other members of the expedition had written an account of it, they, too, could have said that they counted 400 in one herd; Jolliet was not the only man of the expedition who could count up to that number.

---

[43] "The 1674 Account," MA, 26 (1944): 310; "The Discovery of the Mississippi. Primary Sources," *ibid.*, 27 (1945): 223.

[44] At Sillery, the St. Lawrence is 1,650 feet wide, nearly half its width at Quebec, 3,150 feet. The latter is the width of the Mississippi which Jolliet gave to Frontenac; it coincides with the width which he gave to Dablon, namely that the Mississippi "a pour l'ordinaire un quart de lieüe de large," about 0.6 mile.

[45] Cf. "The Discovery of the Mississippi. Primary Sources," *loc. cit.*, 224 f.

3) Jolliet's Dedicatory Letter to Frontenac

The importance of this letter for our knowledge of the voyage of 1673 comes from the fact that it was originally inscribed on the map which Jolliet drew from memory between August and November 1674. The letter, however, is secondary to the map itself, for it contains little information which is not in Dablon's narrative, in Jolliet's letter to Laval, or in Frontenac's letter to Colbert.

There are three extant copies of the lost original of this letter. The handwriting of the oldest copy has not been identified.[46] The second copy appears on the so-called Jolliet "larger map," the author of which is very probably Franquelin, and the third is inscribed on Bernou's reduction of this map.[47]

Since it is clear that Bernou had before him the above-mentioned Franquelin map, the three copies of the dedicatory letter are simply two different reproductions of the same original, the anonymous author transcribing it as Jolliet wrote it, while Franquelin introduced changes which Bernou copied.[48]

We said above that there is little information in the dedicatory letter concerning the voyage of 1673 which is not contained in the other three primary sources. Thus the statement that the Mississippi is located between Florida and Mexico is also found in Jolliet's letter to Laval; that the mouth of the river must be in the Gulf of Mexico is clear from Dablon's narrative. The route to the Vermilion Sea is explicitly mentioned in Dablon's account and in Frontenac's letter to Colbert. In his dedicatory letter, however, Jolliet is more emphatic than the Jesuit and the governor in saying that the Vermilion Sea could be reached by ascending one of the western tributaries of the Mississippi. The route which Jolliet followed when returning from the West in 1674, by way of the Ottawa River, is already indicated in Dablon's letter of August 1, 1674. Dablon says that Jolliet's canoe capsized in sight of Montreal

---

[46] "The Jolliet Lost Map," loc. cit., 69 f.
[47] Ibid., 89–93.
[48] The text of this letter along with the Franquelin and Bernou variants will be found in "The Discovery of the Mississippi. Primary Sources," loc. cit., 226–228.

after having successfully negotiated "more than forty rapids"; in the dedicatory letter, Jolliet notes that the accident occurred after he had passed "forty-two rapids" without mishap.

4) FRONTENAC'S LETTER TO COLBERT

Although this letter contains oral information given to Frontenac by Jolliet shortly after his return to Quebec, the letter is given as the last of the primary sources because, as is clear from its wording, it is posterior to the dedicatory letter.

At the end of a forty-seven page letter in which petty village quarrels are narrated at great length, Frontenac finally mentions Jolliet's return from his voyage.

When I arrived from France, I was advised by M. Talon to send Sieur Jolliet to discover the Sea of the South. He returned three months ago and has discovered admirable countries. The navigation over the beautiful rivers which he found is so easy that from Fort Frontenac on Lake Ontario, one could sail a ship to the Gulf of Mexico. There is only one unloading place—a portage of about half a league—where Lake Ontario falls into Lake Erie. We could have a settlement [on Lake Ontario] and build another ship on the Lake Erie side.

These projects could be carried out when peace is restored and when it pleases the king to exploit these discoveries.

He [Jolliet] went to within ten days' journey of the Gulf of Mexico, and he believes that by way of the western tributaries of the great river which he found, which is as wide as the St. Lawrence before Quebec[49] and which flows from north to south, there may be a water route to the Vermilion Sea or to the Sea of California.

I am sending by my secretary the map which he made as well as the noteworthy details which he was able to recall, for he lost all his memoirs and his journals in the shipwreck [which occurred] in sight of Montreal, after a voyage of 1,200 leagues. He nearly drowned and lost all his papers. A young Indian from these countries whom he was bringing to me was drowned, to my great regret.

He left with the [Jesuit] Fathers of Sault Ste Marie on Lake Superior copies of his journals, which we cannot have until next year. From them you will learn more particulars of this discovery which he accomplished very creditably.[50]

As can be seen, the governor's secretary who wrote this letter was not quite clear with regard to the geography of the Great Lakes, for he makes the St. Lawrence flow from east

---

[49] See *supra*, p. 56, note 44.
[50] Frontenac to Colbert, November 14, 1674, RAPQ, 1927, 76 f.

to west.[51] The same secretary was also confused with regard to the portage. He gives as the length of the portage at Niagara Falls, which Jolliet never saw, the length of the Chicago portage, which the explorer told Dablon was half a league.[52]

The distance between Jolliet's terminal point and the Gulf of Mexico—given as ten days' journey—is different from the distance given in Jolliet's letter to Laval, where he says that when he decided to return he was five days' journey from the sea. The explanation of this discrepancy seems to be as follows. On returning to Quebec, Jolliet told Frontenac that he went within ten days' journey from the sea; later, he may have reasoned that having traveled 9° 30′ in a month, from latitude 42° 30′ to latitude 33°, and since for all he knew the mouth of the Mississippi lay in latitude 31°, he concluded that he could have reached the sea in five days.[53]

We remarked at the end of the preceding chapter that the discovery of a direct waterway to the Pacific Ocean was most wished for in seventeenth century New France. As can be seen, Frontenac's letter testifies to the desire of finding such a communication. Jolliet in his letter to Laval wrote that he had returned from his voyage to the "Sea of the South," although he knew then that the Mississippi emptied into the Gulf of Mexico and not into the Pacific Ocean, the Mar del Zur of contemporary maps; and Dablon who in his narrative of the ex-

---

51 It is apparently the same secretary who wrote the letter of November 13, 1673, in which the same mistake occurs. Speaking of Fort Frontenac which the governor had built in the preceding summer, he says that it commands the whole of Lake Ontario and that Frontenac has given orders to construct a ship which will be used to bring the pelts of the Ottawa country to the French. "Il est même aisé d'aller encore plus avant avec le temps, puisqu'en faisant une habitation à l'endroit que vous pouvez remarquer sur la carte [this map, made by Randin, is lost; cf. "The Jolliet Lost Map," *loc. cit.*, 76] *où le lac Ontario se décharge dans le lac Erié* et où il y a un portage d'un quart de lieue, on pourrait faire bâtir une autre barque sur le lac Erié avec laquelle on irait dans le lac des Hurons et celui des Illinois, dans la Baie des Puans, et jusqu'au Sault Ste Marie où commence la lac Supérieur, qui sont des espaces infinis et où la navigation est partant fort aisée." Frontenac to Colbert, November 13, 1673, RAPQ, 1927, 40. Six years later, La Salle carried out this plan; he built a ship on the Lake Erie side and sailed it to Michilimackinac.
52 "The 1674 Account," *loc. cit.*, 322.
53 Cf. "The 'Récit des voyages ... du Père Jacques Marquette'," MA, 28 (1946): 248 f.

pedition of 1673 had given the reasons why the Mississippi
emptied into the Gulf of Mexico and not in the Vermilion
Sea, nevertheless entitled his narrative: "Relation de la
découverte de la Mer du Sud."

Frontenac's secretary inaccurately speaks of Jolliet's "journals." The explorer did not lose several "journals" when his
canoe capsized. He made mention of only one journal to
Dablon, and in the dedicatory letter on his map as well as in
his letter to Laval he says explicitly "mon journal."

CHAPTER IV

THE DISCOVERY OF THE MISSISSIPPI

Cartographical Evidence

We shall examine in this chapter the cartographical evidence for our knowledge of the voyage of 1673, namely, Marquette's map and five contemporary maps based on that which Jolliet drew from memory after his return to Quebec in 1674.

I. MARQUETTE'S AUTOGRAPH MAP

Marquette's map is not only the oldest source for our knowledge of the expedition of 1673, but it is also the single extant autograph document by a member of the expedition. Its importance is readily realized when we remember, first, that it expresses cartographically what was contained in Marquette's journal, which the missionary had before him when he made the map, and secondly, that in spite of its sketchiness, it is much more accurate than the maps of the same section of the Mississippi River which were drawn during the next twenty-five years.[1]

When discussing Miss Kellogg's opinion that Marquette "began [his] map at St. Ignace before he set forth, and that later he added the courses of the Mississippi,"[2] we showed that such an opinion was untenable.[3] While it is quite possible that a map was made before the expedition started, that map is certainly not Marquette's autograph under consideration. What Sparks wrote of the Thévenot map is much truer of that of Marquette: "It was impossible to construct it, without having

---

[1] "It is refreshing to turn to such a work executed with a strict attention to detail, erected on a firm foundation of fact, and one in which the author attempts to impart his knowledge unadorned by any flights of fancy."—N. M. Crouse, *Contributions of the Canadian Jesuits to the Geography of New France 1632–1675* (Ithaca, N. Y., 1924), 114.

[2] L. P. Kellogg, *The French Régime in Wisconsin and the Northwest* (Madison, Wis., 1925), 200, note 29.

[3] "Marquette's Autograph Map of the Mississippi River," MA, 27 (1945): 30 f.

seen the principal objects delineated";[4] and, we may add, it
would have been impossible to draw such an accurate map of
the Mississippi merely on information derived from the Indians.

Marquette's original manuscript map is preserved in the
archives of the Collège Sainte-Marie, Montreal. A facsimile
of the map was first published by Shea in 1852,[5] and again
in 1861, by Father de Montézon to accompany his edition of
the *Relations inédites*.[6] Thwaites wrote about these reproductions: "The facsimile of Marquette's genuine map, as reproduced by Shea and others is not without blunders, which will
be detected upon comparison with the photographic facsimile
given in the present volume of our series."[7]

I have looked in vain for these "blunders." In some respects Shea's facsimile is better than the photographic copy
in Thwaites' *Jesuit Relations*. Father Steck, who made the
comparison suggested by Thwaites, says that "this latest reproduction shows that since the days of Shea the original has
been mutilated so that the unmistakable handwriting of Marquette no longer appears on it."[8] The truth is that the original
of the map is exactly as it was in the days of Shea, without
the least mutilation.[9] A comparison between the original and
Thwaites' reproduction of it shows that whoever prepared
Thwaites' photographic copy thought that the four original
legends in cursive were too finely written to photograph well,
and therefore rewrote these legends more clearly, pasting his
reproductions of them over the originals. On the Montreal
map, the original legends in cursive—in the "unmistakable

---

[4] Jared Sparks, "Life of Father Marquette," in *Library of
American Biography* (10 vols., 1st series, 2nd ed. New York, 1848),
10: 297.

[5] J. G. Shea, *The Discovery and Exploration of the Mississippi
Valley* (Redfield, N. Y., 1852).

[6] *Relations inédites de la Nouvelle-France*; the map is at the end
of the second volume.

[7] JR, 59: 295.—"Shea's map was traced and in this process
somewhat changed and 'improved'." L. P. Kellogg, "Marquette's
Authentic Map Possibly Identified," *Proceedings* of the State Historical Society of Wisconsin for 1906 (Madison, Wis., 1907), 183,
note 1.

[8] Steck, *The Jolliet–Marquette Expedition, 1673*, 149, note 32.

[9] See the photograph in S. J. Tucker, *Indian Villages of the Illinois Country*, Part I, *Atlas* (Springfield, Ill., 1942), pl. V.

handwriting of Marquette"—may still be seen, which settles the question of the authenticity of the map.

The map measures 467x350 mm. The projection is the simplest and most conventional one: the cylindrical equal-spaced projection. The latitudes from 30° to 48° are numbered on both sides of the map, but the longitudes marked off at the top and bottom are not numbered.

The delineation of Lake Superior is the same as that of the Jesuit map of 1671;[10] except that the northern shore is not shown, for the area represented extends only to latitude 48°. The contours of Green Bay, and of the northern shores of Lake Huron and of Lake Michigan are also derived from the map of 1671. The west shore of Lake Huron and the east shore of Lake Michigan are indicated by a dotted line. The three upper lakes are given their seventeenth century French names. Three legends in cursive and one in block letters, taken from the map of 1671, are inscribed on Lake Superior. On the north shore of Lake Huron, Marquette wrote "SS.Ap-[ostres]" intending to indicate the location of the mission of the Holy Apostles begun by Father Nouvel in the winter of 1671–1672.[11] The center-top of the map, which is torn, originally contained the name of an Indian tribe beginning with "ki"; these are evidently the first two letters of the word "Kilistinons" on the 1671 Jesuit map of Lake Superior.

The names of four Indian tribes are inscribed in the Green Bay–Fox River region. The first, "folle auoine," written in cursive, is located as on the map of 1671, on the Menominee River; but Marquette does not indicate as clearly as Dablon did whether the village of these Indians was on the Wisconsin or on the Michigan side of the Menominee.[12] The name of the three other Indian tribes are written in block letters: 1) the P8te8tami at Point Sable, where the St. Francis Xavier mission was located before it was moved to De Pere, Wisconsin; 2) the 8tagami on the east bank of the Wolf River,[13]

---

[10] This map is described in "Marquette's Autograph Map," *loc. cit.*, 31–35.

[11] JR, 56: 92 ff.

[12] On the site of this village, cf. Kellogg, *The French Régime in Wisconsin*, 125, note 47.

[13] *Id., ibid.*, 127, note 50.

exactly where it is situated on the 1671 map; and 3) the Masc8tens, on the south bank of the Fox River.[14]

The names of the Indian tribes shown in the Mississippi Valley may be divided into three groups. The first group comprises "Kachkaska" on the Illinois River and the names of three Indian tribes on the banks of the Mississippi: "Pe8area," "Mons8pelea," and "Akansea." We cannot be certain whether "Metchigamea" is meant to represent an Indian village on the west bank of the Mississippi, or one located farther inland.[15] The second group comprises five names echeloned east of the Mississippi, which are said to be "Nations dans les terres." The third group, west of the Mississippi, includes two clusters of villages, nine in the north and eight in the south; they are the "Noms des nations eloignees dans les terres."

The legend "Bassin de la Floride" is written along the 31st parallel and one degree below, farther to the east is the word "Floride." The Mississippi is marked "R. de la Conception."[16] From the mouth of the Wisconsin, at latitude 42° 30', it is represented as flowing to the south-southeast, to latitude 41°,

---

[14] J. J. Wood, "The Mascoutin Village," *Proceedings* of the State Historical Society of Wisconsin for 1906 (Madison, Wis., 1907), 167–174; A. E. Jones, "The Site of Mascoutin," *ibid.*, 175–182.

[15] "Marquette's Autograph Map," *loc. cit.*, 45–47.

[16] There is no reason for questioning the authenticity of this name on the ground that it is not written in cursive "like other portions" of the map, "but in Roman capitals" (Steck, *The Jolliet–Marquette Expedition*, 296). At that rate only the four legends in cursive are authentic, for all the other are in Roman capitals, and there is no difference between the style of the Roman capitals "R. DE LA CONCEPTION" and the style of the Roman capitals of the other legends. Neither is it conclusive to argue that because Marquette calls the Mississippi by its Indian name in his autograph journal of the second voyage, he therefore had not called it "R. de la Conception" in his journal of the voyage of 1673. For it is at least possible that, like other seventeenth century explorers, Marquette could have referred to the Mississippi by more than one name. Thus, although Jolliet had called it "Rivière de Buade," he later referred to it as "Mississippi"; and La Salle, who had solemnly christened it "Fleuve Colbert" in April 1682, opens his letter of October of that year by calling it "fleuve Mississipi" (Margry, 2: 288), and "grande rivière" in the last lines of the same letter. *Ibid.*, 301. Moreover, when referring to the Mississippi by its Indian name in the autograph journal of his second voyage, Marquette tells Dablon that he has made copies of his journal of the first voyage. Hence he naturally mentioned the Mississippi by its Indian name, because this was the only name by which Dablon could have known the Mississippi unless he had read Marquette's journal of the first voyage.

and then to the south-southwest as far as latitude 39°. From this point to the confluence of the Illinois, at latitude 38°, its course makes an angle of 140 degrees. From the confluence of the Illinois River the course of the Mississippi is due south for one and a half degrees, to latitude 36° 30'. The river then turns to the southeast and follows this direction as far as the mouth of the Ohio, situated slightly below latitude 36°. From the Ohio to the southernmost point shown on the map, latitude 33° 40', the Mississippi flows southwestward.

The two accompanying drawings show graphically how accurately the course of the Mississippi is delineated on this "rude sketch."[17] On the first drawing, the course of the Mississippi River has been transposed on a modern map, keeping the latitudes as they are on Marquette's map; on the second drawing, all his latitudes have been raised one degree to correct the average error of position of identifiable points. No map of this section of the Mississippi made before 1700 either in France or in Canada is as accurate as that of Marquette; and the exactness of the latitudes is itself enough to prove that this map could not have been made before the voyage on information furnished by Indians.[18]

Four unnamed rivers empty into Lake Michigan between Chicago and the Door County peninsula, Wisconsin, bounded by this lake and Green Bay.

The "R. de la Conception" receives seven tributaries, four coming from the west, and three from the east; of these seven rivers only two are named: the "Pekitan8i" [Missouri], which is shown coming from the west-northwest, and the "8ab8skig8" [Ohio], coming from the east-northeast. These two are shown at their confluence as broad rivers tapering off into a single line.

Of the five unnamed tributaries of the Mississippi, the Wisconsin and the Illinois can be identified with certainty. The whole course of the former, from Portage to Prairie du Chien, is represented by a thin line, the river flowing in a

17 F. Parkman, *La Salle and the Discovery of the Great West* (11th ed., Boston, 1907), 451.
18 Compare Delisle's sketch of the Mississippi (AN, JJ, 75–197, *supra*, p. 39, note 45) based on information furnished exclusively by the Indians with Marquette's map.

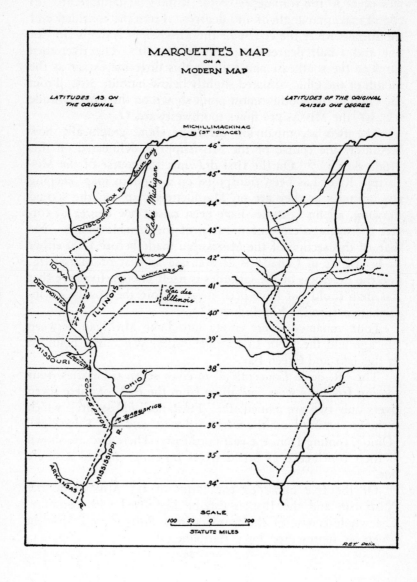

MARQUETTE'S MAP
ON A
MODERN MAP

LATITUDES AS ON
THE ORIGINAL

LATITUDES OF THE ORIGINAL
RAISED ONE DEGREE

SCALE

STATUTE MILES

south-southwest direction. The Illinois is shown at its confluence as a broad stream coming directly from the north for one degree; above this point, it is represented as by a thin line running upward toward the northeast, then toward the east to the headwaters near Lake Michigan. There is no means of identifying the rudimentary river which empties into the Mississippi slightly below latitude 41°. The river on the banks of which the Pe8area dwelt is the Iowa; and the southernmost tributary of the Mississippi represented on Marquette's map is more probably the White River rather than the Arkansas.

II. THE LOST JOLLIET MAP

From Frontenac's letter we know that, after his return to Quebec, Jolliet drew from memory a map of the Mississippi which was sent to France in November 1674. This map is lost, but five maps based on Jolliet's original, which were made in Quebec between the summer of 1674 and the summer of 1678, have come down to us. One of these maps was made by an anonymous draughtsman, another was made by Randin, a third is known as the Manitoumie map, and the fourth and fifth by Franquelin.

By means of these five maps we have tried to reconstruct the lost original and concluded that it had the following appearance. The outline of the continent resembled that on the anonymous map; the Mississippi was drawn clear to the Gulf and the delineation of its course was not much different from that on the Randin map; but we can no more than conjecture what was the shape of the Great Lakes. By a multiple comparison of the nomenclature on the five maps, we attempted to determine the place-names and inscriptions on Jolliet's maps along the route followed by the explorers, and the names of Indian tribes they heard of during their journey.[19]

Since the description, the authorship, the accuracy and the derivation of each of these five maps have been treated in detail,[20] it suffices to give the essential points of this discussion.

---

[19] "The Jolliet Lost Map of the Mississippi," MA, 28 (1946): 130–139.
[20] *Ibid.*, 68–93.

1) THE ANONYMOUS COPY OF JOLLIET'S MAP

Since 1880, when Gabriel Gravier first reproduced it in reduced form,[21] the accepted view has been that this map was made by "Jolliet himself immediately after his return to Montreal."[22] Gravier had no doubt that it was an autograph Jolliet map, which he saw in an atlas of old maps of America, some engraved and others in manuscript. Today, this "hitherto unknown map" is in the John Carter Brown Library, Providence, Rhode Island.

Gravier gives no reason for saying that "it is the oldest map of the Mississippi which we have"; as a matter of fact, Marquette's map antedates it; and there is no reason for attributing it to Jolliet. First, the style of this map is quite different from the style of the genuine Jolliet maps which have come down to us. Secondly, the handwriting of the legends on the map, which is the same as that of the dedicatory letter to Frontenac, in no way resembles the handwriting of Jolliet. Thirdly, there is no known example of Jolliet signing or writing his name with one *l*; on this map however, the letter is signed "Joliet," and a knoll in Illinois is legended "Mont Joliet."

The identity of the draughtsman has not been ascertained, and probably never will be, except by some fortunate accident. Although this anonymous copyist was an incompetent draughtsman and a poor geographer, he did not make any deliberate change in Jolliet's original text when reproducing the dedicatory letter to Frontenac. Hence the presumption is that he did not deliberately tamper with the nomenclature. This alone constitutes the value of the map, for as a representation of North America it is quite useless, and it would be difficult to draw the Great Lakes more inaccurately, even if one were to try.

---

[21] Nouuelle Decouuerte de Plusieurs Nations Dans la Nouuelle France En l'annee 1673 et 1674. Cf. Tucker, *Indian Villages of the Illinois Country*, 2, notes for plate IV.

[22] *Étude sur Une Carte inconnue. La première dressée par Louis Joliet en 1674* (Paris, 1880), 14.—The map accompanying this study is re-issued in JR, 59, facing p. 86.

2) THE RANDIN MAP

Since this map is not signed, we had to explain on what evidence it has been attributed to Randin. We have shown that the Randin map in the John Carter Brown Library is not the same as that which Margry traced, but is a contemporary copy on a smaller scale. We next endeavored to ascertain the identity of this Randin, for at the time there were at least two men of that name in Canada, Antoine and Hugues. The solution of this question of the identity of the author of the map depends on our knowing for certain the first name of the Randin whom Frontenac sent to Acadia in 1674. What we know now is that this Randin was certainly not Hugues; for Frontenac's man was a lieutenant in September 1672, whereas in an official document of November of the same year, Hugues Randin is said to be an ensign.[23]

Randin's map represents the North American Continent[24] from N. latitude 23° to N. latitude 51°, whereas the anonymous copy extends from N. latitude 27° to N. latitude 59°. On the latter the longitudes are not shown, but on the Randin map they are marked off and numbered from 266° to 325°. The projection is a modified equal-spaced cylindrical projection in which the meridians and the parallels are straight lines forming two parallel systems mutually perpendicular, but the ratio between the spacing of the meridians and that of the parallels is the cosine of latitude 38°, the middle latitude of the map. The grid however, is that of the plate-carrée projection. After Randin had drawn his map according to his model, the projection of which was the equal-spaced cylindrical, he super-

---

23 "The Jolliet Lost Map," *loc. cit.*, 72–78. Since I wrote this article, I found in the Archives Judiciaires of Quebec (Greffe Genaple), the deed of June 5, 1684. This deed establishes two facts: first, that Hugues Randin was the brother of Antoine; second, that Hugues was granted a concession in Acadia, not in 1679 as is commonly maintained—for he had been dead two years by this date—but more probably in 1676, after his return from the West. The document, however, does not solve the question of the identity of the author of the Randin map.

24 Carte de l'Amerique Septentrionale Depuis l'embouchûre de la Riviere St. Laurens jusques au Sein Mexique. Reduced reproduction in S. J. Tucker, *Indian Villages of the Illinois Country*, pl. VI.

imposed upon the finished map a set of equidistant and mu-tually perpendicular meridians and parallels.

We cannot determine what basic map the anonymous copy-ist used, for his delineation of the North American Continent is too sketchy and the nomenclature too sparse. On the other hand, Randin's nomenclature makes it clear that he used as a model a Dutch version of a Spanish map. In this basic map Randin inserted the five Great Lakes and the Mississippi with its tributaries as on the anonymous map. Lake Superior is taken from the Jesuit map of 1671; the delineation of the northern part of Lake Michigan and of Lake Huron is taken from the same map; while the south and east shores of Lake Michigan are conjectural. The delineation of Lake St. Clair and the southern part of Lake Huron is derived from the 1656 Sanson map of New France. Lake Erie is given a much larger area than its actual size, and the representation of Lake Ontario is a variant of one of the numerous maps showing this lake.

To dispense with making elaborate comparisons between the actual course of the Mississippi and its course as shown on the Randin map, the river has been transposed twice on a modern map.

The double line represents the first transposition. The Wis-consin-Mississippi confluence has been placed at the same lati-tude as on the Randin map, and at W. longitude 91° 30′. The reason for selecting this longitude is as follows.

Because we do not know where the prime meridian on Randin's basic map was located, we have no means of know-ing where North America would appear on the globe. If we suppose that this prime meridian was the western part of Ferro Island, the Wisconsin-Mississippi confluence would be at A, in Hitchcock County, Nebraska. This is quite unlikely, for the Dutch geographer who made Randin's basic map was not bound by the decree of Louis XIII which obliged all French-men to use Ferro as their prime meridian.

If as a basis of our computations we were to take the longi-tudinal difference between Green Bay and Prairie du Chien, nine degrees of longitude on Randin's map instead of the ac-tual three, the Wisconsin would join the Mississippi six degrees west of longitude 91° 30′, at B, in Nuckoll County, Nebraska.

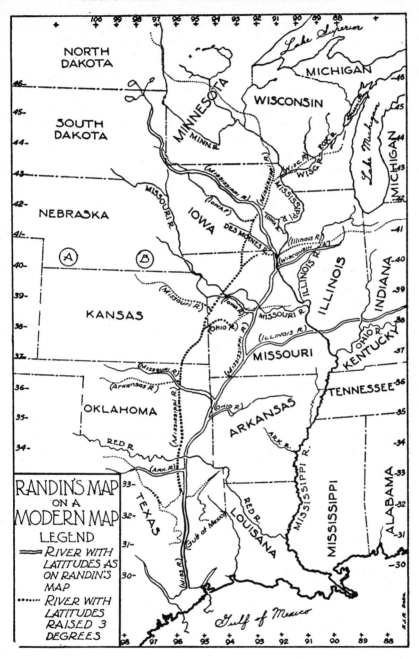

RANDIN'S MAP
ON A
MODERN MAP
LEGEND
— RIVER WITH
LATITUDES AS
ON RANDIN'S
MAP
····· RIVER WITH
LATITUDES
RAISED 3
DEGREES

If, however, one takes as prime meridian that which grazes the east coast of the Floridan peninsula (the 80th West of Greenwich), the longitudinal difference between this meridian and Prairie du Chien is nearly the same on Randin's map as on a modern map. Because this method of calculation approximates the true longitudinal relation between these two points, we have placed the junction of the Mississippi and the Wisconsin at W. longitude 91° 30′, fifteen minutes west of the true longitude of Prairie du Chien.

The difference between the first—the double line—and the second—the dotted line—transposition is that the Mississippi-Wisconsin confluence has been raised three degrees, thus making it nearly coincide with its actual position.

3) THE MANITOUMIE MAP

The third contemporary map based on that of Jolliet is that published by Thévenot in 1681.[25] The original draft of this map, however, was made several years earlier than the date of its publication. Some writers have said that Marquette was the author of the Thévenot map; others, that it was the work of a western Jesuit; and nearly a century ago, Shea surmised that it was a Jolliet map.[26] Though his surmise was correct, Shea could not prove his contention, because he lacked the other four maps based on Jolliet's original as well as the manuscript map used by Liébaux to engrave that published by Thévenot. This manuscript map is available today in two states, which for the sake of convenience, we have called Manitoumie I[27] and Manitoumie II.[28]

---

[25] M. Thévenot, ed., *Recueil de voyages de Mr Thevenot* (Paris, 1681), fontispiece.

[26] When Shea published his facsimile of Marquette's autograph, he wrote that the map in Thevenot's book "is so different from that which still exists in the handwriting of Father Marquette, that it is not probable that it was taken from it. With greater likelihood we may believe it to be Jolliet's map drawn from recollection, which Frontenac, as his despatch tells us, transmitted to France in 1674, and not a blundering copy."—*Discovery and Exploration of the Mississippi Valley,* lxxv.

[27] Reproduced in facsimile in G. Marcel, *Reproductions de cartes et de globes relatifs à la découverte de l'Amérique du XVIᵉ au XVIIᵉ siècle* (Paris, 1892), pl. 30. In the letter-press volume accompanying this atlas, p. 106, and in his *Cartographie de la Nouvelle France* (Paris, 1885), 8, no. 7, Marcel gives as reference the Dépôt des Cartes,

The variants between the Thévenot and the two Manitoumie maps do not mean that Liébaux used a different map as his model, for it is well-known that seventeenth century engravers did not always reproduce exactly the drafts that were given them. This freedom partly accounts for the omissions, changes in spelling, differences of latitudes and inaccurate positions noticeable in those maps of which we have the manuscript and the engraved product.[29]

We have called attention to the fact that the wording of the title of the Manitoumie differs widely from that of Thévenot's map, and we have shown that the more elaborate cartouche of Manitoumie II, the differences in the wording of the text and certain particularities in the appearance of the map, suggest that Manitoumie I is an earlier draft.[30]

On all three maps the latitudes are marked off and numbered on the east side; but as in the case of the anonymous map, the longitudes are not marked. Since there is no scale, use must be made of the degree of latitude to calculate distances and positions.

The only worth while study of the Manitoumie map is that by L. P. Kellogg.[31] At the end of her article, she draws four conclusions from the evidence presented. While her first

---

Bibliothèque Nationale, vol. C., 17701. This volume is the seventh of a collection; the other six have not been found.—A photographic reproduction of the original is in Kellogg, *Early Narratives of the Northwest*, between pp. 228–229. The original is listed in Leland, *Guide to Materials for American History*, 226, with the call-number Rés. Ge. C. 5014.

[28] Photograph of the original (BN, V^d 30, Estampes) in the Karpinski Series of Reproductions. This is the map that could not be found when Harrisse was preparing his *Notes pour servir*, 194, no. 202.—Three tracings of the map were made in the middle of last century. One by P. L. Morin for the Dominion Parliamentary Library, Ottawa; another by Margry, which is now in the Ayer Collection of the Newberry Library, Chicago; the third, which was made for Parkman, is now in the Harvard Library, and is referred to as "Parkman No. 5." This last, an imperfect tracing, was reproduced by L. P. Kellogg, "Marquette's Authentic Map Possibly Identified," *Proceedings* of the State Historical Society of Wisconsin for 1906 (Madison, Wis., 1907), between pp. 184–185.

[29] Compare Delisle's manuscript of his map of 1718 (reproduced in Tucker, *Indian Villages of the Illinois Country*, pl. XV) with the engraved product published in Paris in the same year.

[30] "The Jolliet Lost Map," *loc. cit.*, 82 f.

[31] "Marquette's Authentic Map Possibly Identified," *loc. cit.*, 183–193.

conclusion is untenable,[32] her second conclusion is undoubtedly correct; namely, " 'Parkman No. 5' [i.e., a tracing of Manitoumie II] is a copy of the prototype of the one published by Thévenot in 1681." The third conclusion is that the original of 'Parkman No. 5' is "an authentic work of the explorers"; and the fourth that "while the authorship of the original of which 'Parkman No. 5' is a copy cannot positively be asserted, indications are sufficient to warrant the supposition that this was a genuine map of Marquette, prepared by him to embody the results of his voyage of exploration."[33]

Twenty years later, Miss Kellogg revised these two last conclusions, saying that

Marquette never drew but one map, which is in Montreal . . . The map known as 'Parkman No. 5,' of which there are several variations, was, I believe, prepared under the auspices of the Jesuits . . . Peter A. Porter, of Buffalo, believes that the Manitoumie maps were adapted from an original left in the West by Jolliet. I cannot concur in this opinion, but consider it probable that they were prepared by one of the western Jesuits from data given by Marquette.[34]

Porter's opinion, which is that of Shea, rightly identifies the author of the original; this original, however, had not been left in the West by Jolliet, but is the map which he drew from memory in Quebec between August and November 1674. In the article published in 1907, Miss Kellogg had said that the opinion that Marquette was the author of the map published by Thévenot was discarded when the Montreal holograph came to light. "Shea supposed that Thévenot's chart might have been made by Jolliet; but the latter's original was later found with the dedication to Count de Frontenac, proving its authenticity."[35] The supposed Jolliet original here referred to is the copy made by the anonymous draughtsman.

The question of the origin of the sketch used by the draughtsman of the Manitoumie involves two steps; first, to determine the place where the sketch was made; second, to identify its author.

At the end of the seventeenth century, an album was made

---

[32] "Marquette's Autograph Map," loc. cit., 30 f.
[33] "Marquette's Authentic Map," loc. cit., 192 f.
[34] The French Régime in Wisconsin, 200, note 29.
[35] "Marquette's Authentic Map," loc. cit., 183.

in Quebec which contains drawings of Indians, of plants and of animals, and also includes two maps.[36] One of these shows the course of the St. Lawrence from Sault Ste Marie to the Ocean; the other is a map of the Mississippi River. Although the measurements of the latter are the same as those of the Thévenot map, the following facts prove that the draughtsman had a copy of the sketch used for the Manitoumie.

(1) The title of this second map in the album is a variant of the Manitoumie title; and is quite different from the title of the Thévenot map.

(2) Two legends of the Manitoumie maps—*Mexique* and *Floride*—which are not on the Thévenot map, are marked on the Mississippi map in this album at the same place as on the Manitoumies.

(3) The terminus of the expedition is not indicated on the Thévenot map. On the two Manitoumies there is a cross on the west bank of the Mississippi and the following inscription on the east bank of the river: "On est venu iusques icy a la hauteur de 33 degrez." The "Codex Canadiensis" has: "Les françois ont esté icy lan 1673 a la hauteur de 34 degres."

(4) On the Thévenot map there is a statue under which is the single word: "Manit8." Under the picture of a man on the Manitoumie maps, is found the legend: "Manit8 Statue ou les Sauuages vont faire leurs adorations." On the map in the "Codex Canadiensis," underneath the drawing of the bust of a man the inscription reads as follows: "Manitou ou les Sauuages vont faire Leurs adorations."

From these and other similarities pointed out elsewhere[37] we argue as follows. The above legends and inscriptions are found on only one map, the Manitoumie, and at the end of the seventeenth century the two manuscripts which have come down to us were certainly in Paris. Now, although the draughtsman of a map made in Quebec at the end of the seventeenth century used Thévenot as his model, his inscriptions

---

[36] *Les Raretés des Indes.* "Codex Canadiensis." *Album manuscrit... contenant 180 dessins concernant les indigènes, leurs coutumes, tatouages, la faune et la flore de la Nouvelle France, plus deux cartes...* Précédé d'un Avant-propos par le Baron Marc de Villiers (Paris, 1930).
[37] "The Jolliet Lost Map," *loc. cit.*, 105, 109, 111.

and legends correspond unmistakably with those on the Manitoumie map.   The only reasonable conclusion is that he had
at his disposal a map containing the Manitoumie inscriptions
and legends.   Since the Manitoumie maps were in Paris at this
time, he must have had in Quebec a copy of the manuscript
draft.

The second step concerning the origin of the sketch used
by the draughtsman of the Manitoumie consists in ascertaining
the author of this sketch.

From the title of Manitoumie I and II as well as from the
cartouche of the latter, there is little doubt that the original
manuscript of this map is the work of a Jesuit.[38]   The agreement between the place-names on the anonymous and on the
Randin maps and the nomenclature of the Manitoumie, shows
clearly that this Jesuit used as a basis the same Jolliet map as
was used by the other two designers, supplementing the Jolliet nomenclature with a few names taken from Marquette's
map.

An investigation of the source of the inscription—"Manit8
Statue ou les Sauuages vont faire leurs adorations"—an inscription which was certainly not on Jolliet's map, makes it
possible to identify the Jesuit who was the author of the original manuscript used by the Manitoumie draughtsman.

The reason why the country discovered should be called
"Manitoumie" we read in the title of the map, is "because,
in a beautiful valley, there is a statue which the Indians acknowledged as their god and which they call Manitou, meaning spirit or genius."   This is expressed more briefly on the
map itself: "Manit8, Statue which the Indians worship."   On
the map, however, the position of this statue is not in a "beautiful valley," but some fifty miles east of the Mississippi, half
way between the "8ab8quig8" and the Illinois River. We know
that no Frenchman went as far inland at this point until thirty
years later; hence we must try to locate this statue somewhere
along the route actually followed by Jolliet.

A passage written by Dablon in the Relation of 1670–1671
is relevant here.   In September 1670, when he and Father Al-

---

[38] *Ibid.,* 86.

louez on their way to the Mascoutens village reached the rapids of the Fox River, they "found some kind of idol, which the Indians honor in that place" by making sacrificial offerings when passing by. "This idol is a rock shaped by nature in the form of a man's bust; from a distance one seems to distinguish the head, shoulders, breast, and more especially the face, which passers-by are wont to paint with the brightest colors. To do away with this occasion of idolatrous worship, we ordered our men to remove it and throw it to the bottom of the river."[39] Dablon then launches into a lyrical description of the Fox River Valley which "somewhat resembles the Garden of Eden."

From this we see that the data concerning the statue in the title of the Manitoumie map are contained in the section written by Dablon of the Relation of 1670–1671. Further facts suggest that he is the author of the original manuscript of the Manitoumie. We know that he was intensely interested in the geography of North America,[40] and that he is very probably the author of the famous map of Lake Superior.[41] We also know that he interviewed Jolliet on his return to Quebec and that he wrote down what he learned from the explorer. Sometime after this interview, Jolliet drew a map of the Mississippi, which we know Dablon saw, and it would be most unlikely if Jolliet had not given him a copy or let him make one, considering that others who were far less interested than he was in the geography of North America had occasion to make copies of Jolliet's map. Nor must we lose sight of the fact that the author of the Manitoumie had Marquette's map at his disposal. All these indications coupled with the fact that the draft of the map was made in Quebec point to Dablon as the most likely author of the original manuscript of the Manitoumie.

But why, it may be asked, should the idol on the banks of the Fox River be shown on the map fifty miles inland between the Ohio and the Illinois rivers? Perhaps because the author wished to support his suggestion that the whole country be named "Manitoumie" by placing the statue and the legend in the center of the map.

---

39 JR, 55: 192.
40 *Supra*, pp. 23 ff.
41 "Marquette's Autograph Map," *loc. cit.*, 31–34.

4) THE FRANQUELIN MAP OF 1678

Gravier held that although this map is signed by Franquelin,[42] the sketch on which it is based is Jolliet's. His first reason for this view is childish and need not detain us. His second reason is put forward as conclusive: "Mr. Parkman's description[43] which we checked on the map in the Dépôt des Cartes de la Marine [now BSH], corresponds exactly to the quite characteristic delineation of an hitherto unknown map [the anonymous copy of Jolliet's lost map] of Jolliet which is before us. The result of the close comparison which we made of these two monuments is that the sketch is Jolliet's and the finished product Franquelin's."[44]

The "characteristic delineation" referred to is that of the North American Continent, which is indeed similar on both maps; this would only prove that both the anonymous copyist and Franquelin used the same outline of North America. What needs to be proved is that the map of the voyage of 1673 was furnished by Jolliet to Franquelin. Now the latter specifies that his general map of North America illustrates in particular "the discovery made by Sieur Jolliet of the Illinois country"; and in March 1680, Duchesneau gave as one of the reasons for granting in fief Anticosti Island to Jolliet, "the discovery made by the said Jolliet of the Illinois country, of which he gave us a sketch which served to draw the map which we sent two years ago to my Lord Colbert, Minister and Secretary of State."[45]

The comparative study of these four maps of the Mississippi River yields the following results.

First, the nomenclature of these maps illustrating the voyage of 1673 is closely related, and in the case of the anonymous and Randin maps, the names of Indian tribes and even their

---

[42] Carte Gnlle de la France Septen–Trionnalle Contenant la découuerte du pays des Ilinois Faite Par le Sieur Jolliet. A photograph of the original in BSH, B 4040–11, is in the Karpinski Series of Reproductions.—For the date of this map, see "Franquelin, Mapmaker," MA, 25 (1943): 56 f.

[43] In La Salle and the Discovery of the Great West, 454.

[44] Étude sur Une Carte inconnue, 13.

[45] Gagnon, Louis Jolliet, 200.

grouping and position are identical.[46] This close relation and identity indicate that these four maps must have been based on a common prototype.

Secondly, the nomenclature of the four maps does not essentially differ from that on Marquette's map which we know was based on the journal kept during the expedition of 1673.

Thirdly, the similarity between the nomenclature on Marquette's map and on the other four, shows that their prototype was the work of one who took part in the voyage.

Fourthly, we know that among those who took part in the expedition no one except Jolliet was capable of constructing a map, and that after his return to Quebec in 1674, he actually drew from memory a map of the country explored.

Hence, from the similarity of the basic nomenclature on the four maps, and from the similarity of this basic nomenclature with that on Marquette's map, we conclude that the prototype used by the anonymous copyist, by Randin, by Dablon and by Franquelin was Jolliet's map.

5) THE FRANQUELIN MAP OF 1675

This map represents the St. Lawrence Basin from Montreal to the western end of Lake Superior, and the course of the Mississippi from its supposed headwaters at latitude 47° to the mouth of the Ohio, located slightly below latitude 38°.[47] This map, known as "Jolliet's larger map," was very probably made by Franquelin, who used Jolliet's original as his model.[48] This can readily be seen by comparing the region west of Lake Michigan with the corresponding territory on the anonymous and on the Randin maps. Moreover the title specifies that the map illustrates "la decouuerte du Sr Jolliet," and its main purpose

---

[46] See the tables at the end of "The Jolliet Lost Map," *loc. cit.*, 130–139.

[47] Carte de la descouuerte du Sr Jolliet ou l'on voit la communication du Fleuue St Laurens auec les Lacs Frontenac, Érié, Lac des Hurons, et Ilinois, le Lac Frontenac est separé par un sault de demye Lieue du Lac Érié, duquel on entre dans celuy des Hurons, et par une mesme Nauigation a celuy des Ilinois au bout duquel on va joindre la Riuiere diuine par un portage de Mille pas qui tombe dans la Riuiere Colbert et se descharge dans le sein Mexique. BSH, B 4044–37; photograph in the Karpinski Series of Reproductions.

[48] "The Jolliet Lost Map," *loc. cit.*, 91 f.

is to show graphically how easy it would be to go by boat from Niagara to the Gulf of Mexico. From Dablon's account and from Frontenac's letter, we know that the facility of communication between the St. Lawrence and the Mississippi at Chicago had made a strong impression on Jolliet.

From the title also, we learn that the lakes were shown on Jolliet's original; which in turn is confirmed by the fact that they are shown on the anonymous and on the Randin maps. How the contours of the lakes appeared on Jolliet's original is a matter of conjecture, for, with the exception of Lake Superior, their delineation is different on each of the three maps.

A distinctive mark of Franquelin's map of 1675 consists in the interpolation of the course of the Ohio and of an inscription which reads: "Route du Sieur de la Salle pour Aller dans le Mexique." These interpolations were made by a later, clumsy hand, certainly not by Jolliet.[49]

By 1676, Franquelin's map had reached the hands of Claude Bernou who made a copy of it on a smaller scale.[50] It stands to reason that on this reduced copy the interpolation of the course of the Ohio can no longer be detected; moreover, Bernou changed the interpolated inscription making it to read: "Riuiere par ou descendit le Sieur de la Salle au sortir du Lac Erie pour aller dans le Mexique." The first inscription may simply mean that La Salle knew of this route as a possible route to Mexico. The second inscription asserts that La Salle actually went down the Ohio on his way to Mexico.

It is difficult to understand why Bernou's copy has been so highly praised, although its draughtsmanship is much inferior to the model. Besides changing the interpolated inscription, Bernou omitted five legends or inscriptions, one of which refers to the outgoing journey of Jolliet; he added other legends, such

---

[49] *Some La Salle Journeys*, 32 f; C. H. Hanna, *The Wilderness Trail* (2 vols., New York, 1911), 2: 213 f.
[50] Carte de la découuerte du Sʳ Jolliet..., facsimile in Marcel, *Reproductions de cartes et de globes*, pl. 27, from BSH, B 4044–49. The variant in the title is discussed in "The Discovery of the Mississippi. Primary Sources," MA, 27 (1945): 229; the date when Bernou was in possession of this map is deduced from one of his questionnaires. *Infra*, p. 84.—About 1700, Bernou gave his copy to Claude Delisle, "The Sources of the Delisle Map of America, 1703," MA, 25 (1943): 285.

as a short portage between the Ohio and a river which, from the position of its mouth at the southwest end of Lake Erie, can only be the Maumee.   Finally, he invented a wide water-way between Munising, Michigan, and Little Bay De Noc, thus joining Lake Superior directly to Green Bay.   In view of all this, Bernou's reduction is valueless for studying the cartographical evolution of the Great Lakes and the Mississippi Valley.

It is more difficult to understand how this map could be attributed to Jolliet more than forty years after Marcel's publication of its facsimile.   Unless one had seen specimens of Bernou's handwriting, of which there are hundreds of pages extant, it might have been difficult to identify Bernou as its author, but it should have been easy to compare the handwriting of the letter inscribed in a band below the map itself with specimens of Jolliet's genuine handwriting.   Such a comparison would have made it evident that the explorer had not drawn this map.   Moreover, one wonders why those who have seen photographs of the anonymous map, of Franquelin's map of 1675 and of Bernou's reduction persist in saying that they were all made by Jolliet.   Jolliet might conceivably have drawn one of these three maps, but he cannot have drawn all three.

CHAPTER V

THE DISCOVERY OF THE MISSISSIPPI

Secondary Sources

As we have already said, the secondary sources for our knowledge of the voyage of 1673 comprise the following documents: 1) an anonymous narrative entitled "Relation de la Nouvelle France, 1673"; 2) two questionnaires and a memorial by Abbé Claude Bernou; 3) the "Récit des voyages et des découvertes du Père Jacques Marquette." These documents are all based on the evidence, documentary and cartographical, previously examined.

1) RELATION DE LA NOUVELLE FRANCE, 1673

This abridged narrative of the expedition,[1] which has been erroneously attributed to Jolliet, is in reality a compilation whose anonymous author used Jolliet's dedicatory letter to Frontenac and a copy of the ASH version of Dablon's letter of August 1, 1674.

What first strikes the reader of this narrative is the peculiar interchange of the first and third person singular, the unexpected transitions from "il" to "je" and from "je" to "il." This is queer enough, on the supposition that Jolliet wrote the document. Still queerer, on the same supposition, are the three opening words: "Le nommé Joliet . . . ." These words are mistranslated when they are rendered by "The said Joliet," as though the French text had "ledit Joliet." This latter expression is used when the name has already been mentioned; obviously, it cannot be used at the beginning of a document. The words *Le nommé*, on the other hand, indicate that the person referred to is either a man of no importance, or else that he is unknown to the writer or speaker. Hence the correct translation of "Le nommé Joliet" is "A man named Joliet," or "One

---

[1] BN, Mss. fr., n. a., 7485, part II, 176–177v; printed in Margry, 1: 259–263.

Joliet." The use of this expression is evidence that the document was written in Paris; for in documents originating in Canada after 1674, the explorer is always referred to as "le sieur Jolliet," or even as "Monsieur Jolliet." Finally, as we have observed,[2] Jolliet never wrote his name with one *l*.

The presence of these incongruities in the first three words should, it would seem, have led to a closer examination of this document, however inconvenient to preconceived theories such an examination might have been. Unless Jolliet were an imbecile, he would not have begun with such words "in drawing up this account."[3] He would not have referred to himself as "one Joliet," and he certainly would not have misspelled his name.[4]

This "Relation" contains one sentence not found in any of the extant accounts of the discovery of the Mississippi, thus pointing to the fact that the compiler had access to a presumably lost narrative of the voyage of 1673, or that he inserted in his account some information which is found today on one of the maps illustrating the voyage of discovery.[5] Except for this information the document is worthless.

2) BERNOU'S PAPERS

In the papers of Abbé Claude Bernou[6] there are three documents which contain all that was known in Paris during the late 1670's about Jolliet's voyage.

The earliest of these documents is entitled: "Memorandum concerning Canada. Bernou, M. Barrois' most humble servant, begs for enlightenment about the following items."[7] The addressee was Jacques Barroys or Barrois, Frontenac's secretary,

---

[2] *Supra*, p. 1, note 1.
[3] Steck, *The Jolliett–Marquette Expedition*, 183.
[4] For other incongruities, see "The Discovery of the Mississippi. Secondary Sources," MA, 28 (1946): 6–8.
[5] "The Jolliet Lost Map of the Mississippi," *ibid.*, 111 f; "The 'Récit des voyages et des découvertes du Père Jacques Marquette'," *ibid.*, 246.
[6] On Bernou, cf. *Some La Salle Journeys*, 10–12, 57–58; *Hennepin's Description of Louisiana*, 53–55, 112 ff.
[7] BN, Clairambault, 1016: 396–397v.

factotum and messenger.[8]   Although not dated, internal evidence shows that the questionnaire was sent to Canada in the first half of 1676. Bernou kept two copies of his questionnaire; the title of one copy differs slightly from that given above;[9] the other copy is neater and contains brief interlinear answers to the first four questions.[10]   The copy from which we shall quote is a two-column document; the questions are on the left-hand side, the right-hand column is entitled: "Answers of Sieur St. Martin,[11] lay professor of mathematics at the Jesuit college of Quebec, who is coming over to France this year, 1677."

We are not concerned with the first seven questions which deal with the meteorology of the North Atlantic, and with the tides on the Newfoundland coast, at Quebec and in the Green Bay region, but with the eighth question which reads as follows:

What is the direction and what is the force of the prevailing winds on both banks of the St. Lawrence River, in the Great Lakes region, and in the country north and south of it, as well as in *Colbertie* or *Louisiane*[12] ... Also, how long does the winter last, and when does it begin and end at Plaisance [Placentia, Newfoundland], Port Royal [Annapolis, Nova Scotia], Cape Breton, Chaleur Bay, Tadoussac, Quebec, Montreal, Fort Frontenac, Lake Erie, Sault Ste Marie and Michilimackinac. Is it cold and does it snow as far south as the mouth of the *Riuiere de la Diuine* [Illinois River] and of the *Riuiere Ohio,* and how long does cold weather last in these two places? When does the rainy season begin in *Colbertie* or *Louisiane,* and how long does it last? This last point is important.

---

[8] "The Discovery of the Mississippi. Secondary Sources," *loc. cit.*, 9 f.
[9] Memoire sur le Canada pour Mr. Barrois que iay prié de me faire scauoir les choses suiuantes.—BN, Clairambault, 1016: 168 f.
[10] BN, Clairambault, 848: 695 f.
[11] On Martin Boutet *dit* St. Martin, cf. A. Gosselin, *L'instruction publique au Canada sous le régime français* (Quebec, 1911), 36 f; 326 ff.
[12] This is the earliest appearance of the name "Louisiane," three years before the date of the document published in Margry, 2: 20–22, see p. 21, note 1. The name originally applied to the country bounded by Lake Michigan, the Fox, the Wisconsin, the Mississippi, the Illinois and the Des Plaines rivers, to the section of the United States circled in canoe in 1673 by Jolliet and his companions, the first white men ever to do so. It is fairly certain that Bernou coined the name.—The text disposes of the theory advanced by M. de Villiers du Terrage in *La Louisiane, Histoire de son nom et de frontières successives* (Paris, 1929), 8–10.

This eighth question was left unanswered, for none of Bernou's informants had ever been in *Colbertie* or *Louisiane*, and in 1676, no white man had as yet spent the winter at the mouth of the Ohio or at the mouth of the Illinois River.

Bernou, however, was so interested in these questions that when, early in 1678, he heard of a Lyons merchant, Jean Daleyrac, who was about to leave for Canada, he drew up another questionnaire containing some of the items which had been left unanswered in that sent to Barrois in 1676. In this 1678 questionnaire, he asked for information about the currents in the Strait of Mackinac, at the entrance of Green Bay and elsewhere; he begged Daleyrac to obtain "if possible the full relation with the map of the voyage of Father Marquette and of Sieur Jollyet"; and finally he wished to know whether "some new discovery had been made."[13]

We were unable to find whether Daleyrac answered this questionnaire, but from a passage in the "Récit des voyages et des découvertes du Père Jacques Marquette," in which there is an allusion to supposed tides in Green Bay and a few lines as to the probable cause of this phenomenon,[14] it seems likely that Daleyrac submitted Bernou's questions to Dablon, the author of the *Récit,* to the man who as Frontenac had publicly admitted, "had a better knowledge of the West than anybody in New France."[15]

We conclude that when Bernou wrote the questionnaire of 1676, he had already seen the Franquelin map of 1675. What we know is that he redrew this map on a smaller scale and copied the dedicatory letter of Jolliet to the governor from it. From the questionnaire of 1678, in which he is asking for the "full relation with the map" of the voyage of 1673, we conclude that he had seen or had made a copy of a version of Dablon's letter of August 1, 1674, in which it is said that "a full relation" of the discovery cannot be expected until next year.

---

[13] Monsieur Dalera est suplié par son tres humble seruiteur Bernou de luy faire scauoir les choses suiuantes quand il sera dans la Nouuelle France.—BN, Clairambault, 848: 363–365.

[14] JR, 59: 98.

[15] *Jugements et délibérations du Conseil Souverain,* 2: 671.

Among Bernou's papers there is another document containing references to the voyage of 1673. Sometime after 1674, Bernou became acquainted with Diego Dionisio de Peñalosa Briceño y Verdugo.[16] The visionary plans of Peñalosa are embodied in numerous memorials, some in French and some in Spanish, some autograph and some in copy form, which are today among the papers of the abbé.[17] One such undated memorial, but written between 1676 and 1677, is entitled: "Memorial for the discovery and conquest of Quivira and Theguayo in North America."[18] The document, analyzed at length elsewhere,[19] is here briefly summarized.

Since the conquest of Quivira and Theguayo, two of the richest "kingdoms" of America, is very difficult and nearly impossible for the Spaniards, Peñalosa [*i.e.*, Bernou] devised a plan for reaching these countries by way of New France. Acadia, we are told by the memorialist, is better than Canada, which is described as a poor and sterile country, but better still is

the country beyond the Great Lakes, where the work of ten men would suffice to sustain five hundred, because of the fertility of the soil which produces two crops a year, and because the lakes and rivers teem with fish and the country abounds in game. The various products can be transported over the Great Lakes or over the beautiful river recently discovered which disembogues into the Gulf of Mexico, or over many of its tributaries, one of which the author [Peñalosa, *i.e.* Bernou] has many reasons to believe that it comes from New Mexico. Finally, a large colony could be established [in the country beyond the Great Lakes], and because of its location, might one day be the starting point for the conquest of the rest of America.

It would take time before a colony founded west of the Great Lakes would be sufficiently developed to serve as a base of operations against "the rest of America," whereas if the plan of the author is adopted, the conquest of Theguayo would

---

16 C. F. Duro, *Don Diego de Peñalosa y su descubrimiento del reino de Quivira* (Madrid, 1882) ; W. E. Dunn, *Spanish and French Rivalry in the Gulf Region of the United States, 1678–1702* (Austin, Tex., 1917), 13 ff.
17 *Some La Salle Journeys*, 65 ff.
18 Bernou's autograph in BN, Clairambault, 1016: 211–219.
19 "The Discovery of the Mississippi. Secondary Sources," *loc. cit.*, 13–21.

be a matter of two or three years at the most. One of the objections that might be raised against this "plan" is that many men would be needed to carry out the undertaking. This objection is disposed of by saying that a small force is sufficient, because the Indians of these parts are kind and sociable. "Father Marquette and Sieur Jolliet have recently experienced this, they traveled over vast countries through unknown nations to a point near the Gulf of Mexico, without being molested."

Another obstacle is the distance from New France to Theguayo and the difficulties of the route. The main difficulty, we are told, is between Montreal and Fort Frontenac, on account of the rapids of the St. Lawrence, but beyond this point, once one has reached the entrance of Lake Ontario

one can go to the end of Lake Superior, or to the Gulf of Mexico and to the Northwest by way of the great river and those which come from the west and empty into it. These rivers come from so far away that no one knows where their headwaters are; in fact, the author is persuaded that one of them arises in Theguayo itself. But even if some overland journey were necessary, he knows that it will not be very long, and that not far beyond the Great Lakes will be found the horses and the mules with which the Spaniards have stocked all the western countries. Father Marquette and Sieur Jolliet have known of these horses and mules, although vaguely, because in the course of their voyage, they traveled through the middle of the country lying south of the Great Lakes.

After answering several other objections against the "plan" which have no bearing on the voyage of 1673, the memorialist proceeds to recount the advantages to be derived from the conquest of Theguayo.

The sixth [advantage] would be the discovery of the Sea of the South or of the West, if one wishes to call it thus, which forms the boundary of the kingdom of Theguayo and which would supply an easy route for the much talked about trade with China and Japan, a route which all the nations of Europe have [thus far] unsuccessfully tried to find.

Bernou had doubts whether the royal approval and support of the Theguayo expedition would be forthcoming in spite of the dazzling advantages he had so eloquently set forth. The sequel proved that his misgivings were well founded. The memorial was examined by some ignorant government official;

his verdict, couched in the form of "observations," was unfavorable.[20]

According to the memorial, the idea of reaching Theguayo
via New France arose in the mind of Peñalosa when he heard
of western discoveries made by the French. In the third of his
"observations," the critic flatly denied that any such discoveries
had been made, and asserts that all those who went into the
interior had nothing else in view except fur trading. "Sieur
Jolliet alone was led by curiosity [in contradistinction to trade]
to travel to the southeast. All we know about the West is
that ice and rocks are found there."

Bernou countered the last statement by appealing to the
description of the Fox River Valley in the Relation of 1670–
1671,[21] and answered the first statement by saying that "Sieur
Jolliet is not the only one who traveled through curiosity to the
southeast. M. de la Salle, governor of Fort Frontenac, reached
the Mississippi River and discovered the Ohio which empties
into the former. M. de Galinée went to the end of Lake
Erie."[22]

In his next "observation" the critic undertakes to defend
Canada, which the memorialist had disparaged. In his answer
to this "observation," Bernou readily admitted that Acadia and
"the country south of the Great Lakes" had everything that is
found in Canada and even more; "no other proof for this is
needed than the relation of Sieur Jolliet which shows the dif-

---

[20] The original document containing these "observations" has
not come to us. All that we have is a manuscript among the Delisle
papers which gives the remarks of the critic, eleven in all, and the
answers of Bernou: "Response aux observations ftes sur le memoire
touchant ladecouverte des Royes de Quivira et de Theguayo par le
Comte de Pennalossa 1684." ASH, 115–9: no. 11. Who dated this
memorial and the answers is not known; a passage in one of Bernou's
answers establishes that they were written in 1677.—On the Delisle
papers, see "The Sources of the Delisle Map of America, 1703," MA,
25 (1943) ; 277 f.
[21] JR, 55: 190 ff.
[22] La Salle did not "discover" the Ohio; he never descended it;
he saw the mouth of this river for the first time in February 1682.
Cf. *Some La Salle Journeys*, 20 ff; "The Jolliet Lost Map of the Mississippi," *loc. cit.*, 90.—In 1669–1670, MM. Dollier and Galinée went
much farther than "the end of Lake Erie." They ascended the Detroit River, Lake St. Clair, the River St. Clair, whence they followed
the shore of Lake Huron to Sault Ste Marie.

ference" between these two sections of the North American continent.

We have already quoted the passage of the memorial in which mention is made of the fertility of the country beyond the Great Lakes and of the means of communication between these lakes and the Gulf of Mexico *via* the "beautiful river recently discovered." On this paragraph of the memorial the critic comments as follows:

Sieur Jolliet did not find any means of communication between the lakes and that great river; he believes that the river itself, instead of emptying into the Gulf of Mexico, disembogues into the Vermilion Sea, beyond California. He went down this river, and heard about Spaniards from a nation in the vicinity who trade with them.

As can be seen the critic says exactly the opposite of what Jolliet wrote; and one can understand Bernou's surprise on reading this "observation." He said:

Sieur Jolliet found not one but two means of communication between the Great Lakes and the Mississippi River. The first by way of a river [the Fox] which empties into Green Bay; for from this river, after a portage of half a league, they entered into another river [the Wisconsin] which led them to the Mississippi. The second means of communication is by way of the St. Louis River, which has since been called *La diuine;* it flows so near Lake Michigan that if one cuts [digs a canal] through half a league of prairie, it is possible to go by bark from Lake Erie to the Gulf of Mexico.

This shows that when answering his critic, Bernou had a copy of Dablon's letter of August 1, 1674, which gives the length of the portage between the Fox and the Wisconsin rivers, the length of the Chicago portage, and Jolliet's original name (Rivière St. Louis) for the Illinois-Des Plaines.

The third paragraph of Bernou's answer to the same "observation" reads thus:

This [double communication between the Lakes and the Mississippi] is absolutely certain; we can prove it (on le prouuera) by two relations and two different maps of the voyage of Sieur Jolliet, which are in the hands of the author [*i.e.,* Bernou]. Further proof has been given by the voyage of the aforesaid Sieur de la Salle, who has, moreover, found a third route through the Ohio River which flows near Lake Erie and Lake Michigan. The author knows that a map showing this [feature] was given to M. Colbert a few months ago, and also that there is a fourth map in Paris, which, however, is not so accurate, although all these maps agree with one another in general.

One of the two maps which Bernou had in his possession was very probably a copy of Jolliet's original map, and the other was certainly a copy of Franquelin's map, for we know that he himself redrew this latter map on a smaller scale and later gave it to Delisle. From his description of the third map which, he says, was given to Cobert a few months previously, we conclude that it was very likely an earlier state of the map known today as "Parkman No. 3."[23] The fourth map which was then in Paris cannot be identified, since Bernou does not give sufficient data about it. As for Bernou's two relations of the voyage of 1673, one was certainly a copy of Dablon's letter of August 1, 1674; and the other may possibly be the already mentioned lost account of the discovery of the Mississippi.

The eighth "observation" is the last one in which there is a reference to the voyage of 1673. The critic begins by saying: "Neither Father Marquette nor Sieur Jolliet saw a single horse or mule," and elaborated on this statement in his second last paragraph: "Sieur Jolliet during his voyage saw a great number of domesticated and wild animals, but he did not see even one horse; although, as his account proves beyond question, he visited tribes who trade with the Spaniards."

This last statement shows that the critic had seen Jolliet's dedicatory letter to Frontenac, for this is the only source that mentions Jolliet's passing through a village which had been visited by Indians who traded with those of California, and so, indirectly with the Spaniards. The proof referred to is a present of four hatchets which had been brought by the visiting Indians.

Bernou answered this "observation" as follows: "On one of the two maps a place is marked to indicate the presence of horses. The relations also speak of them although in a vague manner, because the explorers, who made the journey by water, only heard of horses through the Indians."

When Bernou wrote that the relations (and he had two, as we saw) vaguely refer to horses, he was very likely thinking of Dablon's letter of August 1, 1674, which says in part: "There [in the Illinois country in particular] a settler would

---

[23] Described in *La Salle and the Discovery of the Great West*, 450 f.

not have to spend ten years cutting down and burning trees. On the very day of his arrival, he could begin plowing; and if he had no oxen from France, he could use those of this country, or even the animals which the western Indians ride as we ride horses."[24] Unless, of course, as in another answer to an "observation," Bernou is taking advantage of the ignorance of his critic.

We have seen that when he wrote these answers, Bernou had in his possession copies of the two maps of the voyage of 1673, and we know that one of these was a copy of Franquelin's map on which, as can be seen today, there is no legend indicating horses. Hence this legend must have been on the other map. Of the various maps illustrating the voyage of 1673 which have come down to us, the only one which indicates the presence of horses is the Manitoumie. On this map a legend inscribed west of the Mississippi at latitude 36° reads thus: "Nations qui ont des cheuaux et des chameaux." We discussed elsewhere the reasons why we are not certain whether "the other map" is an earlier state of the Manitoumie.[25]

3) The "Recit des Voyages et des Decouvertes du Pere Jacques Marquette"

Most of the information contained in this document is derived from the primary sources and the cartographical evidence listed in the two preceding chapters; but in addition the author of this account of the voyage of 1673 embodied in the narrative information which he learned from Jolliet or from some other members of the expedition.

Until 1927, Father Marquette was unanimously believed to be the author of the Récit. In that year, however, Father Francis Borgia Steck questioned its authenticity in the sixth chapter of his doctoral dissertation and reached the conclusion that Marquette was not the author of the Récit as we have it today.

Besides this conclusion, he formulated the following hypothesis: "In its present form [the Récit] is in substance Jol-

---

[24] "The 1674 Account of the Discovery of the Mississippi," loc. cit., 323 ff.

[25] "The Jolliet Lost Map of the Mississippi," loc. cit., 107 f.

liet's journal recast and amplified by Dablon with the aid of other sources which he had at his disposal."[26]

Father Steck's conclusion is certain, but the hypothesis for which he claims great probability is most improbable and thoroughly unacceptable.

The above mentioned sixth chapter of Father Steck's doctoral dissertation has been the object of much ill-advised criticism. One of his critics arbitrarily rejected arguments from external evidence as unconvincing and maintained that "the internal evidence quoted by Father Steck is even less conclusive"[27] than external evidenc. There is some ground for the latter contention. Why such weak arguments should have been advanced is difficult to understand, considering that textual analysis furnishes conclusive proof that Marquette did not write the Récit. It will suffice to outline this proof which was developed at length in two articles.[28]

On October 25, 1678, Father Dablon, then superior of the Jesuit missions in New France, sent a letter to Father Claude Boucher, the French assistant to the general of the Jesuits in Rome. In this letter he says that he is sending to Father Ragueneau in Paris a "little work" in which Dablon had embodied "all the memoirs of the discoveries of the late Father Marquette after setting them in order," and in which he had inserted "all the rarities and curiosities" of the voyage of 1673.[29] In the same little work there is also an account, added by Dablon, of the establishment of the Illinois mission. From the title and from the opening words of the Relation of 1677–1678, we know that this "little work" is the "Récit des voyages et des découvertes du Père Jacques Marquette."[30]

26 Steck, *The Jolliet–Marquette Expedition*, 310.
27 A. Repplier, *Père Marquette* (Garden City, N. Y., 1929), 260.
28 "The 'Récit des voyages ...'," MA, 28 (1946): 173–194, 211–258.
29 Dablon to Boucher, October 25, 1678, Jesuit Archives, Rome, *Gallia*, 110, I fo. 62v.
30 "Pour Relation de Lannée 1678 ‖ Recit des voyages et des Descouuertes du Pere Jacque Marquette ‖ de la Compagnie de Jesus en l'année 1673 et autres suiuantes ‖ Au R. P. Pierre de Verthamont Prouincial de la Compa ‖ gnie en la Prouince de france
Mon Reuerend Pere
Pax christi
Auant que de commencer ce recit je prie vostre Reuerence ..."—
Archives of the Province of France, Fonds Brotier 159, Canada–5,

Several copies of this Relation were made in Quebec and at least one was made in Paris. But of these copies only one is complete, namely Canada–5, an in–8o manuscript of 68 pages numbered 1 to 67 on the verso of each page.[31] The whole manuscript is in the same handwriting which is not that of Marquette, Dablon or Ragueneau, but probably that of a Jesuit lay-brother in Paris.

Canada–5 may be conveniently divided into four parts, A, B, C, D. The first part, A, includes pages 1–[22] and treats of all missions of Canada. Pages 23–[24] are blank. From pages 25–[52] is found the Récit with its preamble. This part, B, of Canada–5, which bears a separate title,[32] is ordinarily referred to as Marquette–5. Pages [52]–61, part C, contain the narrative of Marquette's second voyage to the Illinois country and an account of his death. Pages 61–67, part D, contain a narrative of a "third voyage to the Illinois country" which consists of the copy of a letter of Father Allouez with a few lines of introduction by Father Dablon. The three parts B, C, D, are of very unequal length and are divided respectively into ten, three and two sections.

Besides Canada–5, there are four fragments of the Relation of 1677–1678 which are bound together in one volume, Fonds Brotier 158, of 148 pages in–8o, and is designated as Canada–4.

The first fragment comprises the whole of A and the first

---

1. Compare this title with that in the *Relations inédites*, 2: 195, and in JR, 61: 18.

[31] The reason why this complete copy is called Canada–5 is as follows. In the Archives of the Province of France this document is one of the volumes of the Fonds Brotier, a collection named after Father Gabriel Brotier, the last librarian of the Collège Louis-le-Grand. At the time of the suppression of the Society of Jesus in France in 1762, Father Brotier saved what manuscripts he could from the pillagers who descended en masse on the Jesuit libraries in that country. After the restoration of the Society, these manuscripts were first housed in the École Sainte–Geneviève, and were sent to Canterbury, England, in 1901, to save them from further damage. In the meantime, the various bundles of manuscripts had been bound into volumes, each of which was given a number. The whole collection comprises 199 volumes. Twenty-two of these volumes contain documents concerning North America; these are numbered 155 to 176 in the collection, but they are also numbered Canada 1 to 22. Thus Canada–5 is volume 159 of the Fonds Brotier.

[32] Recit ‖ Des voyages et des Descouuertes du Pere ‖ Jacques Marquette de la Compagnie de Jesus ‖ en 1673 et autres. ‖

seven pages of B down to the middle of page 31 of Canada–5. This is the same as sections 1 and 2 of Marquette–5, and half of section 3.

The second fragment of Canada–4 begins with the last six lines of the music score of the Illinois song, that is, with the end of section 6 (pages [42]–43) of Marquette–5 and covers the rest of the Relation of 1677–1678, namely, the remainder of B, the whole of C and D. The handwriting of this second fragment is not the same as that of the first and differs from the handwriting of Marquette–5.

The third fragment contains the first sixteen pages of A, down to the end of the relation of the Lorette mission. The handwriting resembles that of the second fragment.

The fourth fragment covers the beginning and the end of D, that is, the narrative of Allouez' voyage to the Illinois country. The handwriting resembles that of the first fragment.

As can be seen, the contents of Canada–4 are very disparate; these four fragments of the Relation of 1677–1678 were bound together in the middle of the nineteenth century by someone who evidently had not read them..

There is another copy of B, C, and D, in the archives of the Collège Sainte-Marie, Montreal. This manuscript as it exists today is mutilated:—two of the original leaves are lost and their place is taken by pages from the Thévenot printed version.

The existence of these various copies of the Relation of 1677–1678 and the differences between them can be accounted for as follows. When the copy or copies of Dablon's original relation reached Paris at the beginning of 1679, Ragueneau had another copy made which he sent to Rome.[33] This is Canada–5, which contains Marquette–5. Father de Montézon, Rochemonteix and others call it the Roman manuscript, because it was in Rome until the middle of the nineteenth century when it was brought to Paris. The four fragments of Canada–4 are evidence that there was more than one copy in Paris in 1679; and

---

[33] "I am sending this little work to Father Ragueneau, who will show it to your Reverence." Dablon to Boucher, October 25, 1678, Jesuit Archives, Rome, *Gallia*, 110, I, f. 62v.

Thévenot's published version of the Récit must have been based ultimately on one of these Paris copies.[34]

Thévenot's published version of the "Récit des voyages et des découvertes . . ." (that is, of part B), has been severely criticized since Shea's publication of the Montreal manuscript. Such criticism is unjustified, since for all that pertains to the voyage, Thévenot's text is not essentially different from the manuscript published by Shea in 1852.[35] This was re-issued by De Montézon in 1861,[36] and by Thwaites in his edition of the *Jesuit Relations*.[37] Father Hamy published Marquette–5 in 1903.[38]

As is to be expected, there are numerous variants in the different manuscript copies of the Récit, but these variants do not affect the substance of the contents. The copies sent to France were made in Quebec on Dablon's original, and Canada–5, the only complete extant copy of the Relation of 1677-1678, was made on one of these copies.

Since there is no doubt that Dablon wrote the Relation of 1677–1678, of which the Récit is an integral part, our main problem is to ascertain what material he had at hand for composing the Récit in 1678.

First, he certainly had his own letter of August 1, 1674, for in the Récit there are passages taken word for word from this letter. It is incredible that Dablon should use the same terms after a four year interval, or that these passages should have been identically expressed by Marquette in his journal written during the Mississippi voyage of 1673.[39]

Secondly, Dablon had a copy of Jolliet's map as well as a copy of Jolliet's dedicatory letter to Frontenac which today is inscribed on a copy of this map.[40] Furthermore, it is not only probable but quite certain that Dablon had further talks with Jolliet between August 1674 and the autumn of 1678 when the Récit was composed. Both were living in the same small

---

[34] M. Thévenot, ed., *Recueil de voyages de Mr Thevenot*, 1–43.
[35] *Discovery and Exploration of the Mississippi Valley*, 231–257.
[36] *Relations inédites*, 2: 241–289.
[37] JR, 59: 86–162.
[38] A. Hamy, *Au Mississipi* (Paris, 1903), 224–255.
[39] Cf. "The 'Récit des voyages . . .'," *loc. cit.*, 233, 239, 250–252.
[40] *Ibid.*, 230, 235, 245, 250.

town,[41] and there is not the slightest evidence to support Father
Steck's contention[42] that Jolliet did not remain friendly with
the Jesuits after his return from his voyage of discovery or
after 1682, when Thévenot's *Recueil* may have reached Canada.[43]   And Dablon certainly questioned Jacques Largilier who
had taken part in the expedition and who after his return to
Quebec in 1675, became a Jesuit *donné*[44] and was again in
Quebec in 1676.[45]   It is probable that Dablon also interviewed
Thiberge and Plattier, two other members of the expedition,
who returned to Quebec in 1674,[46] but we have no evidence
that he did so.

Thirdly, Dablon had Marquette's map,[47] and from Dablon's autograph note on the fly leaf of Marquette's journal of
his second voyage to the Illinois country, we know that he also
had this journal.[48]

Finally, if Dablon did not have at his disposal in Quebec
a complete set of the *Jesuit Relations,* he certainly had those
which had been published since his arrival in Canada in 1655,
in particular those which he himself had edited and the manuscript of those written since the publication of the Relations
had been suspended.[49]

We have shown in detail that there was no essential fact
concerning the voyage of 1673 in the Récit that could not be
traced to these written or oral sources, and in the case of one
important point we have been able to test the trustworthiness

[41] In 1681, the population of Quebec was 1,345 persons. Sulte,
Histoire des Canadiens–Français, 5: 88.

[42] *The Jolliet–Marquette Expedition,* 237.

[43] In 1679, Father Silvy went with Jolliet as far as Nemiskau,
and Father André spent the summer with Jolliet on Anticosti Island.
—Registre des baptêmes, mariages et sépultures des Sauvages du
Lac St. Jean, Chicoutimi, et Taduussac de 1669 à 1692. Archives of
the Séminaire of Quebec (Laval University), 54v, 61v.

[44] The year when Largilier became a *donné* is deduced from the
following notarial acts in the Archives Judiciaries, Quebec: 1) July
31, 1675, Greffe Becquet, minute; 2) August 16, 1675, Greffe Becquet,
cahier 23; 3) October 20, 1675, Greffe Rageot, no. 1357; also from
the letter of Father Cholenec to Father de Fontenay, October 10,
1675, in Rochemonteix, *Les Jésuites et la Nouvelle–France au XVII*e
siècle, 3: 607.

[45] JR, 60: 128.

[46] *Jugements et délibérations du Conseil Souverain,* 1: 864.

[47] "The Jolliet Lost Map of the Mississippi," *loc. cit.,* 103, 105.

[48] JR, 59: 182.

[49] "The 'Récit des voyages ...'," *loc. cit.,* 227, 228, 234, 237.

of the oral testimony given to Dablon by his informants.[50]
Our analysis of the Récit indirectly showed that the document
is not Marquette's journal, that it is not based on Marquette's
notes edited by Dablon, and that the latter had no need of a
Jolliet journal as a source of information.

It may be objected that the parts of the Récit for which
we have no written sources may have been taken by Dablon
from Marquette's journal of his first voyage. If this were true,
Dablon would not have written to Boucher that he had "gathered all the writings of the late Father Marquette to the best
of his ability."[51] Instead, he would have mentioned Marquette's journal. His failure to mention Marquette's journal
of the second voyage does not at all indicate that he would
have failed to mention the journal of the first if he had possessed it.

We know that his interest in the geography of North
America led him to collect all possible data which would make
the continent better known. We also know that he directed
his subordinates to compute latitudes whenever they could do
so. That latitudes were computed during the voyage of 1673
is certain. We know this from the fact that in July 1674,
Jolliet told Dablon the position of the mouth of the Wisconsin,
that of the mouth of the Missouri, and the latitude of the terminus of the expedition.[52] We also know that they computed
latitudes from Marquette's letter of August 4, 1673;[53] and
from Gravier's journal of his descent of the Mississippi in 1700,
we know that two other latitudes were entered in Marquette's
journal of the voyage of 1673:—the latitude of the mouth of
the Ohio and that of the terminus of the expedition.[54] These
two latitudes are at variance with those given in the Récit because Dablon took them not from Marquette's journal but from
Marquette's map. Now it is unbelievable that he should have
relied on the map for this information, if he had in his pos-

50 *Ibid.*, 251.
51 Dablon to Boucher, October 25, 1678, Jesuit Archives, Rome,
Gallia, I, 110, fo. 62v.
52 "The 1674 Account of the Discovery of the Mississippi," *loc.
cit.*, 317, 318, 319.
53 C. W. Alvord, "An Unrecognized Father Marquette Letter,"
The American Historical Review, 25 (1919–1920): 678.
54 JR, 65: 106, 116.

session Marquette's journal in which the exact latitudes were entered.

The chief reason why many have believed Marquette to be the author of the Récit is because the document is written in the first person singular. They failed to see that the use of this pronoun is a literary device employed by Dablon, the real author of the Récit. Because his concept of history did not differ from that of his contemporaries, Dablon made use of the written and oral documentation at his disposal and composed the Récit according to the canons of history-writing prevalent in his day. His honesty is no more involved[55] than is the honesty of Livy or Tacitus for putting speeches in the mouth of the characters of their histories. If anything, Dablon's honesty is even less involved than that of the two Latin historians, for, whereas in many cases it is doubtful whether any speech at all was made, it is certain that Marquette went down the Mississippi, that he saw, and heard and experienced all that Dablon narrates about the voyage.

The fact that Marquette has been regarded as the author of the Récit for 250 years does not make him its author. The acceptance of authorship by historians does not affect the fact itself. Otherwise an erroneous ascription would become true merely because historians have for centuries believed it to be true. Furthermore, this unanimous consent is much less impressive than is generally thought; for among the numerous writers who have made use of the document not one has taken the trouble to investigate its authenticity. Previous to the publication of Father Steck's dissertation, everyone took for granted that Marquette wrote it. Some went so far as to call it the "journal" of the expedition, and others, going farther still, have called the Montreal manuscript Marquette's *autograph*.

The style of the narrative as an argument against Marquette's authorship must also be considered. Dablon's style is very distinctive: his use of words, his expressions, and even his sentence structure are so individualistic that one can recognize his contributions in the earlier Relations, even though these contributions have been "edited" or "revised" by the editor of

---

[55] Repplier, *Père Marquette*, 264.

the Relations in Quebec or in Paris. Because of its importance in this connection we must insist on the following statement: the Récit is an integral part of the 1677–1678 Relation. No one has ever doubted that those parts of this Relation which are not transcriptions of letters from missionaries in the field, were written by Dablon. In particular, no one denies that Dablon wrote the chapter describing Marquette's second voyage to the Illinois country and his death on the return journey. The same characteristics of style are so obviously present in the Récit of the voyage of 1673 and in the Relation's narrative of the second voyage to the Illinois country that, if some student ignorant of the question of authorship were given both documents, he would, I confidently believe, recognize that they were written by the same man.

CHAPTER VI

THE VOYAGE OF 1673

The present chapter contains an account of the voyage of 1673 based on the evidence previously analyzed. Anyone comparing the present account of the discovery of the Mississippi with Dablon's Récit will see that the two narratives do not substantially differ, because both are based on the same documentation. In quite a few particulars, we can correct Dablon's narrative or add to it, because we now have a better knowledge of the route followed by the explorers.

1) Preliminaries

In the summer of 1672, Talon officially commissioned Jolliet to search for a water route to the Sea of the South and for "the great river which [the Indians] call Michissipi, and which, it is believed, discharges itself into the Sea of California."[1]

There is no evidence whatever from which we can learn the reasons for Talon's choice. We only know that six years previously, the intendant "presented very good arguments" in a philosophy disputation in which Jolliet was one of the defendants. The following considerations show that Gagnon had no reason for saying that the intendant "never lost sight" of Louis Jolliet between 1666 and 1672.[2] The latter went to France in the autumn of 1667 and returned to Canada in the summer of the following year, that is, at the time when Talon himself was about to leave for France. The intendant arrived at Quebec to begin his second term on August 18, 1670, when Jolliet was about to leave or had already left for the West, whence he did not return until September 1671.

We simply do not know why Jolliet was selected to lead

---

[1] The opening words of the passage in Frontenac's letter to Colbert, November 2, 1672 (AC, C 11A, 3: 243v), read as follows: "Il [Talon] a aussi jugé expedient ... d'envoyer le Sr Joliet ..." This sentence is inaccurately transcribed in RAPQ, 1927, 18, "Il a aussi été jugé expedient ... d'envoyer le Sr Joliet ..."

[2] Gagnon, Louis Jolliet, 63.

the expedition of 1673, any more than we know why Talon
chose Paul Denis, Sieur de Saint-Simon,[3] to lead the expedition
sent two years earlier to ascertain whether the Sea of the North
was "the bay to which Henry Hudson gave his name."[4] Perhaps the discerning eye of the intendant had recognized, as
Dablon wrote in the Récit, that Jolliet "possessed all the necessary qualifications for such an undertaking."[5]

Nor do we know when Dablon learned that Jolliet was
being sent to search for a route to the Sea of the South; but
from Marquette's letter of *post* March 25, 1673,[6] we learn that
Dablon had ordered the missionary to accompany Jolliet:
"Meanwhile I am preparing to leave it [the mission at St. Ig-
nace] in the hands of another missionary to go according to the
order of your Reverence and seek toward the Sea of the South
new nations that are unknown to us, to teach them to know our
great God, of whom they have hitherto been ignorant."[7] From
Marquette's letter to Father Le Mercier, which had been inserted in the Relation of 1669–1670, Dablon knew that Marquette fully intended to visit the Illinois on the Mississippi in
the autumn of 1670 and to descend the river as far as he could.[8]
But, as we have seen, this voyage did not take place owing to
the hostility of the Sioux.[9]

Since Lorin published his doctoral dissertation fifty years
ago, it has been the fashion to elaborate a theory according to
which the Jesuits did everything in their power to keep from

---

3 Talon to Louis XIV, November 2, 1671, RAPQ, 1931, 158.
4 JR, 56: 148; 54: 134.
5 JR, 59: 88; cf. "The 1674 Account of the Discovery of the Mississippi," MA, 26 (1944): 317.—After saying that Talon had judged
expedient to send Jolliet, Frontenac goes on to say: "C'est un homme
fort entendu dans ces sortes de découvertes et qui a déjà été jusques
auprès de cette grande rivière de laquelle il promet de voir l'embouchure." Frontenac to Colbert, November 2, 1672, RAPQ, 1927, 18.
In 1671, Jolliet's nearest approach of the Mississippi was 375 miles
away in a straight line; and the distance from Sault Ste Marie to
the Mississippi along the route which he followed in 1673, is more
than 550 miles.
6 For the date of this letter, see "The 'Récit des voyages et des
découvertes du Père Jacques Marquette'," MA, 28 (1946): 220, note
26.
7 JR, 57: 262.
8 JR, 54: 184, 186, 188. See how Dablon made use of this letter
to write the opening paragraph of the Récit, JR, 59: 86; and cf.,
"The 'Récit des voyages ...'," *loc. cit.*, 212.
9 *Supra*, p. 27.

Frontenac the fact that a Jesuit had accompanied Jolliet, for if he had known it, the governor would certainly have blamed them.[10]

In his letter transmitting the Relation of 1671–1672, after mentioning Albanel's journey to Hudson Bay, Dablon goes on to say:

We expect no less result from the expedition which M. the Count de Frontenac and M. Talon, in deference to the wishes of His Majesty, have sent for the discovery of the Sea of the South, which will probably give us access to the great China and Japan seas. *The Father* and the Frenchmen who are being sent on that hazardous expedition have need of much courage and prudence in their quest of unknown seas over an entirely new route of three or four hundred leagues and through nations which have never seen any European.[11]

This letter, written in November 1672, was printed in the first months of 1673, and the Relation in which it appears may have reached Quebec by the autumn of this year or at the latest early in the summer of 1674. Frontenac may not have read the whole Relation, but he certainly read Dablon's letter in which his own name appears in the second and fourth paragraphs, and the latter contains the reference to *the Father* and the Frenchmen sent to search for a route to the Sea of the South. When Dablon wrote this letter, he knew that it would come back in print to Canada, and that Frontenac would see it. This is certainly not doing everything in one's power to keep from Frontenac the knowledge that a Jesuit accompanied Jolliet. Moreover, we have shown that by the autumn of 1674 Frontenac not only knew that a Jesuit had taken part in the discovery of the Mississippi, but that he also knew his name.[12]

We can be quite sure that if Frontenac had been opposed to a Jesuit's going with Jolliet, he would have protested in his letter to Colbert when he heard of it. Finally, since Frontenac failed to realize the importance of the discovery of the Mississippi and the route to the Gulf,[13] it is hardly to be expected that he would have blamed the Jesuits or shown resentment

---

[10] H. Lorin, *Le Comte de Frontenac* (Paris, 1895), 74, 77, 95.
[11] JR, 56: 234.
[12] "The 1674 Account," *loc. cit.*, 312–314.
[13] "The Discovery of the Mississippi. Primary Sources," MA, 27 (1945): 220 f.

toward Jolliet,[14] because Marquette had taken part in the expedition.

We have already called attention to the fact that although the expedition of 1673 was officially sponsored, it was not subsidized by the government, and that the expenses would be defrayed by trade profits.[15]   As was the custom, Jolliet entered into partnership with other Canadians, pooling their resources and determining beforehand the share of each in the profits.   The contract was duly legalized on October 1, 1672, on which day

Before Giles Rageot, notary ... were present Sieur Louis Jolliet, François Chavigny, escuyer, Sieur de la Chevrotière, Zacharie Jolliet, Jean Plattier, Pierre Moreau, Jacques Largilier, Jean Tiberge, all now in this town, who of their own free will have entered into partnership and society to make together the voyage to the Ottawa country, [there to] trade with the Indians as profitably as possible.[16]

Although the contract says that they will leave on October 2, we know from another notarial act determining the respective shares of three of the partners that they were still in Quebec on October 3.[17]

Referring to the act of October 1, 1672, M. P.-G. Roy asks whether Jolliet's partners are not the men who took part in the discovery of the Mississippi.[18]   By itself, the fact that they were Jolliet's associates does not mean that they went to the Mississippi with him.   For instance, we are certain that Chavigny was not one of them, for he was with Frontenac at Catarocouy in July 1673,[19] that is, at the time when Jolliet and his companions were traveling on the Mississippi.

Jolliet himself told Dablon that he and Marquette set out "with five other Frenchmen";[20] and in the Récit, Dablon added

---

[14] Steck, *The Jolliet–Marquette Expedition*, 237.

[15] *Supra*, p. 18.

[16] AJQ, Greffe Rageot, no. 939.

[17] *Ibid.*, no. 943.

[18] P.-G. Roy, *Toutes petites choses de notre histoire* (Quebec, 1944), 201.

[19] "Journal of Count de Frontenac's Voyage to Lake Ontario in 1673," NYCD, 9: 113.

[20] "The 1674 Account," *loc. cit.*, 317.—On the omission of Marquette's name in the "Relation de la Nouvelle France 1673" (*Supra*, p. 82), see "The Discovery of the Mississippi. Secondary Sources," MA, 28 (1946): 6.

"in two canoes."[21]   Of these seven men we know the names
of two: Jolliet and Marquette; and it is practically certain that
Largilier was a member of the expedition.   We say "practically
certain" because his name is not specified in Father Cholenec's
letter of October 10, 1675.   After speaking with the two men
who had assisted Marquette in his last moments, Cholenec goes
on to say: "The Reverend Father Superior of the Ottawa missions . . . sent him [Marquette] two of our servants [Jacques
Largilier and Pierre Porteret], one of whom had made the
journey [down the Mississippi] with him."[22]   That this man
was Largilier and not Porteret is deduced from the fact that
he had been hired by Jolliet in Quebec.

In virtue of the contract of October 1, 1672, Jolliet had full
control over Moreau, Plattier and Thiberge. Since it seems quite
improbable that he hired three new hands at Sault Ste Marie
or at Michilimackinac before setting out for the journey, we
can be reasonably sure of the names of six of the seven men
who took part in the discovery of the Mississippi.

In the contract of October 1, 1672, the name of Louis'
brother, Zacharie Jolliet, also occurs; but there is reason to
think that he was not the seventh member of the expedition of
1673.   Although Jolliet is very reticent when it comes to giving
the names of those who accompanied him in his journeys, yet
he would hardly pass over, it seems, the fact that his brother
had taken part in the discovery of the Mississippi.   Moreover,
when Jolliet set out to find the great river, it is unlikely that he
would have left unguarded the pelts which had been gathered
during the winter of 1672–1673 as well as those which had
been left at Sault Ste Marie in 1671.[23]   It must have occurred
to him that it would be safer to leave his forge, the merchandise
brought to the West and the pelts in the keeping of his brother,
who had invested money in the enterprise, than to leave a comparative stranger in charge while he went in search of the
Mississippi.

To sum up, we are certain of the identity of two of the

---

21 JR, 59: 90.
22 Rochemonteix, *Les Jésuites et la Nouvelle–France au XVII*e
siècle, 3: 607.
23 See "Louis Jolliet. Early Years," MA, 27 (1945): 26 f, Appendix B.

seven men who took part in the expedition of 1673: Louis Jolliet and Jacques Marquette; we are practically certain that Jacques Largilier was one of them; and we have good probability with regard to the identity of three more: Pierre Moreau, Jean Plattier, and Jean Thiberge. As for the unknown seventh, he may have been one of the two men who were drowned in the rapids above Montreal while returning with Jolliet in 1674.[24]

We saw that Jolliet was selected by Talon to make the voyage of discovery; Dablon, however, states that the choice was made by Frontenac and Talon,[25] and in his dedicatory letter to Frontenac, Jolliet says that he undertook the voyage conformably to the "first orders which you gave me when entering on your administration of New France."[26]

These statements are not contradictory. As is clear from Frontenac's letter, Talon had chosen Jolliet for the expedition before the arrival of the governor at Quebec on September 7 or 8, 1672;[27] but it belonged to the governor to ratify this choice. After saying that Talon had judged expedient for the service to send Jolliet to search for the Sea of the South, and after mentioning that other canoes have been sent to investigate the copper mine of Lake Superior,[28] Frontenac says in conclusion: "In this as well as in all that regards the affairs of this country, I followed the advice of M. Talon and acted on the information which he gave me."[29] Again, in his letter notifying Colbert of Jolliet's return from the Mississippi, Frontenac says: "When I arrived here from France, I was advised by M.

---

24 Jolliet to Laval, October 10, 1674, in Harrisse, *Notes pour servir*, 322.

25 In "The 1674 Account," *loc. cit.*, 317, and in the Récit, JR, 59: 86.

26 "The Discovery of the Mississippi. Secondary Sources," *loc. cit.*, 227.

27 On November 2, 1672, Frontenac wrote to Colbert (RAPQ, 1927, 10) that he arrived at Quebec on the seventy-first day after leaving La Rochelle; he left this port on July 1 or July 2 (Colbert de Terron to Colbert, June 30, 1672, BN, Mélanges de Colbert, 106: 606). The king's letters appointing Frontenac governor of New France were engrossed in the registers of the Sovereign Council on September 12. *Jugements et délibérations du Conseil Souverain*, 1: 689.

28 Cf. JR, 55: 236.

29 Frontenac to Colbert, November 2, 1672, RAPQ, 1927, 18.

Talon to send Sieur Jolliet to discover the Sea of the South."[30] The fact that by the latter part of 1674, Talon had been out of Canada for nearly two years seems to explain why Jolliet makes no mention of the intendant in his dedicatory letter to Frontenac.

The primary objective of the expedition was not the discovery of the Mississippi, but "above all to find out in what sea it emptied itself."[31] Although the Gulf of Mexico is an alternative when they speculate as to where the great river had its mouth, it was hoped that it emptied into the Gulf of California. In 1670, St. Lusson's secondary objective was to find some means of communication between the St. Lawrence and the Sea of the South; and in the following year, Talon expressed the belief that from Sault Ste Marie there were no more than 300 leagues to the shores of the Vermilion or South Sea; and we have just seen that he sent Jolliet to discover the Sea of the South by way of the great river, "which, it is believed, empties into the Sea of California."

In spite of Jolliet's conviction that the Mississippi emptied into the Gulf of Mexico, he nevertheless wrote to Laval that "not long ago he had returned from his voyage to the Sea of the South,"[32] and Dablon entitled the account of the voyage of 1673: "Relation of the discovery of the Sea of the South." It is clear from this account that the fact that the Mississippi emptied into the Gulf of Mexico was disappointing.[33] As a consolation, Dablon hoped that a direct water route to the Pacific, "which is what we are looking for," might be found by way of one of the western tributaries of the Mississippi.[34]

We do not know the exact date of Jolliet's departure from Quebec, but we know that he was still there on October 3, 1672. As the season was already far advanced, we may presume that he and his companions left shortly after this date. Nor do we know which route they took, although it seems probable

---

[30] Frontenac to Colbert, November 14, 1674, *ibid.*, 76.
[31] "The 1674 Account," *loc. cit.*, 317.
[32] Harrisse, *Notes pour servir*, 322.
[33] "The 1674 Account," *loc. cit.*, 321.
[34] See also Frontenac's letter to Colbert, November 14, 1674, RAPQ, 1927, 76, and Jolliet's dedicatory letter in "The Discovery of the Mississippi. Secondary Sources," *loc. cit.*, 227 f, 230.

that they went up the Ottawa River, portaged to Lake Nipissing, and then went down the French River to Georgian Bay.

According to the Récit, Jolliet arrived at Michilimackinac on December 8, 1672. Dablon may have received this information from the explorer or, as we have observed, the date may be an inference.[35] Considering that Jolliet left Quebec after October 3, 1672, he cannot have reached Sault Ste Marie before the middle of November. From Sault Ste Marie he may have gone to Michilimackinac, or he may have gone first to Michilimackinac and then to Sault Ste Marie, for he was bringing Dablon's order to Marquette that the latter should accompany him.

2) THE VOYAGE OF DISCOVERY

It seems quite probable that Jolliet spent the winter at Sault Ste Marie where he had his business headquarters. In the spring of 1673, he left with his men for Michilimackinac where Marquette was waiting for him. According to the Récit, their provisions consisted of Indian corn and some smoked meat.[36] Although Dablon makes no mention of beads, needles, hatchets, it is quite certain that they must have taken them along as presents for the Indians. In all the extant documentation concerning the expedition of 1673, there is not one word about any equipment that would enable the explorers to calculate their position. From Marquette's map, however, it is clear that they had a compass. From the accuracy of the latitudes, it is evident that they had an astrolabe, and in view of the time of the year, they must also have had declination tables. Since it was further customary for explorers to carry a map, there is no reason to suppose that they lacked this part of the usual equipment. Indeed, on the basis of the two coordinates mentioned in Marquette's letter, it is very likely that this map was the Sanson map of Florida of 1656 or 1657.

According to Dablon, before their departure the explorers obtained all the information they could from Indians who had frequented the unknown regions toward which they were bound, and they embodied this information in a map. Dablon either learned this detail from Jolliet or else took for granted

---

35 "The 'Récit des voyages...'," loc. cit., 220.
36 JR, 59: 90.

that the explorers followed the common practice in this respect.[37]   We have given the reasons why if a map was made,
this map is certainly not Marquette's autograph map.[38]

We only know approximately the date when the expedition
left Michilimackinac, toward the middle of May 1673.[39]   They
followed the northern shore of Lake Michigan, then down the
west shore of Green Bay[40] and a week or ten days later arrived
at the St. Francis Xavier mission, near present-day De Pere,
Wisconsin.   From the St. Francis Xavier mission they ascended
the Fox River to the Mascoutens village, in the vicinity of what
is now Berlin, Wisconsin.[41]   This was "the limit of the discoveries which the French had made, for they have not yet
gone any farther"[42] westward on the Fox River.   "Toward the
beginning of June 1673," the party left the Mascoutens village
"to enter countries wherein no European had ever set foot."[43]

They had previously learned or learned at the Mascoutens
village that by ascending the Fox River, they would find "a
portage of half a league beyond which was another river which
came from the northwest"[44] and which emptied into the Mississippi.   It is quite probable that guides from the Mascoutens
village showed them the way up the Fox River to the portage.[45]
They crossed over from the Fox River to the Wisconsin, south
of present-day Portage, and must have learned the name of the
latter river—Meskousing—from the Indians of the Mascoutens
village or from their guides.[46]

---

[37] Cf. JR, 44: 236 ff; La Salle's letter of *post* September 29,
1680, in Margry, 2: 52 f; Journal of the *Badine, ibid.*, 4: 178; Journal of the *Marin, ibid.*, 269.

[38] "Marquette's Autograph Map of the Mississippi River," MA,
27 (1945): 30 f, 40.

[39] "The 'Récit des voyages...'," *loc. cit.*, 221.

[40] It is improbable that they went up the Menominee River, *ibid.*,
224.

[41] A. E. Jones, "The Site of Mascoutin," in *Proceedings* of the
State Historical Society of Wisconsin for 1906 (Madison, Wis., 1907),
175–182.

[42] JR, 59: 100.

[43] "The 1674 Account," *loc. cit.*, 317.—The date of their arrival
at, and that of departure from Mascoutens in the Récit are inferences.
"The 'Récit des voyages...'," *loc. cit.*, 226, 228.

[44] "The 1674 Account," *loc. cit.*, 317.

[45] "The 'Récit des voyages...'," *loc. cit.*, 228 f.

[46] For the variants of this name, see "The Jolliet Lost Map of
the Mississippi," MA, 28 (1946): 130 f, 99; and cf. "The 'Récit des
voyages...'," *loc. cit.*, 230 f.

The distance from Portage to the mouth of the Wisconsin (118 miles) was computed as forty leagues. When they were about three-fourths of the way down, they noticed on the left bank of the river what appeared to them an iron mine.[47] When they arrived at the mouth of the Wisconsin on June 15, they ascertained their position and found that they were at latitude 42° 30'[48] (true latitude 43°).

Six years earlier, Allouez had made known to the world the Indian name of the great river on which they now were, but Marquette christened it "Rivière de la Conception." We know for certain that he did so from the legend on his map;[49] that he did so at this time is inferred from the fact that he dated his letter of August 4, 1673, "From the River of the Conception."

In his interview with Dablon, Jolliet corrected some misinformation with regard to the width of the Mississippi which some Indians had reported was twice as wide as the St. Lawrence before Quebec.[50] The explorer said that it was one fourth of a league wide but much wider where there were islands, and found that it was ten fathoms deep.[51]

Proceeding down the Mississippi they saw large herds of buffaloes, in one such herd they counted as many as four hundred head of cattle;[52] they noted the changes in direction of the river and computed their position at latitude 41°.[53] The country through which they were passing was deserted; the first Indians whom they met were Peoria who were gathered in a large village of several thousand people[54] lodged in 300 cabins.[55] This village was situated a few miles up a western

---

[47] See the anonymous copy of Jolliet's map.
[48] "The 1674 Account," *loc. cit.*, 317.
[49] *Supra,* p. 64.
[50] *Supra,* p. 41.
[51] "The 1674 Account," *loc. cit.*, 317 f.
[52] *Ibid.*, 319; and cf. *supra*, p. 56.
[53] On Marquette's map, the Mississippi which, until this latitude is represented as flowing S.E. by S., abruptly changes its direction and is shown to flow south one and a half points to the west.
[54] On the population of the Peoria village, see "The Discovery of the Mississippi. Primary Sources," *loc. cit.*, 224.
[55] This figure is inscribed on every map derived from that of Jolliet; it is also found in Dablon's account and in Jolliet's letter to Laval.

tributary of the Mississippi and is identified as the Iowa River.[56]
Here they saw large wooden canoes hewn out of a kind of
cotton-tree, measuring fifty feet in length and three in width,
in which thirty men with all their baggage could embark.[57]

The Peoria, who belonged to the Illinois confederacy,
"were affable and obliging and received the explorers well.
They gave in present a calumet of about three feet long
adorned with feathers of various kinds, which was to serve
them as a safeguard in their journey."[58]   It was probably in
this village that Jolliet was given the young Indian who was
drowned two years later in the St. Lawrence.[59]

With regard to the customs of these Indians, Jolliet remembered that "the women were very modest, and that when they
did wrong, their noses were cut off.   Women and old men
till the soil, and after sowing time, all go together to hunt buffaloes.   The meat supply them with food; and the hides are
made into garments after tanning them with a certain kind
of earth, which they also use as [war] paint."[60]

We do not know the date of their arrival at the Peoria
village nor do we know the date of their departure,[61] and the
documents supply no information whatever about the voyage
until they were below the mouth of the Illinois River. Between
the latter and the mouth of the Missouri, on the left bank of
the Mississippi, they noticed petroglyphs which very much impressed Jolliet.   After his return to Quebec in 1674, he drew
from memory and inserted on his map a picture of the piasa,[62]
a fabulous animal of Indian mythology which is supposed to be
the "thunderbird."   We have explained why we are unable to
determine how successful Jolliet was in representing the petroglyphs.[63]

Jolliet was also much impressed by the tumultuous waters
of the Missouri.   Its waters, he told Dablon, greatly increase

56 Cf. "The Jolliet Lost Map," loc. cit., 102 f.
57 "The 1674 Account," loc. cit., 318.
58 Ibid.
59 Jolliet to Laval, October 10, 1674, Harrisse, Notes pour servir,
322; Frontenac to Colbert, November 14, 1674, RAPQ, 1927: 76.
60 "The 1674 Account," loc. cit., 319.
61 "The 'Récit des voyages...'," loc. cit., 235, 241.
62 Cf. JR, 59: 140.
63 "The Jolliet Lost Map," loc. cit., 116–120.

the swiftness of the Mississippi current,[64] and later said that at the confluence "the disturbance was so great that the waters were very muddy and could not become clear."[65] From Dablon's letter of August 1, 1674, it is clear that they took the latitude of the mouth of the Missouri,[66] but Jolliet did not remember the name of the river, which Dablon only learned when Marquette's map reached him.[67]

The Récit is the only document which mentions the whirlpool between the Missouri and the Ohio.[68] We have observed that Dablon's source of information for this detail may have been Jolliet or some other member of the expedition.[69]

Three leagues from "8ab8skig8" they computed the latitude and found 36° 47′, which Marquette inserted in his journal.[70] "8ab8skig8," the earliest form of "Wabash," was given to the lower course of the Ohio because the French conceived the hydrography of the Ohio basin differently from ourselves. They looked upon the Ohio as a tributary of the main stream which for them was the Wabash. It seems more probable that the latitude was computed while encamped below the mouth of the Ohio, because the discovery of so large a river would suggest the advisability of recording its position by computing their latitude at this point rather than above the mouth. We have explained the reason for the difference between the latitudes in Marquette's journal and the position of the mouth of the Ohio and that of other identifiable points on his map.[71]

Beyond the Ohio, on the left bank of the Mississippi, they noticed a second iron mine[72] and some sticky red clay with which they dyed a paddle.[73] The voyage continued uneventful to the end. The southernmost point reached by the explor-

[64] "The 1674 Account," *loc. cit.*, 318.
[65] JR, 59: 140.
[66] "The 1674 Account," *loc. cit.*, 318.
[67] "The Jolliet Lost Map," *loc. cit.*, 105.
[68] JR, 59: 68.
[69] "The 'Récit des voyages...'," *loc. cit.*, 245.
[70] JR, 65: 106.
[71] "Marquette's Autograph Map," *loc. cit.*, 49, 51.
[72] The inscription is on the various maps based on that of Jolliet. "The Jolliet Lost Map," *loc. cit.*, 136 f.
[73] Dablon very likely learned this last detail from Jolliet. "The 'Récit des voyages...'," *loc. cit.*, 245.

ers was questioned by two seventeenth-century pamphleteers,[74] and a writer of last century found it "difficult to believe that the explorers could have been as far south—the mouth of the Arkansas River—as has been contended." He believed that the Arkansas village visited by Jolliet "was not very far below the mouth of the Ohio."[75]

This conclusion is based on the following "facts": the time La Salle took in going from the mouth of the Illinois River to the sea, a distance of 1,430 miles in fifty-three days; the time Tonti took to go from Fort St. Louis to the Gulf, a distance of 1,690 miles in fifty days; and the time required by M. de St. Cosme in 1699 and by Father Gravier in 1700 to go from Tamaroa to the mouth of the Arkansas, about 600 miles in twenty-two days.

This is all very interesting, but why these particular "times" are selected is not clear. Instead of computing La Salle's time from the mouth of the Illinois to the sea, and Tonti's time from Starved Rock to the Gulf, why not take the time needed for La Salle and Tonti to go from Quebec or Montreal to the mouth of the Mississippi? The only time worthy of comparison here is the time it took these explorers to go from the mouth of the Illinois River to the Quapaw village. The accounts of their respective journeys show that La Salle covered this distance in 17 days of actual traveling,[76] Tonti in 18 days,[77] M. de St. Cosme in 16[78] and Gravier in 19. The last named traveler, however, noted that although the current

<hr>

[74] "The Jolliet Lost Map," *loc. cit.*, 119 f.

[75] J. Moses, *Illinois, Historical and Statistical* (2 vols., Chicago, 1889–1892), 1: 59, 60.—Father Steck's argument (*The Jolliet–Marquette Expedition*, 164, note 74) against this theory is inconclusive. He says: "That the explorers reached the thirty-third degree, *i.e.*, the Arkansas River, is certain only from Jolliet's report to Governor Frontenac whom he would not have ventured to deceive." No latitude is given in Jolliet's dedicatory letter to Frontenac, and the governor does not mention any latitude in his letter to Colbert. The documents which mention this latitude are Dablon's account and Jolliet's letter to Laval. We also know that the explorers went near the Arkansas River from Marquette's map and from the Manitoumie map.

[76] "A Calendar of La Salle's Travels," MA, 22 (1940): 300.

[77] "The Voyages of Tonti in North America," MA, 26 (1944): 275.

[78] Kellogg, *Early Narratives of the Northwest*, 355–358.

THE VOYAGE OF 1673—DISTANCES IN MILES

The Voyage Of Discovery

Sault Ste Marie to Michilimackinac	90	
Michilimackinac to the St. Francis Xavier Mission	225	
St. Francis Xavier Mission to [Portage, Wis.]	175	
[Portage, Wis.] to the mouth of the Wisconsin	118	
Total from Sault Ste Marie to the Mississippi		608
Mouth of the Wisconsin to the mouth of the Iowa	197	
Mouth of the Iowa to the mouth of the Missouri	250	
Mouth of the Missouri to the mouth of the Ohio	211	
Mouth of the Ohio to [Memphis]	227	
[Memphis] to Quapaw	200	
Total on the Mississippi		1,112
Total (round numbers) from Sault Ste Marie to Quapaw		1,700

The Return Journey

Quapaw to the mouth of the Illinois	661	
Mouth of the Illinois to Kaskaskia	230	
Kaskaskia to the Chicago Portage	97	
Chicago Portage to [Sturgeon Bay]	225	
[Sturgeon Bay] to the St. Francis Xavier Mission	50	
Total from Quapaw to the St. Francis Xavier Mission		1,263
Total from Quapaw to the St. Francis Xavier Mission (round numbers)		1,250
GRAND TOTAL (round numbers)		2,900

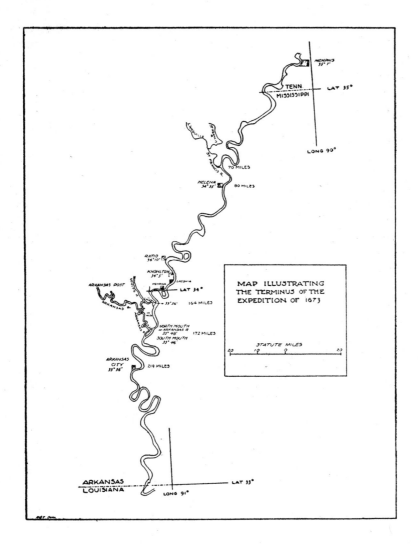

MAP ILLUSTRATING
THE TERMINUS OF THE
EXPEDITION OF 1673

STATUTE MILES

of the Mississippi was strong, they were only able to cover 35 leagues in the first five days owing to the illness of the pilot.[79]

We shall see that in 1673, the explorers arrived at Quapaw about July 25, or forty days after entering the Mississippi. If from this figure we deduct two days for the halt at the Peoria village we see that they covered the distance from the mouth of the Wisconsin to Quapaw in thirty-eight days; simple arithmetic shows that it is not "incredible" that Jolliet and his companions should have traveled over 1,100 miles in thirty-eight days, seeing that the four explorers mentioned above traveled 688 miles in an average of seventeen days.

The first argument confirming these "facts," namely the former name of the Ohio River (Akansea), is ridiculous; the additional "corroborative evidence," namely, "the first map made by Joliet on his return shows the Mississippi only a little below the Ohio River," does not corroborate anything, for this map was not made by Jolliet and its purpose was not to give a map of the voyage, but to show how easily a boat could pass from the St. Lawrence to the Mississippi basin; finally the confirmatory evidence from the pseudo-Douay is no confirmation at all.

In order to follow more readily the discussion of the terminus of the expedition and later the return journey two maps and a table of distances have been inserted.

A comparison between the latitudes of four easily identifiable points on Marquette's map shows that their positions are from 30° to 1° 15′ lower than the true ones.[80]   On Marquette's map also, the mouth of the southernmost tributary of the Mississippi is placed at latitude 33° 40′, which is a few minutes of arc below the latitude of the mouth of the Arkansas River.   Considering, however, the error in the four positions, and specifically the error of one degree for the mouth of the Missouri and that of the Ohio, if we place the mouth of the southernmost tributary one degree higher, at latitude 33° 40′, it will coincide with the latitude of the mouth of the St. Fran-

---

[79] JR, 65: 104.
[80] There are two errors in the figures given for the latitudes on Marquette's map ("Marquette's Autograph Map," loc. cit., 41); the latitude of the mouth of the Wisconsin should be 42° 30′, and that of the Chicago portage 40° 30′.

cis River. On the other hand, Jolliet told Dablon in 1674, and also wrote to Laval in October of the same year, that he had gone as far south as latitude 33°, which is the latitude of the present-day Arkansas-Louisiana boundary line. Actually, the explorers did not reach this boundary line, though they did go below the St. Francis River to a village which stood on the west bank of the Mississippi.

We shall ascertain first, the location of this village in 1673, and second, whether the explorers began their return journey from it or whether they went farther south.

French explorers of the last quarter of the seventeenth century speak of four villages—Uzutiuhi, Tourima, Tongigua, and Quapaw—near the Arkansas River, inhabited by Indians of Siouan stock known to the French under the generic name of Arkansas; and all agree in saying that the northernmost of these four villages, that of the Quapaw, was on the west bank of the Mississippi.[81] Their descriptions of this section of the Mississippi are quite intelligible if we remember that they conceived the confluence of the White River and the Arkansas River quite differently from ourselves. We distinguish the mouth of the White River from that of the Arkansas, ten miles farther south; we call the channel west and south of Big Island the lower course of the Arkansas, and we call the river east of Big Island the Mississippi. In the seventeenth century, the junction of the branch of the White River with the Arkansas was considered the mouth of the Arkansas River, the lower course of the Arkansas was regarded as the western branch of the Mississippi, and our Mississippi was the eastern branch of the river.

From accounts of seventeenth century travelers, we can ascertain the location of the four Arkansas villages. Uzutiuhi was five or six leagues up the Arkansas River; Tourima was in the northwest corner of Big Island, two leagues from Tongigua, which was situated on the east bank of the Mississippi, slightly above the mouth of the White River; and the Quapaw village was on a bluff eight leagues farther up on the west

---

[81] The details will be found in "Marquette's Autograph Map," *loc. cit.*, 42 f.

bank of the Mississippi, that is, between Knowlton, Arkansas, latitude 34° 5′ and Ratio, Arkansas, latitude 34° 10′.

This location of the Quapaw village is confirmed by the journal which Father Gravier kept during his descent of the Mississippi River in 1700.   On October 27, they "passed the St. Francis River, at the point of a bend on the northern bank, eighteen leagues from the Akansea."[82]   There is no entry for October 28.   On the 29th, at noon, the French met "four pirogues of Akansea."

On the 30th [of October] we encamped one league lower [than the place where they had met the Arkansas pirogues], half a league above the old village of the Akansea—where they formerly received the late Father Marquette—which is now recognized only by the old outworks, for not a hut remains.   On the 31st, at about 9 o'clock in the morning, we arrived at the village of the Kappa Akansea, located according to the estimate of Father Marquette at latitude 24°.[83]

Gravier inquired from the chief of the village whether he remembered having seen a Frenchman clad like himself, in black.   The chief said that he did, but that it was long, long ago.

I told him that it was more than twenty-eight [i.e., twenty-seven] years ago.   He added that they had danced to him the captain's calumet,— which I did not at first understand, believing that he was speaking of the calumet of the Illinois, which the Kaskaskia had given to Father Marquette to carry with him in the Mississippi country as a safeguard; but I found in the Father's journal that they had indeed danced the calumet to him.[84]

The journal of Marquettte which Gravier mentions is now lost, but from what he says, we see that there is only a difference of a few minutes between the latitude of the Quapaw village as computed by Marquette—24° is clearly an error of transcription for 34°—and the latitude of the same village as calculated from independent accounts.   Moreover, since Indian huts on Marquette's map at latitude 34° indicate the position of a village, we conclude that this village represented by these huts was the one visited by Marquette.

---

[82] JR, 65: 114.   In his journal, Father Gravier invariably calls the west and east banks of the Mississippi, north and south, respectively.

[83] Ibid., 116.

[84] Ibid., 120.

Against this conclusion there are two difficulties: First, on the map, at latitude 34°, the word "Metchigamea" appears instead of "Quapaw," and ends near some huts, which are used by Marquette to designate Indian settlements or villages on the map; second, on the map at latitude 33° 40', on the east bank of the Mississippi, there is another cluster of huts indicating a village named "Akansea."

We have explained that Marquettet seems to have inscribed "Metchigamea" on his map, because he met an Indian or Indians of that Illinois band in the Quapaw village, or because an Illinois-speaking Indian told him that there was a village inland which was called Metchigamea.[85]

The second difficulty coincides with the second point which we are trying to make, namely, which of the two villages was the southernmost point reached by the expedition: Quapaw, the village on the west bank of the Mississippi at latitude 34°, or Akansea, on the east bank, at latitude 33° 40'.

It is of course quite possible that the explorers went down as far as Akansea, but the fact that this village is inscribed on Marquette's map is not sufficient evidence that the party actually went there, for on the map there are many names of tribes about which the French merely heard from the Indians, but did not visit. It might be objected that Akansea is shown on the map to be close to the Mississippi, whereas the names of the other villages which were certainly not visited by the explorers are indicated as being far inland. This objection loses much of its apparent force when we remember that on all the extant variants of Jolliet's lost map, the "Tahensa" are also shown as dwelling close to the banks of the Mississippi; yet it is certain that the explorers did not go as far south as the Taensa villages.

Moreover, if they had gone to Akansea, it is unlikely that Marquette would have failed to give at least some indication of the true hydrography of this part of the course of the Mississippi. All that he indicates on his map at this point is a river coming from the west and emptying into the Mississippi across from Akansea. The inadequacy of this representation

[85] "Marquette's Autograph Map," *loc. cit.*, 45–47.

is easily understood if he had simply been told by a Michigamea Indian at Quapaw that twenty-five miles below there was another Arkansas village located on the east bank of the Mississippi. Last but not least is the fact that Gravier who had Marquette's journal makes no mention of his having visited any other Arkansas village except that of the Quapaw.

In his dedicatory letter to Frontenac, Jolliet wrote: "I saw [i.e., visitetd] a village which was only five days' journey from a nation that trades with those of California; if I had arrived two days earlier, I would have been able to speak with those who had come from there and had brought a present of four hatchets."[86] Commenting on this passage I said that it was impossible to determine the village referred to by Jolliet.[87] Further consideration, however, leads me to believe that he is speaking of the Quapaw village, for in the documentation of the voyage there are only two villages on the west bank of the Mississippi which we are certain were visited by the explorers, Peoria and Quapaw, hence it seems probable that the village mentioned in the dedicatory letter was the later.

After his return to Quebec, Jolliet told Dablon that in the Arkansas country "the soil is so fertile that it produces wheat [alias, corn] three times a year. Excellent fruits, which are unknown to us, grow naturally. Grapes, plums, apples, mulberries, chestnuts, pomegranates and many other fruits are gathered everywhere and amost at all times, for winter is only known there by the rains."[88] At Quapaw they inquired about the distance to the sea and were told that they were ten days' journey away.[89] We have attempted to explain what led Dablon to write in the Récit that they "could have covered the distance in five days."[90] As a matter of fact, the lowest point reached was still more than 700 miles from the sea; and if it

---

[86] "The Discovery of the Mississippi. Primary Sources," loc. cit., 228. See Dablon's interpretation of this passage in "Marquette's Autograph Map," loc. cit., 46 f.
[87] "The Discovery of the Mississippi. Primary Sources," loc. cit., 230.
[88] "The 1674 Account," loc. cit., 319.—The passage is misplaced, for Dablon makes it appear as though Jolliet is speaking of the Iowa country. Cf. the parallel passages in "The 'Récit des voyages...'," loc. cit., 250 f.
[89] Frontenac to Colbert, November 14, 1674, RAPQ, 1927, 76.
[90] "The 'Récit des voyages...'," loc. cit., 248 f.

took them more than a month to travel over the thousand miles from the mouth of the Wisconsin to the Arkansas village, at the same rate of travel the voyage from this village to the sea would have taken them close to four weeks.

In the evening, we read in the Récit, the elders of Quapaw held a secret council; some wanted to put the strangers to death and rob them. But the chief of the village intervened, sent for the explorers, "danced the calumet dance before us . . . , and in order to banish all fear, made me [Marquette] a present of the calumet."[91]

The passage from Gravier's journal quoted above shows the trustworthiness of the oral testimony given to Dablon. In view of this, we can also accept as substantially correct what we read in the Récit about the hostility of the Indians when the expedition first came in sight of the Quapaw village, their change of attitude when they saw the calumet, and the outcome of the encounter.[92] As in the case of the chief dancing the calumet dance, the source of Dablon's information is oral testimony.

Jolliet explained to Dablon why, although they were so close to the sea, they decided to return:

Toward the end of their journey they learned from the Indians that they were approaching European settlements which were on the left hand [i.e. in the east]; that they themselves were at first only three days and later only two days distant from them and that they were only fifty leagues from the sea.

In this juncture the Father and Sieur Jolliet deliberated as to what they should do, namely, whether it were advisable to go on. They had no doubt that, if they advanced farther, they would fall into the hands of the Spaniards of Florida and would expose the Frenchmen who were with them to the manifest danger of losing their lives. Moreover, the good results of their voyage would be lost if—as seems very probable—they were taken prisoners, for then they could not give any information about it.

These reasons made them resolve to retrace their steps, after having obtained full information about everything that a person would care to know in this sort of situation.[93]

---

91 JR, 59: 158.
92 Ibid., 150–152.
93 "The 1674 Account," loc. cit., 319 f.

We learn from the same letter of Dablon what this "full information" was.

The Father and Sieur Jolliet have no doubt [that the Mississippi has its mouth] in the Gulf of Mexico, that is, in Florida. Its mouth cannot be in the east, in Virginia, for the lowest latitude of the Virginia coast is 34°, and they went as far down as latitude 33°, being then still fifty leagues from the sea. Nor [can the river have its mouth] in the west, in the Vermilion Sea, because their route which was always southward took them away from that sea. There remains, therefore, only Florida which is midway between both; and the Mississippi which our Frenchmen navigated is very probably the river which geographers mark [on their maps] and call [rivière] du St. Esprit.[94]

3) THE RETURN JOURNEY

We have very little information concerning the return journey. All that Dablon says in his letter of August 1, 1674, is that "Ils ne reprirent pas entièrement le mesme chemin . . . s'estans rendus à la baye des puants par des routes differentes sans autre guide que leur boussole."[95] There are details about this route in Frontenac's letter, namely, the easy water communication between the St. Lawrence and the Mississippi basins,[96] and we only know from the cartographical evidence what this different route over part of the way was.

Below the Ohio, says the Récit, the explorers met a party of Indians. Because on Marquette's map a village of Mons8pelea is placed on the east bank of the Mississippi at latitude 35° 15', it is thought that they are the Indians mentioned by Dablon, who, he says, "have guns."[97] I have suggested that Dablon may have obtained this information from a member of the expedition, or that he found it in a lost account of the discovery.[98] I have also observed that on the two Manitoumie maps and on the engraved product published by Thévenot, the Aganalt (Aganahali, Aganatchi) and the Monsoperia (Mons8pelea) are made to appear as though they were in one village,

---

[94] *Ibid.*, 321.—Dablon's "very probable" identification of the Mississippi is discussed in *El Rio des Espíritu Santo* (New York, 1945), 101 f.

[95] "The 1674 Account," *loc. cit.*, 320.

[96] Frontenac to Colbert, November 14, 1674, RAPQ, 1927, 76.

[97] JR, 59: 148.

[98] "The Discovery of the Mississippi. Primary Sources," *loc. cit.*, 8; "The Jolliet Lost Map," *loc. cit.*, 112.

and that immediately below the names of these two tribes is the inscription: "Ils ont des fusils," they have guns.[99] There are several possible explanations with regard to the place of this inscription: it may have been misplaced on Jolliet's original, by the author of the Manitoumie or by the draughtsman of the Manitoumie. The available evidence does not enable one to come to a definite conclusion.

Ethnologists call the Monsopelea "a problematic tribe."[100] Some have identified them with the Chickasaw, others think that they were a tribe akin to the Taensa and Natchez. What is certain is that "Mons8pelea" is an Algonquian vocable and that the explorers heard this name from Algonquian-speaking Indians. We have called attention to the fact that oral testimony is almost certainly the source of the description in the Récit of the appearance of these Indians.[101]

We shall now show that these Indians, whom according to the Récit the explorers met on their journey down the Mississippi, were met on the return journey, and that Marquette gave them a letter.[102]

The authenticity of the original of this letter can hardly be questioned, because it contains a reference to the "Immaculate Virgin," which Alvord rightly considered as particularly significant, and also because it is dated "ad Fluvium Convectionis [Conceptionis]." On this latter point Alvord remarks that "in August 1673, Marquette was the only man in the world calling the Mississippi River by the name of 'Conception'."[103]

That the explorers met these Indians on their return journey, and not on the way down as Dablon says, is deduced from the following facts: 1) the date of their arrival at the Mississippi, June 15, 1673; 2) the date of their portage at Chicago on their return journey, toward the end of September 1673; 3) the time which it took other seventeenth century explorers to travel by canoe from the Quapaw village to the vicinity of

---

99 "The 'Récit des voyages ...'," loc. cit., 246.
100 Hodge, Handbook of American Indians, s.v. Mosopelea.
101 "The 'Récit des voyages ...'," loc. cit., 246.
102 C. W. Alvord, "An Unrecognized Father Marquette Letter," The American Historical Review, 25 (1919–1920): 676–680.
103 Ibid., 677.

present-day Memphis. Thus in 1682, La Salle made the journey in less than ten days,[104] and in 1687, Joutel went from the
Quapaw village to the mouth of the Ohio, more than double
the distance from Quapaw to Memphis, in eighteen days.[105]

The data pertinent to the identification of the Monsopelea
as the Indians whom they met on the return journey are contained in the dateline at the end of the letter: "Dat[ae] ad
Fluvium Convectionis [Conceptionis] ad ‖ altitudinem Poli 35ª
‖ ad Longitud[inem] forte 275ᵈ ‖ 4th August 1675 [*i.e.*,
1673]."[106]

Latitude 35° is the Tennessee–Mississippi boundary line,
whereas on Marquette's map, the position of the Monsopelea
is at latitude 35° 15', the site of present-day Memphis. We
have given the reasons why when any latitude on Marquette's
map differs from the corresponding latitude in a Marquette
document, the preference is to be given to the latter.[107] Since
on the map only the Monsopelea are indicated near latitude
35° and since Marquette gave to the Indians a letter in which
this latitude is specifically mentioned, we conclude that these
Indians were those whom he calls Mons8pelea.

The date of Marquette's letter, August 4, also gives a clue
as to the date when the explorers began their return journey.
We have just seen that it took about ten days to go from Quapaw to Memphis, hence they must have left the Arkansas village about July 25.

We have no details at all about the voyage from Memphis
to the mouth of the Illinois River. They passed again by the
mouths of the Ohio and of the Missouri, and above the latter
saw the piasa for the second time. One cannot satisfactorily
explain why the explorers returned to the St. Francis Xavier
mission *via* the Illinois River.

---

104 "A Calendar of La Salle's Travels," MA, 22 (1940) : 302 f.
105 Margry, 3: 464, 469.
106 The month and the day were clearly not in English in the
original; "4th August" is the copyist's translation of Marquette's
"4ª [die] Augusti." The date, 1675 instead of 1673, the signature
"Macput" instead of "Marquette," are also attributable to the copyist,
whose ineptitude is evident from his nonsensical garbling of the Latin
text of the letter. These errors do not affect the authenticity of the
original, nor invalidate Alvord's main argument.
107 "Marquette's Autograph Map," *loc. cit.*, 49 f.

In the Relation of 1673–1674, Allouez speaks of the Illinois returning to their former habitat "near the lake that bears their name [Lac des Illinois, Lake Michigan], at six days' journey from Mascoutens. . . . Those who are called Kaskaskia have been there for a year or two, as they had promised Father Dablon when I went with him to the Miami mission."[108]

If we could be sure that the above information is correct, and if we knew for certain that it was in the report sent by Allouez in 1674,[109] we could conclude that Jolliet and his companions learned of the migration of the Kaskaskia to the Illinois River when they passed through the St. Francis Xavier mission on their way to the Mississippi, for it is practically certain that Allouez was there at the time.[110]   Moreover, if by 1673, the Kaskaskia had actually migrated from the banks of the Mississippi to those of the Illinois, the explorers could have obtained from the Peoria in whose village they stopped on their way out the necessary directions to return by way of the Kaskaskia village, after they had ascertained into what sea the Mississippi emptied.

The Illinois River Valley is the only section of the voyage which is fully described in the primary sources.   Jolliet told Dablon:

The river which we have christened St. Louis[111] rises near the lower end of the Lake of the Illinois [Lake Michigan],[112] and seemed to

---

[108] JR, 58: 264.—Allouez is here referring to his voyage with Dablon to the Mascoutens village in 1670.

[109] In the paragraph following the passage quoted in the text, Allouez says that he "has already visited the village of the Kaskaskia and has baptized several of their children." L. P. Kellogg (*The French Régime in Wisconsin*. 166) gives this text of the Relation of 1673–1674 as a proof that Allouez went "to the Kaskaskia village, reaching there before Marquette's return from his voyage of discovery," *i. e.*, before the middle of September 1673.   That the part of the Relation in which these passages occur is a later revision by an unknown hand of the original report will be shown in a forthcoming study.

[110] Allouez left the Mascoutens village on May 22, 1673, and went to De Pere by way of the Fox village. JR, 58: 62.

[111] In his interview with Dablon Jolliet refers three times to the Illinois–Des Plaines as "Rivière St. Louis" or "Rivière de St. Louis"; this may be taken as an indication that he had originally so christened the river.—For the subsequent names of the Illinois–Des Plaines, see "The Jolliet Lost Map," *loc. cit.*, 121–123.

[112] From this passage as well as from the drawing of the river on Marquette's map and on the variants of Jolliet's lost map, it is apparent that they looked upon the Illinois–Des Plaines as one river.

me the most beautiful and most suitable for settlement. At the place where we entered the lake is a harbor, very convenient for receiving vessels and sheltering them from the wind.[113] This river is wide and deep, abounding in catfish and sturgeon. For a distance of eighty leagues, not a quarter of an hour passed without my seeing game, which is abundant in those parts; oxen, cows, stags, does and turkeys are found there in much greater number than elsewhere. There are prairies three, six, ten, and twenty leagues long, and three wide, surrounded by forests of the same extent; beyond these, the prairie begin again, so that there is as much of one sort of land as of the other. Some of the grass is very short, but some grows as high as five or six feet; hemp grows wild here and reaches a height of eight feet.

A settler would not have to spend ten years in cutting and burning trees; on the very day of his arrival he could put his plow into the ground. And if he had no oxen from France, he could use those of this country, or even the animals on which western Indians ride as we do on horses. After sowing grains of all kind, a settler could devote himself to planting vine, and grafting fruit-trees; to tanning ox-hides, wherewith to make shoes, and with the wool of these oxen,[114] he could make finer cloth than that brought here from France. Thus he would easily find in the country his food and clothing, and nothing would be wanting except salt; however, by taking proper measures, it should not be difficult to remedy this deficiency.[115]

About two hundred miles up the Illinois River, the explorers came upon the village of Kaskaskia Indians about which they may have heard at the St. Francis Xavier mission. From the introductory note to the journal of his second voyage, we learn that Marquette christened the mission among the Kaskaskia, "mission de la Conception,"[116] the same name he had given to the Mississippi. From subsequent events, we deduce that like the Peoria, the Kaskaskia received the Frenchmen kindly, but we do not know how long the explorers remained in this village.

From the Kaskaskia village they continued their journey ascending the Illinois to its junction with the Des Plaines, then up the latter river to the Chicago portage. If the location of the minerals on the various copies of Jolliet's map can be trusted, all the minerals and stones, with the exception of the two iron mines, were seen along the Illinois River, between

---

113 The mouth of the Chicago River.
114 That is, the buffaloes.
115 "The 1674 Account," loc. cit., 323 f.
116 JR, 59: 164. Cf. "The 'Récit des voyages...'," loc. cit., 223.

the Kaskaskia village and Chicago, and along the west shore
of Lake Michigan to present-day Milwaukee. All these minerals and stone are enumerated in one paragraph of Jolliet's
dedicatory letter to Frontenac: "The iron mines and the bloodstones, which are never found except with red copper, are not
rare. Slate is not scarce, nor are salpeter, coal, marble, and
millstones. As to copper, the largest piece I saw was as big
as a fist and quite pure. It was found near some bloodstones
which are much better than those of France and are found in
great quantity."[117]

Jolliet described the Chicago portage to Dablon and called
attention to its importance as a gateway to the Gulf of Mexico:

The fourth remark concerns the following very great and important
advantage which perhaps will hardly be believed:—we could easily
sail a ship to Florida; all that needs to be done is to dig a canal through
half a league of prairie from the lower end of Lake Michigan to the
River of St. Louis. Here is the route that we would follow: the ship
should be built on Lake Erie, which is near Lake Ontario; from Lake
Erie it would easily pass to Lake Huron and thence to Lake Michigan.
The canal which I mentioned would be dug at the end of the latter
connecting it with the River of St. Louis, which empties into the
Mississippi, which the ship could easily descend to the Gulf of Mexico.[118]

Although Jolliet undoubtedly exaggerated the ease with
which one could navigate from Lake Michigan to the Gulf *via*
the Des Plaines and the lower course of the Illinois River then
down the Mississippi, his description of the Chicago portage
is not much different from that of later travelers.[119]

From Chicago the explorers went up the west shore of Lake
Michigan to Sturgeon Bay where they portaged into Green
Bay,[120] and then down to the St. Francis Xavier mission. We
do not know why they went to St. Francis Xavier instead of

---

117 "The Discovery of the Mississippi. Primary Sources," *loc.
cit.*, 227.—Cf. "The Jolliet Lost Map," *loc. cit.*, 99, no. 14, and 113, no.
64; 126, nos. 80 and 82; 128, nos. 86, 87, 88; 129, no. 90. On Jolliet's
mistaking red hematite for the bloodstone, see *ibid.*, 123, no. 76. Allouez' report of 1677 mentions copper on the west shore of Lake
Michigan, red copper and slate in the Illinois country. JR, 60: 154,
162.
118 "The 1674 Account," *loc. cit.*, 322.
119 "The Jolliet Lost Map," *loc. cit.*, 127 f.
120 JR, 59: 180.

continuing to Michilimackinac which was Marquette's mission.
We cannot even be certain whether Jolliet parted company with
Marquette at Sturgeon Bay and went to Sault Ste Marie, or
whether, as seems probable, they all went first to St. Francis
Xavier. There is no proof whatever to support Charlevoix'
statement that "on arriving at Chicago on Lake Michigan, they
separated."[121]

In his letter of August 1, 1674, Dablon wrote that the explorers reached the St. Francis Xavier mission "toward the end
of November";[122] whereas in the Récit the date of their arrival is said to be "toward the end of September."[123] The
latter date is more nearly correct for the following reasons.
We are fairly certain that the expedition reached the Mississippi
on June 15; as we have seen, they began their return journey
about July 25, and we know that they portaged at Chicago at
the end of September.[124] The distance along the west shore
of Lake Michigan from Chicago to Sturgeon Bay is 225 miles,
and from Sturgeon Bay to the St. Francis Xavier mission
another fifty miles, in all a two weeks' journey. Accordingly,
the party must have arrived at the St. Francis Xavier mission
toward the middle of October.

The last months of Marquette's life are well known. He
spent the winter of 1673–1674 at the St. Francis Xavier mission, where he became ill at the end of May, 1674.[125] Sometime in the summer, he wrote to the local Superior, Father
Nouvel, for orders as to where he would spend the coming

---

121 Charlevoix, *Histoire et description generale de la Nouvelle-
France*, 1: 446. Cf. "The Jolliet Lost Map," *loc. cit.*, 70 f.
122 "The 1674 Account," *loc. cit.*, 320.
123 JR. 59: 162.
124 JR, 59: 180.—Even though we do not know how long they
remained in the Kaskaskia village, it is apparent that the explorers
of 1673 traveled slower than later travelers. In 1687, Joutel left the
Quapaw village, the terminus of the expedition of 1673, on August
2, and reached Starved Rock on September 14. In the following year,
he left Starved Rock on March 21 and was at the Chicago portage
by the 29, or fifty days of actual traveling (Margry, 3: 463, 477,
508, 509). In 1682, Tonti made the journey from Quapaw to the
Illinois village in thirty-six days ("A Calendar of La Salle's Travels,"
MA, 22 [1940]: 302 f; "The Voyages of Tonti in North America,"
ibid., 26 [1944]: 270 f), and in 1686, Tonti made the same voyage in
forty days ("The Voyages of Tonti," *ibid.*, 278).
125 Lettre circulaire [obituary] du P. Jacques Marquette, October 13, 1673. Jesuit Archives, Rome, *Gallia*, 110, II, fo. 195.

winter. At the beginning of October, the two men who had been sent brought Nouvel's permission to go to "the mission of the Conception of the Illinois." In the interval between the return of these two men and his departure for the Illinois country, he made or had copies made of his journal of the voyage down the Mississippi.[126] On October 25, 1674, toward noon, he set out with Pierre Porteret and Jacques Largilier, the two men who had been sent to Father Nouvel.

From the St. Francis Xavier mission to Chicago, they went over the same route as that followed on the return journey from the Mississippi, namely, along the east shore of Green Bay to Sturgeon Bay where they portaged to Lake Michigan, and down the west shore of this lake to Chicago, where they arrived on December 4.[127] Marquette's illness forced them to spend the winter at Chicago. They resumed their journey on March 31, 1675, and arrived at the Kaskaskia village during Holy Week.

Marquette preached to the assembled Indians and said Mass on Holy Thursday, and again on Easter Sunday,[128] April 14, 1675. A recurrence of his illness forced him to leave shortly after this date. Accompanied by Illinois Indians, Marquette and his two companions returned to Lake Michigan by way of Chicago. From this place they went along the south shore of Lake Michigan then up the east shore of this lake to near present-day Ludington, where Marquette died on May 18, 1675.[129]

---

[126] JR, 59: 164. Cf. "The 'Récit des voyages ...'," *loc. cit.*, 186 f.
[127] JR, 59: 172.
[128] JR, 59: 188.
[129] See Kellogg, *Early Narratives of the Northwest*, 276, note 1.

CHAPTER VII

JOLLIET'S ACTIVITIES BETWEEN
1674 AND 1679

As was noted at the end of the preceding chapter, we do not know whether Jolliet parted company with Marquette at Sturgeon Bay and went to Sault Ste Marie, or whether, as seems probable, he first went to the St. Francis Xavier mission and then to Sault Ste Marie; but we can be sure that he went to the latter place, for he had his trading headquarters there. Besides attending to his business from which he had been away six months, Frontenac's letter to Colbert suggests that he made copies of his journal during the winter, and the governor states positively that he left copies with the Jesuits at Sault Ste Marie.[1]

Toward the last part of May 1674, he set out for Quebec with two men and the young Indian who had been presented to him by a Mississippi chief. From Dablon's letter of August 1, 1674, which declares that he negotiated "more than forty rapids,"[2] and from Jolliet's own dedicatory letter to Frontenac which speaks of "forty-two rapids"[3] along the route from the West to Montreal, we know that he went down the Ottawa River, the ordinary route followed by seventeenth century travelers.

The accident which occurred at Sault St. Louis, the last rapid above Montreal, is mentioned in all the primary sources,[4] but because there are more details in Jolliet's letter to Laval, the passage from this document is translated here:

My Lord:
It is not long[5] since I am back from my voyage to the Sea of the

---

[1] Frontenac to Colbert, November 14, 1674, RAPQ, 1927, 77.
[2] "The 1674 Account of the Discovery of the Mississippi," MA, 26 (1944): 320.
[3] "The Discovery of the Mississippi. Primary Sources," MA, 27 (1945): 228.
[4] "The 1674 Account," *loc. cit.*, 320; "The Discovery of the Mississippi. Primary Sources," *loc. cit.*, 228; Frontenac to Colbert, November 14, 1674, *ibid.*, 221.
[5] More than two months.

South.[6] I was favored with good fortune during the whole time, but on my return, when I was about to reach Montreal,[7] my canoe capsized and I lost two men and a box wherein were all my papers, my journal[8] as well as some curios from those far off countries. I am much grieved over the loss of a ten year old slave who had been presented to me.[9] He was of a good disposition, quickwitted, diligent, and obedient. He could express himself in French, and was beginning to read and write. I lost consciousness, and after four hours in the water,[10] I was found by fishermen who never go to this place and who would not have been there if the Blessed Virgin had not obtained for me this grace from God, Who stayed the course of nature in order to rescue me from death.

Except for this shipwreck, Your Excellency would have had a quite interesting relation, but all I saved is my life.[11]

The accident occurred at the end of June or the beginning of July 1674. As soon as Mathurin Normandin *dit* Beausoleil heard of Jolliet's arrival in Montreal, he had papers served on the explorer, demanding that the claims of his wife, Jeanne Dodier, widow of Adrien Jolliet, Louis' elder brother, be submitted to arbitration. Louis Jolliet agreed to compromise, and on July 6, 1674, an amicable settlement was arrived at before Bénigne Basset, the royal notary of Montreal. This settlement was submitted to two members of the Sovereign Council then in town who were chosen as arbiters of the case, and who rendered their decision on July 7, 1674.[12]

On the verso of the document containing this decision there is a declaration by Normandin and his wife before the same notary that Jolliet, in conformity to the above verdict of the arbiters, has given them satisfaction. This declaration was "made and legalized in above-mentioned Montreal, in the house of Sieur Jacques Leber, merchant, in the year 1674, on

---

6 *Supra,* p. 59.

7 The dedicatory letter has "a quarter of an hour" from Montreal; Dablon says that the accident occurred at Sault St. Louis.

8 Dablon mentions a map; Frontenac says that "he lost all his papers."

9 There is no mention of the men or of the young Indian in Dablon's account; Frontenac wrote that Jolliet was bringing the Indian to him.

10 This detail is also in Dablon's account.

11 "A peine a t'il pu sauver sa vie," Dablon; "Il ne me reste que la vie," Jolliet's dedicatory letter.

12 The document is printed in "Louis Jolliet. Early Years," MA, 27 (1945), 27 f.

the twentieth . . ." at this point the document is torn, and hence gives no clue to the month in which it was written. The important fact, however, is that the document refers to Jolliet as absent.

Whatever may have been the date of this declaration, we know from a postscript to it that Jolliet was still in Montreal on July 13, 1674, and from Dablon's letter of August 1, 1674, which contains the earliest account of the discovery of the Mississippi, we know that Jolliet had arrived in Quebec before this date. Since the latter document and the various copies derived from it, directly or indirectly, have been discussed in a previous chapter, it suffices to point out here that the existence of the ASH copy is an indication that Jolliet had heard of the fire at Sault Ste Marie,[13] where he had left copies of his journal; otherwise he would not have given this variant of Dablon's narrative to Frontenac, but would have waited for the copy or copies of his journal which he had left at the house of the Jesuits (chez le Pères) of Sault Ste Marie. Another indication that he had learned of the fire which destroyed the Jesuit house is his redrawing of the map of the Mississippi, for if he had not known that the map based on his journal had perished, he would not have attempted drawing another one from memory.

Against this reasoning the following objection might be raised. We have shown that Marquette kept a journal of the expedition, and that he made copies of it at Green Bay,[14] hence it might be said that Jolliet knew of Marquette's journal, and that it was not necessary to jot down the "few noteworthy details he was able to remember."[15] Such an objection is not very cogent. From Jolliet's letter to Laval and from his dedicatory letter to Frontenac, it is clear that he wanted to bring out how he himself carried out the enterprise, for it was he who had been sent to find out where the Mississippi emptied its waters, and it was only natural that he would want to send an account of his own rather than wait for Marquette's journal, even though both were journals of the same journey. As for Mar-

---

[13] "The 'Récit des voyages et des découvertes du Père Jacques Marquette," MA, 28 (1946) : 191-193.
[14] *Ibid.*, 185-188.
[15] Frontenac to Colbert, November 14, 1674, RAPQ, 1927, 77.

quette's map, it is clear from Dablon's account of August 1, 1674, and especially from his letter of October 25 of the same year,[16] that Jolliet did not know of Marquette having drawn one, because it was made at the St. Francis Xavier mission after Jolliet had departed for Sault Ste Marie.

As after his return to Montreal, so two months after his arrival at Quebec, Jolliet was haled into court and forced to give an account of his trading activities in the West between 1672 and 1674.[17]

This reception tendered to the discoverer of the Mississippi on his return is quite different from that imagined by Gagnon. According to this author, Jolliet's arrival was greeted by the "ringing of the churches' bells and he was met by the people [of Quebec] amidst enthusiastic acclamations."[18]   Although there is not one shred of evidence for this "triumphal reception," the note by the editor of the fourth reprint of Gagnon's book shows that he is loath to discard this legend.   The welcome of Jolliet by "the bells of the churches ringing a full peal"[19] is all the more unlikely for the following reason.   At that time, hardly a year went by but some explorer returned to Quebec with news of new countries discovered, new lakes seen, new rivers navigated.   We know the importance of Jolliet's discovery, but in 1674, few men in New France realized its meaning; and the population of Quebec certainly had no idea that their fellow townsman had opened the way to the richest valley of North America.

From Frontenac's letter to Colbert and from Jolliet's dedi-

----

16 Dablon to Pinette, October 25, 1674, Jesuit Archives of the Province of France, Fonds Brotier, 157, Canada-3, 2.

17 See the account of this lawsuit in "Louis Jolliet.   Early Years," loc. cit., 24 f.

18 Louis Jolliet, 121.—Martin originated this pious legend.   He wrote: "This important discovery filled all Canada with joy, and the inhabitants of the capital followed the constituted authorities of the colony to the cathedral church, where the bishop [who was in France in 1674], surrounded by his clergy, sung a solemn Te Deum." F. X. Martin, The History of Louisiana from the Earliest Period (2 vols., New Orleans, 1827), 1: 78.—Monette repeated it: "The discoveries of M. Joliet and Father Marquette filled all New France with rejoicing. A Te Deum was chanted in the Cathedral." J. W. Monette, History of the Discovery and Settlement of the Valley of the Mississippi (New York, 1846), 127.

19 A. Grandbois, Né à Québec ... Louis Jolliet (Paris, 1933), 201.

catory letter inscribed on the map which he drew from memory between August and November 1674, we know that the explorer reported to the governor. Even if we lacked this positive evidence, we could surmise that he did so, for he had been sent as an official agent of the government, and it was his duty to report to the authorities. From Frontenac's letter we also learn that the governor was very satisfied with the manner in which Jolliet acquitted himself of the task.[20]

From July to November 1674, we can follow Jolliet's movements. We know that he was in Montreal from before July 7 to after July 13, and that he arrived in Quebec before August 1. On October 3, he appeared before the Sovereign Council,[21] and a week later he wrote to Bishop Laval who was then in France. Although Frontenac does not say so in his letter to Colbert, it is likely that Jolliet was in Quebec in November 1674, and it is unlikely that he left town between this date and the following October when his marriage took place.

On October 1, 1675, in drawing up the marriage contract, Romain Becquet, the notary, wrote that the bridegroom was "Sieur Louis Jolliet, domiciled in this town of Quebec," and that the name of the bride was Claire–Françoise Bissot. Among those who signed the contract were Jacques de Lalande, who had married the widowed mother of Claire Bissot three weeks earlier;[22] Louis Rouer de Villeray, first councillor of the Sovereign Council; Jacques Leber, a Montreal merchant; Charles Bazire, collector general of the king's revenues in the colony; and Denis-Joseph Ruette d'Auteuil, the king's attorney general. Villeray and Leber are said to be the friends of the bridegroom, while Bazire and Ruette d'Auteuil are mentioned as the friends of the bride.[23] The contract was signed on Tuesday, and the marriage itself took place on the following Monday in the

---

[20] Frontenac to Colbert, November 14, 1674, RAPQ, 1927, 77. See also what Dablon wrote in his letter of August 1, 1674, "The 1674 Account," *loc. cit.*, 317; and the encomium of Jolliet in the Récit, JR, 59: 88.

[21] *Jugements et délibérations du Conseil Souverain*, 1: 864.

[22] The marriage contract drawn on August 20, was filed on September 5, 1675. AJQ, Greffe Becquet, minute.

[23] The marriage contract is in AJQ, Greffe Becquet, minute; photographic reproduction in RAPQ, 1925, facing p. 240; printed in Gagnon, *Louis Jolliet*, 162-165.

cathedral of Quebec.   M. Henri de Bernières, vicar-general of
the Bishop of Quebec and parish priest of the cathedral, offi-
ciated.[24]

"One of those who brought the most glory, if not the most
affluence" to the Bissot family, wrote J.-E. Roy, "was certainly
Louis Jolliet . . . What Canadian family does not seek the hon-
or of being in some way related to this daring explorer? All
the great names of the colony are connected with this illustrious
man, the son of a poor wheelwright who worked for a company of merchants."[25]   Before his voyage to the Mississippi,
Jolliet himself had traded in the West, and the minutes of a
law-suit that dragged on through January and February 1676[26]
show that after his marriage, he too, like his friends and relatives, became a merchant, and other notarial acts show that he
spent the winter of 1675–1676 in Quebec.[27]   Here his eldest
son, Louis, was born on August 11, 1676;[28] and on October
20, he was one of the inhabitants present at a meeting called
by Duchesneau, the intendant, for the purpose of regulating
the price of beaver pelts.[29]

It was about this time that Jolliet petitioned Colbert
through Duchesneau for leave to go to the Illinois country. The
exact date is not known because the letters of Duchesneau for
the years 1676–1678 have not come to light. That a petition
was sent, we know only from the minister's answer dated April
28, 1677, in which he says: "His Majesty is unwilling to grant
the leave asked by Sieur Jolliet to go to the Illinois country
with twenty men in order to begin a settlement there. The
number of settlers in [Lower] Canada should be increased be-

---

24 Photograph of the entry in the register of the cathedral of
Quebec in RAPQ, 1926, facing p. 224; printed in Gagnon, *Louis Jolliet*, 165.
25 J.–E. Roy, *Histoire de la seigneurie de Lauzon* (5 vols., Lévis,
1897–1904), 1: 452.
26 *Jugements et délibérations du Conseil Souverain*, 2: 34–39,
41, 45.
27 Partnership contract of April 23, 1676, AJQ, Greffe Rageot,
no. 1430; renting of Denis Guyon's ship and hiring of the crew, May
2, 1676, *ibid.*, no. 1433.
28 Tanguay, *Dictionnaire généalogique des familles canadiennes*,
1: 324.
29 AC, F 3, 2: 32v–42.

fore thinking of settlements elsewhere; this should be your
guiding principle with regard to newly made discoveries."[30]

It was only logical that Jolliet should have asked for a concession in the Illinois country where, as he had told Dablon in
July 1674, "a settler would not have to spend ten years cutting
down and burning trees, for on the very day of his arrival he
could put his plow into the ground."[31] Gagnon comments[32]
on Colbert's refusal by saying that it was consistent with what
the minister had written to Talon in 1666,[33] but fails to call
attention to Colbert's inconsistency in granting to Frontenac's
protégé, La Salle, in 1678, much more than he had refused to
Jolliet in 1677.

Quite improbable theories have been elaborated to explain
Frontenac's attitude toward Jolliet between 1675 and 1682;
yet the explanation of the governor's antagonism is quite
simple—the friends of the explorer and his protectors were
Frontenac's political opponents. On returning from his voyage of discovery, Jolliet had paid his respects by naming the
great river and a section of the Mississippi Valley after the
governor,[34] but he did not feel that he had to espouse Frontenac's petty quarrels and thus turn his back upon those who had
befriended and helped him when he was in need. It is to the
credit of Jolliet that he did not imitate La Salle's ingratitude
towards his benefactors.[35]

Among the witnesses who signed Jolliet's marriage contract on October 1, 1675, were, as we saw, Louis Rouer de
Villeray and Denis-Joseph Ruette d'Auteuil. Those who have
studied the history of Frontenac's first administration, especially
the events of 1675, can easily imagine what the irascible governor must have thought of one whose prominent friends were
men whom he considered his "enemies." Jolliet was also obli-
gated to Laval who returned to Canada in that year. Besides,
he was protected by Duchesneau during the seven years that

30 Colbert to Duchesneau, April 28, 1677, AC, B 71: 76.
31 "The 1674 Account," loc. cit., 323.
32 Louis Jolliet, 170.
33 Colbert to Talon, January 5, 1666, RAPQ, 1931, 43.
34 "The Jolliet Lost Map of the Mississippi," MA, 28 (1946):
100 f.
35 Frontenac and the Jesuits, 213.

the intendant remained in Canada, and contrary to assertions of theorists, he always remained in good terms with the Jesuits.

We do not know what share Frontenac had, directly or indirectly, in Colbert's refusal to allow Jolliet to found a settlement in the Illinois country which he had discovered four years earlier; but we do know that in the following year, La Salle, who had the support of the governor's agents in Paris, was granted what had been refused to Jolliet, although La Salle had as yet made no discoveries. We also know that at the beginning of 1677, shortly before Colbert sent his "guiding principle" to Duchesneau, these same agents were very active in Paris, and although La Chesnaye had offered to defray the initial expenses for the Illinois project, "Jolliet's petition was not granted."[36]

The news of this refusal reached Quebec in the summer of 1677. Gagnon writes that after his petition had been thus rejected, "Jolliet devoted himself to a project dear to his new family, that is, to the exploitation of the resources of the lower St. Lawrence and of the gulf.[37] From the Canadian archives we learn that he sometimes served as a public functionary in Quebec. We shall pass these details over in silence, and shall be satisfied with mentioning that on one occasion he was called to give his advice on a particularly delicate subject."[38]

We do not know what Gagnon means by "these details" concerning Jolliet's activities in behalf of the welfare of the community, unless he is referring to two notarial documents showing that Jolliet acted as tutor of the younger children of François Bissot, the deceased father of his wife.[39] Gagnon may also be thinking of the meeting of the inhabitants called by Duchesneau to regulate the price of beaver pelts. This

---

[36] D. Brymner, ed., *Report on Canadian Archives 1885* (Ottawa, 1886), cxvi.

[37] Jolliet seems to have doubted all along that his petition to found a settlement in the Illinois country would be granted. On November 2, 1676, he bought, jointly with his father-in-law, from Michel Le Neuf de la Vallière "une Quesche de present dans le haure de cette ville"; he made a part payment on this day and promised to pay the balance "aussy tost le Retour de la de Quesche du voyage premier quelle doibt faire aux Sept Isles l'an prochain [1677] au printemps." AJQ, Greffe Duquet.

[38] Gagnon, *Louis Jolliet*, 170.

[39] 1677, May 1 and May 12, AJQ, Greffe Becquet, minutes.

meeting, however, took place in 1676, before the unfavorable answer to Jolliet's petition reached Quebec.

Between the summer of 1677 and the "brandy parliament" (Gagnon's "particularly delicate subject"), Jolliet's name appears several times in notarial acts and in legal records. On November 8, 1677, he renewed the contract of partnership passed with his father-in-law in the preceding year;[40] on March 5, 1678, acting as tutor of the children of François Bissot, he made a land grant to Étienne Landeron;[41] in the following month, he hired a shoemaker for one year;[42] on April 21, 1678, he sold to his brother Zacharie a share in the ship which he had bought in 1676 from Michel Le Neuf de la Vallière;[43] on June 5, Madeleine Macart sold to "Louis Jolliet, a house in the lower town of Quebec, situated at the end of the rue Sous-le-Fort";[44] and on June 18, one week after the birth of his second child, Charles, Pierre Norman summoned "Louis Jolliet, bourgeois of this town [Quebec]," to appear before the Sovereign Council.[45]

Before we discuss the "brandy parliament," a few words should be said about a document written in Paris in 1678, wherein is found an echo of Frontenac's antagonism to Jolliet. When analyzing this document,[46] we showed that, besides being sprinkled with egregious blunders, the text had been carelessly edited and tampered with by Margry, and we called attention to his erroneous attribution of authorship. Margry calls it a letter of Frontenac, although it is actually one of Claude Bernou's memoirs, which he composed in 1678, using as his sources a letter of Frontenac and information received from the latter's partisans in Canada. In a footnote at the beginning, Margry says that his main reason for publishing the document is because "it contains very important statements relative to Cavelier de la Salle and Jolliet."[47] In the entire memoir there is only one "important statement" which Margry had already

40 1677, November 8, *ibid.*, Greffe Rageot, no. 1696.
41 1678, March 5, *ibid.*, Greffe Becquet, minute.
42 1678, April 5, *ibid.*, Greffe Becquet, minute.
43 1678, April 21, *ibid.*, Greffe Rageot, no. 1769.
44 1678, June 5, *ibid.*, Greffe Becquet, minute.
45 *Jugements et délibérations du Conseil Souverain*, 2: 204.
46 *Frontenac and the Jesuits*, 175 ff.
47 Margry, 1: 301.

given as the third "proof" for his contention that La Salle had discovered the Mississippi before Jolliet.[48]   What follows is the translation of the passage reproduced elsewhere in its original form.[49]

Here is the reason, my Lord, why they [the diocesan clergy and the Jesuits] together with M. Duchesneau and Sieur Bazire have launched two projects.   The first consists (in asking for the concession of Lake Erie and of Lake Michigan) [*the words in parentheses are deleted; the following passage in the margin takes their place*]. Their first project [took shape] when they learned that M. de la Salle intended to ask for the concession of Lake Erie and of Lake Michigan; for the first is a necessary adjunct of his commercial privilege at Fort Frontenac, since most of the trading is carried on between the latter place and Lake Erie, at the entrance of which he must necessarily build a fort to keep the English out.   Even the Reverend Jesuit Fathers report that the English [*four words so deleted as to be illegible*] have recently sent as a scout a deserter by the name of Turquet.   As I have said above, when they got wind of M. de la Salle's project, they themselves resolved to ask this concession for Sieurs Jolliet and Leber, two men entirely devoted to them.   As a preparation, they have extolled the first of these two men, although Sieur de la Salle's travels antedate his. Sieur de la Salle will prove to you that (Sieur Jolliet lied) [*the words in parentheses are deleted and are replaced by the following sentence written between the lines*] the relation of Sieur Jolliet is false in many particulars. Their second project is the reestablishment of congés . . .[50]

Among the changes made by Bernou in copying the material out of which this document was compiled, two are of special interest: his softening of the very strong statement about Jolliet's veracity, and his altering his petition for leave to begin a settlement in the Illinois country into a petition for the exclusive privilege of trading in the region around Lake Erie and Lake Michigan.   Bernou's statement that La Salle was thinking of asking for this privilege is quite gratuitous.   There is no trace of any such intention before 1678,[51] that is, two

---

48 Margry to Draper, July 4, 1879, *Report and Collections* of the State Historical Society of Wisconsin for the years 1880, 1881, and 1882 (Madison, Wis., 1882), 111.

49 "Louis Jolliet. The Middle Years," MA, 27 (1945): 72.

50 BN, Clairambault, 1016: 48v.

51 The earliest mention of La Salle's "dessein" occurs in an undated Bernou memoir (BN, Clairambault, 1016: 50v, printed in Margry, 1: 336).   Internal evidence shows that it was composed sometime between January and May 1678.

years after Jolliet had asked for the Illinois concession. In 1676, La Salle had his hands so full with Fort Frontenac that he obviously would not think of asking for the exclusive privilege in the huge area mentioned in the memoir. Moreover, as La Salle must have known, the discoverer of a territory had a prior right to trade or settle in it. Strictly speaking, La Salle "had traveled" westward before Jolliet; for, as we have shown, Louis Jolliet's first western journey took place in 1670, while by 1669, La Salle had gone to the western end of Lake Ontario. It is certain, however, that Jolliet discovered and traveled in the Illinois country more than six years before La Salle.[52]

It would be interesting to know the grounds for La Salle's assertion that "Jolliet lied," or as Bernou expresses it more politely, that "the relation of Sieur Jolliet is false in many particulars." In 1678, La Salle had not come within 400 miles of seeing the territory described by Jolliet in that relation.

While La Salle was telling his fairy tales in Paris, the nomenclature of Jolliet's map of the Mississippi was being revised in Quebec.[53] On Franquelin's map of 1678 the great river is called "Riviere de Messisipi," and not "Riviere Buade" as on

---

[52] At the beginning of 1682, Bernou, then better informed, wrote as follows: "Pendant que le sieur de La Salle travailloit à la construction de son fort, les envieux, jugeant par de si beaux commencements de ce qu'il pourroit faire dans la suite, suscitèrent le sieur Jolliet à le prévenir dans ses descouvertes. Il alla par la baye des Puans [Green Bay] à la rivière de Mississipi, sur laquelle ils descendit jusqu'aux Illinois, et revint par le lac des Illinois en Canada, sans avoir essayé pour lors ny depuys d'y faire aucun establissement." Bernou's "Relation des descouvertes ...," in Margry, 1: 438 f. On this document, cf. Hennepin's Description of Louisiana, 55–64.

Although Jolliet's priority with regard to the discovery of the Illinois country is here clearly set forth, there are five errors in this short passage. First, Jolliet went to the Mississippi in 1673, that is more than three years before La Salle even began to "travailler à la construction de son fort" ("A Calendar of La Salle's Travels," MA, 22 [1944]: 288). Second, Talon, not "les envieux" of La Salle, sent Jolliet to the Mississippi. Third, the intendant did not "susciter" Jolliet "pour prévenir le sieur de La Salle," but commissioned the Canadian at the time when La Salle was somewhere in the Iroquois country, after the fiasco of an expedition to which he had been sent in 1670 by Courcelle and Talon ("A Calendar of La Salle's Travels," loc. cit., 286). Fourth, not only did Jolliet go down the Mississippi "jusqu'aux Illinois," but went 600 miles below the mouth of the Illinois River. Fifth, Jolliet did try "depuys d'y faire un establissement," but was refused by Colbert.

[53] "The Jolliet Lost Map," loc. cit., 101 f.

the anonymous copy of Jolliet's map; "Frontenacie" is not
mentioned at all; and Lake Ontario is given its Indian name
only, instead of having also the alternative "Lac Frontenac"
as on the anonymous copy, or of being simply called "Lac
Frontenac" as on Franquelin's map of 1675, the so-called Jolliet "larger map."

The question is whether Jolliet was a party to these changes,
and whether he was led to approve of them because of Frontenac's antagonism.

The map of 1678, which is dedicated to Colbert by Duchesneau, has a title which emphasizes one of its purposes:
"Carte Gnlle de la France Septen-Trionalle Contenant la découuerte du pays des Ilinois Faite Par le Sieur Jolliet." In 1680,
two years after this map was made, Duchesneau wrote that
Anticosti Island was granted in fief partly "in consideration
of the discovery made by Sieur Jolliet of the Illinois country,
of which he has given us [Duchesneau] a sketch which served
as a basis for making the map sent two years ago to my Lord
Colbert, Minister and Secretary of State."[54]   In view of this
it seems quite likely that on the sketch which Jolliet gave
Duchesneau, he himself eliminated Frontenac's names.

It is unlikely that Frontenac saw Duchesneau's map.   The
governor, however, was soon to learn unequivocally what was
Jolliet's stand with regard to the thorniest problem which agi-
tated Canada during the French régime:—the unrestricted sale
of hard liquor to the Indians.[55]   The contradictory reports sent
to France about the evils resulting from this trade had led the
king to issue an order that a meeting of the *habitants* be called.
They were to give their opinion as to whether the selling of
liquor to the Indians should be abolished or continued.   This
meeting, sometimes called the "brandy parliament," took place
on October 26, 1678.   Jolliet was one of the twenty who were
summoned to give their opinion. "Unfortunately, most of those
who had been chosen were interested in the nefarious traffic.
Fifteen maintained that the brandy trade was absolutely neces-

---

[54] P.–G. Roy, ed., *Inventaire de Pièces sur la côte de Labrador*
(2 vols., Quebec, 1940–1942), 1: 8.
[55] *Frontenac and the Jesuits*, 101 ff.

sary for the welfare of the colony, five acted as men of character and voted against its continuation."[56]

This is not quite correct, for only three voted for complete abolition. The other two, Leber and Jolliet, gave a different opinion. Leber was in favor of selling brandy to the Indians, but was opposed to its being brought for sale to their villages. Jolliet's opinion is as follows:

To transport liquor to the woods, to bring it to the Indians who trade with the French, must be forbidden under pain of death. The same penalty should be meted out to Indians carrying liquor [to the villages], but the *habitants* should be allowed to sell them [brandy] in the houses and other places where trade is carried on; with moderation, however, being careful to prevent drunkenness, and if some disorder arises, the culprits should be punished. It is not true to say that all the Indians get drunk, for some, like those who live among us, use liquor in moderation. There are some other Indians who are engaged in the liquor trade; they buy brandy in the French settlements and bring it to the woods where they sell it for beaver pelts, in turn exchanging these for brandy and other merchandise. It must be said, however, that these are few, and they number no more than three for every two hundred.[57]

It has been said that Frontenac's antagonism to Jolliet sprang from his having learned that Marquette accompanied the explorer to the Mississippi.[58] There is no basis for this assertion. As early as the autumn of 1674, Frontenac knew that a Jesuit had gone with Jolliet and that this Jesuit was Marquette;[59] and yet in a letter of November 14, 1674, he shows not the slightest trace of resentment against Jolliet.

The author of this erroneous hypothesis also declares that Jolliet "took this to heart" and that a "number of facts seem to indicate that the affair caused estrangement between him [Jolliet] and the Jesuits."

Three of the "facts" mentioned can hardly be said to indicate this very clearly: the fact that two of Jolliet's nephews joined the Recollects during the eighteenth century, after the death of their uncle; the further fact that a Franciscan, *i.e.,* a

---

56 "La traite de l'eau-de-vie avec les Sauvages," BRH, 12 (1906): 375 f.
57 AC, F 3, 5: 78; printed in Margry, 1: 418.
58 Steck, *The Jolliet–Marquette Expedition,* 237.
59 *Supra,* p. 101 ff.

Recollect, was chaplain at Anticosti in 1681; and the third fact that the year 1679 is the last time that a Jesuit accompanied Jolliet.

I had no idea that the vocation of nephews to a branch of the Order of St. Francis could be cited as a proof of avuncular preferences. At that rate the present writer should be a Franciscan, for an aunt of his had long been a nun of St. Francis when he entered the Society of Jesus. The census of 1681 shows that there was no chaplain, Recollect or other, on Anticosti Island in that year,[60] and there is no evidence that a chaplain was ever permanently stationed on the island. The year following the brandy parliament (1679), "Jolliet undertook an expedition to Hudson Bay. On this occasion he was accompanied by the Jesuit Father Antoine Silvy, then missionary at Tadoussac. This is the last time so far as records show that Jolliet united with a Jesuit in any public endeavor."[61] Records for the year 1684 show the following: "During the summer Reverend Father [Louis] André [went] to Ka8 and Anticosti with M. Jolliet."[62]

---

[60] Sulte, *Histoire des Canadiens-Français*, 5: 88. For his statement that in 1681 there was a Recollect chaplain on Anticosti Island, Father Steck refers the reader to Gagnon, *Louis Jolliet*, 204. Although the latter writer does not give any source, it is clear that he used Sulte's book for this paragraph, but does not, of course, mention a Recollect as being then on the island. This Recollect, we are further told by Father Steck, was "probably Simon [Gérard] de la Place, whose services he [Jolliet] engaged as chaplain and missionary." Simon de la Place could not have been at Anticosti in 1681, for he came to Canada two years later, in 1683 (I. Caron, "Prêtres séculiers et Religieux qui ont exercé le ministère en Canada [1680–1690]," BRH, 47 [1941]: 260). Father Steck's authority for this statement is also Gagnon, *op. cit.*, 227, note 1. In this note Gagnon vaguely refers to "le Père Sixte Le Tac" for saying that Simon de la Place was in Anticosti not in 1681, but in 1689. The reader may judge for himself whether the text—not given by Gagnon—but on which he bases his assertion, proves his point: "Il [Jolliet] s'y [Anticosti] est retiré avec sa famille & un Père Recollect pour y hyverner, mais comme il n'y a point de bois dans cette isle il a fait dresser une maison en la grande terre [*i. e.*, at Mingan on the mainland]; le Père Simon de la Place, Recollect, qui y est actuellement, a soing d'instruire les sauvages qui s'y rendent pour cet effect & mesme est allé cette année 1689 exposer sa vie pour anoner l'evangile aux Esquimaux."— [Sixte Le Tac?], *Histoire chronologique de la Nouvelle France*, E. Réveillaud, ed., (Paris, 1888), 37 f.

[61] *The Jolliet-Marquette Expedition*, 237.

[62] Registre des baptêmes, mariages et sépultures des sauvages du Lac St Jean, Chicoutimi, et Tadoussac de 1669 à 1692, Archives of the Séminaire of Québec (Laval University), fo. 54v.

More worthy of comments is the first fact brought forward as indicating an estrangement between Jolliet and the Jesuits; namely: "There is nothing on record to show that he ever again in his later career visited the Illinois country." How this indicates "estrangement" is not quite clear. "In his later career" Jolliet's business was in the north. What with his fisheries at Mingan, his seignioral grant of Anticosti, his mapping of the St. Lawrence, and his class of hydrography at Quebec, he had not much time to "visit" the Illinois country, even if he had felt so inclined. Moreover, "in his later career," when Jolliet wanted not only to "visit" the Illinois country but begin a settlement there, Duchesneau was told by Colbert that the king "was unwilling to grant the leave asked by Sieur Jolliet."

The second "fact" is no fact at all. "[There is nothing on record to show] that he at any time espoused the cause of the Jesuits in their controversy with La Salle." The Jesuits never had any "controversy" with La Salle. If Father Steck had studied La Salle's letters instead of taking his cue from Parkman, Margry, Lorin, and other secondary sources, he would have seen that in these letters there are two passages which imply that the Jesuits were carrying on a lucrative beaver trade in their missions, and a critical examination of the contemporary evidence would have shown him that these implications are unfounded, and that La Salle was employing the familiar underworld practice known as "framing" to give some color to his accusations.[63]

The third "fact" has to do with the stand taken by Jolliet in the "brandy parliament."

In 1678, a year after he had been refused permission to settle in Illinois, he and La Salle were among the twenty men summoned to Quebec by the civil authorities to present their view concerning the sale of liquor to the Indians. On this occasion Jolliet recommended that a moderate sale be permitted in the French settlements, but that the transportation of liquor into the forest be prohibited.[64]

In a note to this passage Father Steck refers the reader to Gagnon, on which he comments as follows: "Now this was certainly not in line with the attitude of the Jesuits toward the

---

[63] *Frontenac and the Jesuits*, 247–251.
[64] *The Jolliet–Marquette Expedition*, 237.

vexing problem, but a concession to the stand taken by the government." The truth is that Gagnon, although quoting only a part of Jolliet's point of view, made it a point to underline the penalty—death—demanded by Jolliet for those who transportetd liquor to the forest; and Gagnon also called attention to the fact that this was in keeping with the compromise advocated by M. Dudouyt, the vicar-general of the Bishop of Quebec in Paris.[65] Now the Jesuits were at one with the bishop and his priests in all that pertained to the selling of hard liquor to the Indians. As the following passage shows, all that Jolliet did was to repeat in Quebec, in October 1678, exactly what Dudouyt had told Colbert at Sceaux, in May 1677; with the difference that the priest did not ask the death penalty for those who transported hard liquor to the Indian villages.

I [Dudouyt] told him [Colbert] that it would be easy to preserve moderation in the liquor traffic, inasmuch as the principal obstacle has already been removed by the decree prohibiting the bearers of congés to go into the woods. If trade is carried on in the settlements, the transactions will come to the public's notice and it will thus be easy to detect any disorder and use the proper means to remedy it ... I told him that it was the transportation of liquor into the forest that was the cause of the greatest disorders.[66]

The actual significance of these "facts" can be left to the judgment of the reader. There can be no objection to an author interpreting facts according to his own personal views, but such facts should be first ascertained from primary evidence, especially in a doctoral dissertation. Unless I am greatly mistaken, one of the main purposes of such a work is precisely to establish the facts on a solid evidential basis.[67]

Jolliet spent the winter of 1678–1679 in Quebec. On November 17, 1678, he signed the marriage contract of his brother Zacharie;[68] on February 2, 1679, he hired two sailors, the contract was to last from the time when the St. Lawrence would be navigable in the spring until the autumn of 1679;[69] and

---

[65] Gagnon, *Louis Jolliet*, 178.
[66] Dudouyt to Laval, May 22, 1677, Archives of the Séminaire of Québec (Laval University). Lettres, Carton S, no. 93; printed in Brymner, ed., *Report on Canadian Archives 1885* cii.
[67] Cf. also "The 'Récit des voyages...'," *loc. cit.*, 185–194.
[68] 1678, November 17, AJQ, Greffe Duquet.
[69] 1679, February 9, *ibid.*, Greffe Duquet.

on March 10 of the same year, Duchesneau granted jointly to him and to his wife's stepfather, Jacques de Lalande, all the "isles and islets called Mingan situated along the northern bank [of the St. Lawrence] down the bay named Lance aux Espagnols [Bradore Bay]."[70] The concession also gave them leave to establish anywhere on these islands cod and seal fisheries.

In order to understand the difficulties that arose in the following year, it is necessary to explain briefly the conditions governing land grants on the Lower St. Lawrence.

In the early years of the colony, the fur trade in the Saguenay country was called *Traite de Tadoussac,* because it was mainly to this post, where an annual fair was held, that the Indians came to exchange their pelts for European goods. The profits of the trade first went to a society of Rouen merchants, and later to the *Compagnie des Habitants* (1645–1664) to which these profits had been made over by the Company of the One Hundred Associates (also known as *Compagnie de la Nouvelle-France* and as *Compagnie de Richelieu*), who were the proprietors of Canada from 1627 to 1663. In order to simplify the exploitation of the *Traite de Tadoussac,* the *Compagnie des Habitants* sold to the highest bidder the exclusive right of trading in the Saguenay region, and the men who bought this right were called *Fermiers de la Traite de Tadoussac.*

On October 10, 1663, Charles Aubert de la Chesnaye bought the exclusive privilege of exploiting the *Traite de Tadoussac.*[71] The money paid for the privilege, however, went to the *Compagnie des Indes Occidentales* to which the king transferred the proprietorship of Canada in 1664. After the dissolution of the latter company, Louis XIV detached the Saguenay territory from the colony and erected it into a *Domaine du Roy,* the King's Domain. Thereafter the Crown sold to an individual the exclusive right to trade in that territory, and since, as a rule, the principal shareholders of such com-

---

[70] *Inventaire de Pièces sur la côte de Labrador,* 1: 5 f.
[71] *Jugements et délibérations du Conseil Souverain,* 1: 19.

panies lived in France, they usually appointed a business manager who resided in Canada to look after their interests.[72]

It should be noted that at first the *Traite de Tadoussac* contained no reference to specified boundaries, for it merely entitled its holder the privilege of trading at Tadoussac and of levying a tax on transactions carried on there during the annual fair; and it should further be noted that later on, when the One Hundred Associates handed over the *Traite de Tadoussac* to the *Compagnie des Habitants,* they retained their right of making seignioral grants where they pleased and to whom they pleased.

Thus on February 25, 1661, the One Hundred Associates granted to François Bissot, the father of Jolliet's wife, trading and hunting rights as well as the right of founding fishing establishment on the mainland wherever convenient from "Isle-aux-Oeufs [Egg Island] to Seven Islands and in the Grande Anse, toward [the country of] the Eskimo where the Spaniards usually [come] to fish." For these privileges Bissot had to pay an annual tax of two beaver pelts or ten livres tournois to the treasurer of the Company of the One Hundred Associates, plus the usual tax to the "community of this country," *i.e.,* to the *Compagnie des Habitants.*

A glance at a map will make it abundantly clear that in 1679, in virtue of his wife's inheritance of her father's rights, and in virtue of the grant made to him by Duchesneau, Jolliet was co-seignior of the islands and the mainland from Egg Island to Seven Islands, and of all the islands that fringe the northern bank of the St. Lawrence from Mingan to Bradore Bay. Jolliet, however, and his heirs at a later date included in their seigniory the hundred miles of coast between Seven Isands and Mingan.[73] Thus on the 1678 map showing the landholdings in New France, Franquelin wrote all along the northern bank of the St. Lawrence from Seven Islands to Bradore Bay: "Seigneurie du Sieur Bissot."[74] In 1685, Marie Couillard,

---

[72] For all that precedes, see Société Historique du Saguenay, *L'histoire du Saguenay depuis l'origine jusqu'à 1870* (Chicoutimi, 1938), 84–87.
[73] *Inventaire de Pièces sur la côte de Labrador,* 1: 3 f.
[74] Carte pour seruir a l'eclaircissement du Papier Terrier de la Nouvelle France. ASH, 125–1–1.

acting in her capacity of Bissot's widow and tutrix of his younger children as well as by the power of attorney which she had from her present husband Jacques de Lalande, leased to her son-in-law, Louis Jolliet, "all the shoreland which belonged to them for Lisle aux Oeufs jusqu'a Lance aux Espagnols, as well as their share [of rights] to the Mingan Isles and islets extending from the Rivière St. Jean to the said Ance aux Espagnols."[75]

On March 11, 1679, that is, on the day after Jolliet received the Mingan concession jointly with Lalande, they both entered into partnership with Denis Guyon and Marie Laurence, to open a fishery and a trading center at Seven Islands.[76] On May 9, Jolliet paid Charles Cadieu *dit* Courville for the house situated in Quebec, rue Sous-le-Fort, which he had bought in the preceding year.[77] Four days later, he left Quebec for Hudson Bay.

---

[75] *Inventaire de Pièces sur la côte de Labrador*, 1: 252 f, 282.

[76] "Acte d'association entre Denis Guyon, J. Lalande, Marie Laurence et Louis Jolliet au sujet d'une entreprise de pêche et de traite aux Sept Isles." I did not find this document in the Archives Judiciaires, but there is a copy of it in the Archives de la Province de Québec, Collection Pierre–Georges Roy, *Carton* Louis Jolliet.

[77] 1679, May 9, AJQ, Greffe Becquet, minute. Madeleine Macart (*supra*, note 44) who had sold the house on June 5, 1678, was the wife of Charles Cadieu.

CHAPTER VIII

THE VOYAGE TO HUDSON BAY

In contradistinction to that to the Mississippi in 1673, Jolliet's voyage to Hudson Bay in 1679 was not one of discovery. This being so it will suffice to recount the voyages of discovery and exploration to Hudson Bay by the English and the French previous to 1679 and to bring out those points which serve to explain the antecedents of the struggle between France and England for the possession of the "Sea of Destiny."

This struggle was preceded by a diplomatic debate, wherein each side tried to prove priority of discovery; but there was too much at stake to expect a solution from an exchange of notes by envoys, ambassadors or plenipotentiaries. We are not concerned with the war which inevitably followed nor even with the period after 1679. We have made use of documents posterior to this date only insofar as they refer to events which took place previously.

1) Voyages to Hudson Bay before 1679

The fourth attempt made by the French to reach Hudson Bay took place in 1671. Paul Denis, Sieur de Saint-Simon, who led the expedition was accompanied by Sébastien Pennasca and Father Charles Albanel.[1] After his return to Quebec, Father Albanel wrote toward the end of his journal:

Hitherto this journey had been deemed impossible for the French who had already thrice attempted it, but, unable to overcome the obstacles on the way, had been forced to abandon it in despair of success ... It is true this journey is extremely difficult, and all that I write about it is but half of what the traveler must endure. There are 200 saults or water falls, which means 200 portages ... There are 400 rapids. ... I say nothing of the difficulties of the road, they must be experienced to be understood.[2]

The French in Canada had long speculated about this overland route to Hudson Bay. In June 1640, an Englishman—

---

[1] On this Jesuit, cf. Rochemonteix, *Les Jésuites et la Nouvelle-France au XVIIe siècle*, 2: 373, note 1; JR, 34: 246 f; BRH, 25 (1919): 111; 33 (1927): 183.

thought to be Sir Thomas Yonge or Young[3]—who had been brought to Quebec by Indians, related to Father Le Jeune "wonderful things about New Mexico." For two years he had sought along the Atlantic Coast, from Virginia to the Kennebec River, for some great lake or river that would lead him to the sea which is north of Mexico. "Not having found any, I came to this country to enter the Saguenay, and penetrate, if I could, with the Indians of this country, to the Sea of the North."

The comments of Father Le Jeune on the exploration contemplated by this Englishman are in sharp contrast with the subsequent attitude of his Jesuit brethren in Canada, and indicate that the overland journey to Hudson Bay, or, as it was then called, the Sea of the North, was looked upon as an almost superhuman feat:

This poor man would have lost fifty lives, if he had had so many, before reaching this Sea of the North by the way he described; and if he had found this sea, he would have discovered nothing new, nor found any passage to New Mexico. One need not be a great geographer to recognize this fact.[4]

Seven years after the discovery of Lake St. John by Father De Quen in 1647,[5] the Jesuits having heard of Indian villages on the "shores of the Sea of the North,"[6] began to think of means of reaching these tribes; and in 1658 several possible overland routes to this sea were mentioned in the Relation. One of these routes was described as leading up the Saguenay to Lake Piouakouami [St. John]; sixty leagues farther was Lake Outakouami,[7] and another sixty leagues' travel from this lake would bring one to the sea.[8] These distances were inferences from vague data supplied by the Indians and no account was taken of the numerous rapids or portages on the way.

---

2 JR, 56: 212.
3 Nute, Caesars of the Wilderness, 284.
4 JR, 18: 234–236.
5 JR, 31: 251–253.
6 JR, 41: 182.
7 According to the annotator of this passage in JR, 44: 323, this was Lake Ouichtagami, the headwaters of the Peribonka River. Crouse (Contributions of the Canadian Jesuits to the Geographical Knowledge of New France, 148 f) identifies this lake as Lake Mistassini.
8 JR, 44: 238–240.

In 1660, an Indian who had made the journey told a Jesuit[9] of an overland route from Hudson Bay to Tadoussac by means of "two rivers [which] flow into Lake St. John, whence the Saguenay takes its rise."[10]

From the wording of Father Albanel's journal quoted above, it would seem that before his voyage to Hudson Bay there had been three attempts by the French to make the journey overland. The records, however, mention three attempts in all, one by sea and only two overland. The earliest, by sea, was made by Jean Bourdon, who, according to the Relation of 1657–1658, returned to Quebec after reaching latitude 55°,[11] namely, the latitude of Cape Harrison on the Labrador coast. The second voyage took place in 1661, when four Canadians under the command of Michel Le Neuf, Sieur de la Vallière, together with the Jesuit Fathers Druillettes and Dablon, went as far as Necouba (Lake Nikabau), near the summit of the St. Lawrence watershed.[12] Two years later, in May 1663, Guillaume Couture, who had taken part in the 1661 expedition, was given a permit by Governor d'Avaugour to take five other Frenchmen and travel with "the Indians dwelling in the north as far and as long as he will deem proper for the service of the king and the good of the commonwealth."[13]

None of these expeditions reached Hudson Bay; although in later years, when the French became aware of the importance of the territory adjacent to the bay as an inexhaustible supply of valuable pelts, they claimed on the strength of these three voyages that according to international law they had a right to the territory in virtue of prior discovery and of having taken possession of the bay through these three voyages.

The events that led to the diplomatic exchange of notes, memorials, and reports containing the claims and counterclaims of the two countries involved must be mentioned briefly, for in this exchange specific reference is made to the three voyages

---

9 *Supra*, 24–26.
10 JR, 45: 232.
11 JR, 44: 188.
12 JR, 46: 272.
13 "Ordre de M. d'Avaugour au Sr. Couture pour aller au Nord," BRH, 7 (1901): 41.

before that of Saint-Simon as entitling the French to the Hudson Bay territory.

The Frenchman Médard Chouart *dit* des Groseilliers,[14] after difficulties with the authorities in Canada, went to England and thence led the English to Hudson Bay in 1668. Seeing the great number of pelts brought back from this expedition, prominent men in England determined to form a trading company, and on May 2, 1670 (O.S.), received a charter from Charles II incorporating them under the title of "The Governor and Company of Adventurers of England tradeing into Hudsons Bay."[15] For four years, Chouart and his brother-in-law, Pierre-Esprit Radisson, who had entered the service of the English at the same time, worked for the Hudson's Bay Company. In 1674, however, as a result of Radisson's quarrel with Charles Bayly, the governor of the bay for the Company, the two renegades went to France where their desertion was pardoned.

In 1682, Radisson made the voyage from Quebec to the bay in the service of Canadian merchants, who had founded a trading company in that year under the title of "Compagnie de la Baie du Nord."[16] Besides seizing an enormous amount of pelts from his former employers, Radisson also brought to Quebec on his return from this voyage a ship belonging to the Hudson's Bay Company. The capture of this ship was disapproved by La Barre, the governor of New France, who returned it to its captain, Benjamin Gillam. Radisson went to Paris to enter a complaint against La Barre, and obtaining no satisfaction, crossed over to England, where he again entered the service of the Hudson's Bay Company. Sailing for Hudson Bay in May 1684, he handed over to the English at Port Nelson all the pelts which his former companions had collected there for the Canadian merchants, and persuaded these companions to take service with the Hudson's Bay Company. Then, after presenting to the Company the fort which had been built at

---

[14] G. Frégault, *Iberville le Conquérant* (Montreal, 1944): 34, note 32.

[15] The charter is printed in E. E. Rich, ed., *Minutes of the Hudson's Bay Company 1671–1674* (Toronto, 1942), 131–135.

[16] This trading company is also known as Compagnie de la Baie d'Hudson, and Compagnie du Nord de Canada.

the mouth of the Nelson River, he left for England at the beginning of September.

It was only in 1685 that the Compagnie de la Baie du Nord in Quebec learned of the new treason perpetrated by their former employee. Incensed at the losses sustained by Radisson's defection, the stockholders obtained leave from Denonville to send an expedition to dislodge the English.[17] This expedition effected the forcible expulsion of the English from all the posts on the shores of James Bay. When this news reached England, it was the turn of the stockholders of the Hudson's Bay Company to complain. Whereupon a committee composed of French and English plenipotentiaries met to discuss the prior rights of their respective sovereigns to Hudson Bay. The "Transactions betweene England and France Relateing to Hudson Bay, 1687,"[18] contain the claims and counterclaims submitted by the English and by the French. The main feature of these "transactions" is their remarkably economical use of truth whenever it suited the purpose of the contestants.

What interests us here is the reference made to the above mentioned three attempts by the French to reach Hudson Bay. Among the documents presented by the Compagnie de la Baie du Nord de Canada are the following:

An act from the Registers of the Sovereign Council of Quebec, dated April 26, 1656, signed Peuvret, secretary of the said Council, wherein it is proved that the man called Jean Bourdon, commanding a ship of the said company [the One Hundred Associates], followed the whole length of the northern coast of Canada, entered the said [Hudson] bay and took anew possession of it.[19]

The certificates of Sieur de la Vallière, officer, and of Father Dablon, missionary, proving that in 1661, Indians [living on the shores] of the Baye du Nord de Canada [Hudson Bay], came to Quebec for the express purpose of confirming their desire of continuing

---

[17] I. Caron, ed., *Journal de l'expédition du Chevalier de Troyes à la Baie d'Hudson, en 1686* (Beauceville, 1918).

[18] Printed in D. Brymner, ed., *Report on Canadian Archives 1883* (Ottawa, 1884), note C, 173–301.

[19] The earlier "prises de possession" consist in an edict of Francis I of 1540 authorizing Roberval to take possession of the country discovered by Verrazano in 1525; the letters patent of Henry IV of 1598 to the Marquis de la Roche; the acts of the Compagnie de Caen; and the letters patent of Louis XIII of 1627 to the Company of the One Hundred Associates.

to live under French rule, and of asking for a missionary. The said Father Dablon was sent overland with the said Sieur de la Vallière and five soldiers.

A commission of Sieur d'Avaugour, the governor of New France, dated May 10, 1663, ordering and permitting Sieur Couture to go with five men to the foot of the Baye du Nord de Canada, to accompany and help the Indians who had once more come to Quebec to ask the governor for assistance. To this commission is attached a certificate of the said Couture, saying that he made the journey in the year 1663, and that in the country around the foot of the said bay, he again erected a cross, and buried the arms of His Majesty, engraved on copper, between two lead sheets at the foot of a large tree.[20]

We must inquire into the validity of these proofs, for the possession of Hudson Bay was to be the cause of much bloodshed, which is unjustified if the English had actually taken formal possession of the bay before the French succeeded in reaching its shores.

Fifty years ago, J.-E. Roy proved that Bourdon made no voyage to Hudson Bay in 1656, and he came to the conclusion that the above-mentioned act of April 26 was a forgery.[21] The voyage, we know, actually took place in 1657; and when we consider the date of Bourdon's departure from Quebec, May 2, and that of his return, August 11,[22] it is obvious that he cannot have gone to Hudson Bay. We have, besides, the positive statement in the Relation of 1657–1658 that he did not go farther than latitude 55° and the sworn statement of Laurent Dubocq who was wounded in a skirmish with the Eskimo, a statement which agrees in every particular with the account in the Relation just referred to and with a letter of Mother Marie de l'Incarnation.[23] In all these accounts there is no indication whatever that Bourdon went to Hudson Bay in order to take possession of it, or that he actually took possession of the Labrador coast at the place where he landed.[24]

---

[20] *Report on Canadian Archives 1883*, 182.
[21] "Jean Bourdon et la baie d'Hudson," BRH, 2 (1896), 2–9, 21–23.
[22] *Le Journal des Jésuites*, 209, 218.
[23] *Lettres de ... Marie de l'Incarnation*, 671.
[24] As will be seen in the course of this chapter, the argument of J.-E. Roy (*Histoire de la seigneurie de Lauzon*, 1: 218) is invalid. Even if the mere fact of Bourdon's landing on the Labrador coast—which the French themselves thought insufficient to give them possession of Hudson Bay—were enough to establish prior rights,

We know from the Relation of 1659–1661 that La Vallière and Dablon did not go farther than Lake Nikabau; that is, they were still 300 miles southeast of Hudson Bay, in a straight line. The only evidence we have of their "certificate" is an extant copy purportedly signed by Dablon and La Vallière and dated Montreal May 3, 1662;[25] this copy, like the copies of Jean Bourdon's declaration, is a forgery which neither Dablon nor La Vallière ever saw.[26] The permit given by d'Avaugour to Couture is authentic enough, but the certificate said to be attached to it is as worthless as the Bourdon declaration and the Dablon-La Vallière certificate.[27]

The first mention of the "prises de possession" of Hudson Bay by Bourdon, Dablon-La Vallière, and Couture, seems to be in a memorial which Hector de Callières sent to Seignelay in 1685,[28] but no certificates are referred to. In this memorial Callières says that two expeditions went to Hudson Bay in 1663, and that both took possession of it by setting up the king's arms there. Now, we know that there was only one expedition that year, and as we shall see presently, the men

Thomas Button was in Hudson Bay and took formal possession of it in 1613, and Thomas James repeated the ceremony in 1632, that is, forty-four and twenty-four years, respectively, before the voyage of Jean Bourdon. In view of this, the opening sentences of Roy's discussion (op. cit., 217) are simply not true: "Mais s'il est exact de dire que Cabot, Frobisher, James, Davis, Button ont devancé les Français sur les mers glacées du pôle il faut avouer aussi que ces navigateurs dans leurs courses audacieuses n'avaient d'autre but que de trouver un passage vers l'ouest et non pas l'intention louable de prendre possession au nom de leurs maîtres, les rois d'Angleterre, des terres désolées ... qu'ils apercevaient du pont de leurs navires." Button and James not only had such a praiseworthy intention, but they actually took formal possession of Hudson Bay, the first half a century, the second a quarter of a century before the voyage of Jean Bourdon. Hence if Roy "demonstrated" anything (Frégault, Iberville le Conquérant, 74), he demonstrated that the English had prior rights to Hudson Bay.

25 Archives des Affaires Étrangères, Mémoires et Documents, Amérique, 5: 28–28; printed in "The Voyage of Louis Jolliet to Hudson Bay in 1679," MA, 26 (1944): 227, note 24.

26 Cf. "The Voyage of Louis Jolliet to Hudson Bay," loc. cit., 227; Roy, Histoire de la seigneurie de Lauzon, 219.

27 The document (Archives des Affaires Étrangères, Mémoires et Documents, Amérique, 5: 95) is printed in Roy, op. cit., 221; its spurious character is discussed ibid., 22 f, and in "The Voyage of Louis Jolliet to Hudson Bay," loc. cit., 228.

28 "Memoir of Sieur de Callières for My Lord, the Marquis de Seignelay," NYCD, 9: 268.

who were supposed to have led the second expedition, Pierre Duquet and Jean Langlois, actually made the voyage under Couture.

The opening paragraph of the same Callières memorial contains an important statement with regard to the question of priority. He wrote: "It is a custom established, and a right recognized among all Christian Nations, that the first who discover an unknown country no inhabited by other Europeans, and who plant in it the arms of their Prince, secure the propriety thereof to that Prince, in whose name they have taken possession of it."[29]

Callières himself admits that the English first went to Hudson Bay with the two French renegades, Messrs. Chouart and Radisson[30] in 1667 (i.e., 1668). He probably did not know that in 1613, Thomas Button had taken possession of Hudson Bay at the mouth of the Nelson River and that in token thereof he had erected a cross to which he affixed the arms of the king of England; nor does he seem to have known that Thomas James was in the bay that now bears his name in 1632 and had taken possession thereof on July 1, of the same year.[31]   But in the 1680's James' book as well as that of Fox had long been known in France, as is evident from an examination of the 1650 Sanson map of North America. The delineation of Hudson Bay on this map is merely a variant of that in *The Strange and Dangerovs Voyage*, and the nomenclature of the bay is borrowed from the map in James' book and from the map in the book of Luke Fox.[32]   That the English realized this may be seen from their answer to one of the memorials presented by the French:

---

29 *Ibid.*, 265.

30 The reason why Radisson did not go to Hudson Bay in 1668 is given in Nute, *Caesars of the Wilderness*, 119 f.

31 In *The Strange and Dangerous Voyage of Captaine Thomas Iames* (London, 1633), 112, is "The copie of the Letter I left at Charleton, fastened to the Crosse the first of *Iuly*, 1632." Besides this letter were also "The two Pictures which are wrapt in lead, and fastened vppermost on this Crosse, are the liuely pictures of our Soueraigne Lord and Lady, *Charles*, the first; and Queene *Mary* his wife; King and Queene of *England, Scotland, France* and *Ireland*, &c. The next under that, is his Maiesties Royall Armes: the lowermost is the Armes of the City of Bristoll." *Ibid.*, 119.

32 *North-VVest, Fox, or, Fox from the North-west passage* (London, 1635).

There is noe intention of Establishing a Right by Maps, yet the names given in them to Places and Countrys are convincing arguments of the Propriety.

It would seeme very strange that had they some years before had any thoughts of makeing pretentions to this Colony they would have permitted ye printing Mapps at Paris (licensed by the King's authority and dedicated to the Dauphin of France) in which are seen none but English names for all that part of America.[33]

The reference in this passage is to the Sanson-Jaillot map of North America published in Paris in 1674, which, for all that pertains to the delineation and the nomenclature of Hudson Bay, repeats the previous Sanson maps of North America, 1650, and of Canada, 1656.

The French flatly denied that Thomas Button took possession of Hudson Bay at the mouth of the Nelson River, and that the ceremony was later repeated by Luke Fox. About Fox's replanting of the cross at the mouth of the river, they blandly said that "cette croix n'a pu estre plantéee que par les François"; but they prudently refrained from saying who these Frenchmen might have been.

In 1667 [1668], we read in one of the English memorials, Zachariah Gillam ("Old Zack"), an Englishman, entered the mouth of a river which he called Rupert River, built a fort near its mouth, which he called Fort Charles, and took possession of the said river as well as of the adjacent territory. The French admitted this, but argued that the English were so little acquainted with the country that they had to be guided by Chouart and Radisson, and that it was "unseemly that the treason of these two men should be used as a title against the rights of the Compagnie Françoise." This drew a very pointed answer from the English:

The expedition made in 1667 is alone solemn enough to establish the Right of the English, and is not the less valid for the service they reaped from Grosseliers and Radisson said to be French men. The Venetians might as well pretend to the English Colonies, because Cabot made the discovery and the Genoese might demand reasons of Spaine for their Possessions in the Indies, because Colomb was a native of that State. There are few expeditions or Voyages, and scarce any Conquests made where there is not a mixture of Forreigners 'tis

---

[33] *Report on Canadian Archives 1883*, 186.

sufficient that those people were not forced but hired into the service of the English nation.[34]

Hence according to the principle of international law appealed to by Callières, the English and not the French had a right to Hudson Bay. The French certainly were not at the mouth of the Nelson River before Button or Fox, nor in James Bay before Thomas James, nor on the shores of James Bay before Gillam, who had taken possession of the Rupert River and of the adjacent territory fully four years before Saint-Simon reached the mouth of that river. It is astonishing that the English plenipotentiaries overlooked the Relation of 1671–1672, in which Dablon and Albanel distinctly state that all the attempts made by the French before 1672 had been unsuccessful.[35]

The exchange of notes between the diplomats of both countries went on from March to December 1687, when a truce was agreed upon which was to last until January 11, 1689 (N.S.). During the interval inquiries were to be made in the colonies with regard to the limits of the territory which rightfully belonged to France and England. On March 8, 1688, an order from Louis XIV was sent to the governor of New France "to make the most thorough search for the titles which prove the property which the French have over those places [Hudson Bay among them], and send them by the first vessels returning to France."[36]

These "proofs" turned out to be rather disappointing and what is found in them is altogether different from the contents of the copies of the "declaration" and "certificates" previously mentioned. On November 2, 1688, witnesses were called in by René-Louis Chartier de Lotbinière, who had been empowered to this effect by Denonville and Champigny. One of the witnesses was Laurent Dubosc [Dubocq], aged 53, who after taking the oath, said that about thirty-one or thirty years ago,

---

34 *Ibid.*, 186.
35 JR, 55: 234; 56: 212. Cf. also *Lettres de ... Marie de l'Incarnation*, 671. This book had been in print six years at the time of the negotiations.
36 Royal instructions to Denonville in *Collection de Manuscrits relatifs à la Nouvelle-France* (4 vols., Quebec, 1882–1885) 1: 419; NYCD, 9: 371. The circular letter to the governors of the English colonies is in the *Report on Canadian Archives 1883*, 200 f.

he embarked "with the late M. Bourdon on a bark called the *Petit Saint-Jean*[37] . . . the said Bourdon was leaving for the *baye du Nord* with sixteen Frenchmen and two Hurons, and he, the witness, was acting as interpreter for the Indians." On the day following their landing on the Labrador coast in order to trade with Indians, an unprovoked attack resulted in the killing of one of the two Hurons, and the wounding of the other and of the witness himself. The two wounded men were rescued by the other Frenchmen; "the second Huron died five days later, so that Sieur Bourdon seeing him, the witness, incapable of serving and the two Indians dead, resolved to return and in fact came back to this town."[38]

As can be seen, there is no question of coming near Hudson Bay, nor of taking possession of it or of the Labrador coast where they landed. This man had every reason to remember the journey, and his testimony agrees perfectly with what is found in the Relation of 1657–1658 and with what Marie de l'Incarnation wrote in 1671.

Peculiarly enough, no inquiry was made about the first overland attempt to reach Hudson Bay. Druillettes, it is true, had been dead seven years in 1688, and La Vallière was in Acadia, but Dablon who had also made the journey was then in Quebec as rector of the Jesuit college there. They probably thought it better not to call in Dablon, for he could simply have referred the examiner to the Relation of 1659–1661, wherein it is specifically stated that the expedition did not go farther than Lake Nikabau.[39]

The first witness actually called in by Lotbinière was Couture, and his testimony leaves no room for doubt about the failure of the second as well as the third attempt. After taking the oath, Couture declared that "about the middle of May of the year 1663, in consequence of the order of M. d'Avaugour, then governor . . . of this country, he left this town with Me Pierre Duquet, who later became a notary and the king's attorney in this provostship, and with Jean Langlois, ship-

---

37 Not the *Saint François–Xavier,* as stated in the forged Bourdon declaration. BRH, 2 (1896): 5.
38 Enquete faite par le Lieutenant general en la Prevoste de Quebec. November 2, 1688, AC, C 11A, 10: 96v–97v.
39 JR, 46: 288.

carpenter, (both of whom died last year), to go to the Sea of the North in company with forty-four canoe-loads of Indians." They reached Lake Mistassini on June 26, and

were astonished to seen more than one foot of snow fall in one night. From this place they went to Lake Nemiskau and to the river [the Rupert] which empties into the Sea of the North. But at this point the Indians whom he had with him refused to go farther; all the more because the Indians who were in the said place, never having seen Europeans, were suspicious of them and gave signs of their dislike, so that he [Couture] felt bound not to go farther; and after trading with them and giving them presents in view of a future alliance, he came back to Quebec. The witness added that about four years earlier [actually two], he went with Fathers Dablon and Druillettes, Jesuits, as far as Lake Nikabau, but at that time they made no alliance with the Indians of the Sea of the North.[40]

This declaration under oath, even though taken long after the journey, clearly shows that in 1663, when the French were nearest Hudson Bay, they were still nearly one hundred miles from the mouth of the Rupert River. It also shows that Couture did not take possession of the country in the name of the King of France, that he erected no cross, that he did not set up the arms of France nor bury any plate of copper or any other metal at the foot of a tree large or small. In fact, his commission did not call for anything of the sort; by its terms he was merely permitted to go with the Indians and to winter with them, if he could do it safely and if he judged that the commonwealth would derive some benefit therefrom.

In all subsequent disputes between England and France with regard to the territorial limits of each in North America, the French, of course, did not produce these damaging declarations, but merely repeated with further embellishments what they had been saying since 1687.[41]

Of the three attempts to reach Hudson Bay from Canada, that of Couture came nearest to the goal. As we saw, he makes

---

[40] Enqueste faite..., November 2, 1688, AC, C 11A, 10: 96–96v.

[41] See for instance the "Memoir on the French Dominion in Canada," of 1706, in which Couture is said to have taken the latitude of the spot when he buried "His Majesty's arms engraved on copper." NYCD, 9: 784. This additional bit of fiction does not become a fact because La Potherie (Voyages de l'Amerique, 1: 142) repeats that Couture took the latitude; the repetition simply means that La Potherie had this memoir when he wrote his book.

no mention of having taken possession of the country at the time of his journey of 1663, although his testimony was taken to establish this fact. Merely to ascertain how far the explorers had gone would have been of no avail unless they could prove to have taken possession of the country in the name of their sovereign at the farthest point of their explorations. Callières, indeed, had clearly stated this to be one of the essential conditions which secured the propriety of the country discovered to that prince in whose name possession had been taken. But even if Couture had set up the king's arms and gone through the ceremony at Lake Nemiskau in 1663, the English would nevertheless be entitled to the mouth of the Rupert River and to the adjacent territory in virtue of Gillam's taking possession of the same in 1668; for, as Bernou wrote in 1685, "a prince who would be the lord of the headwaters of the Danube, would not therefor be the master of its mouth."[42]

In 1667, four years after the date of d'Avaugour's permit to Couture, Father Beschefer wrote from Quebec: "Next spring another attempt will be made to reach the Sea of the North, notwithstanding the great difficulties that have already been experienced."[43] At this very time Allouez, who was then in the West, was hearing more about this Sea of the North, "which we think is in all probability the one designated on the map by the name of Hutson."[44] We saw in a preceding chapter that in 1669 Dablon came to the West, and that one of the geographical problems which he intended to solve was to "discover at last that Sea of the North ... which has not as yet been discovered by land";[45] also to find out whether that sea "is the bay to which Hudson gave his name."[46] Dablon himself did not make the contemplated journey to the Sea of the North; it was Albanel's voyage that solved the geographical problem which had been puzzling so many in New France for a long time.

Accompanied by Paul Denis, Sieur de Saint-Simon, and by

---

[42] Reflexions sur le Memoire de M. l'Abbé de Saint Vallier. BN, Clairambault, 1016: 629.
[43] JR, 50: 176.
[44] JR, 51: 56.
[45] JR, 54: 134.
[46] JR, 56: 148.

Sébastien Pennasca, the government's representatives, Albanel left Quebec on August 6, 1671. They began their journey from Tadoussac in August and were forced to winter on the way. On June 28, 1672, Albanel wrote in his journal,

scarcely had we proceeded a quarter of a league when we encountered in a small stream on our left, a hoy of ten or twelve tons, with its rigging, carrying the English flag and a lateen sail. A musket-shot's distance thence, we entered two deserted houses. A little farther on, we found that the Indians had wintered near there, and had recently taken their departure. We pursued our course, accordingly, as far as a point of land six leagues distant from the house of the Europeans.[47]

They were now at the mouth of the Rupert River; they "considered with pleasure the sea which we had so eagerly sought and this so famous Hudson Bay, of which we shall speak later." The houses mentioned by the missionary were the headquarters of the Hudson's Bay Company, which the English together with Chouart and Radisson had left in July of the preceding year.[48]

In Albanel's journal, which was in print in the first months of 1673, it is clearly stated that this was the first successful journey by the French to Hudson Bay,[49] and that, as we just saw, when they arrived at the mouth of the Rupert River there were unmistakable signs of the English having been there. We have also seen that the reason for the inquiry of 1688 was precisely to prove that the rights of France anteceded those of England; and since the narrative of the expedition of 1671–1672 had been in print fifteen years, there would seem to be no reason for questioning those who had taken part in it. In 1668 Albanel was not available, for he was in the West that year, but Paul Denis was called in by Lotbinière.

In 1671, he testified, he left Quebec by order of Talon "to go to the Baye du Nord in order to set up the arms of the king there." With him were Father Albanel and a Frenchman named Sébastien Pennasca. He went up the Saguenay, crossed Lakes St. John, Nikabau, Mistassini, Nemiskau, and then

descended a great river which led him to the said bay. On the bank of the said river and quite near the said bay, he found two deserted

---

47 JR, 56: 184–186.
48 Nute, *Caesars of the Wilderness*, 138.
49 JR, 56: 212.

houses, which, as he learned afterwards, had been built by the English. He did not notice that anyone had spent the winter there, for the houses were in a very bad state of disrepair, having no doors nor windows, and were built of uprigths and roofed with reeds. They were therefore forced to go farther along the bay toward the north to find the Indians.

Many Indians, who were found at a place called Scoutenagachy,[50] were told by "the said Father Albanel, who speaks their language perfectly,"[51] that the King of France was taking them under his protection and would defend them against the Iroquois provided they embraced the Catholic Faith. Many children were brought to be baptized,[52] and presents were exchanged between the Indians and the French.

Having returned to the said river [the Rupert], he had a post set up to which a plaque of tinned iron bearing the arms of His Majesty was affixed. The return journey was along the same route as that taken coming to the bay, and on the way back he also set up the same arms in the same manner on the shore of Lake Nemiskau and on that of the great Mistassini Lake,[53] for he had brought along the said three tinned iron plaques for this purpose, and at the time, he drew a procès-verbal of all this which he handed over to M. Talon on arriving at Quebec.[54]

Talon, as is well known, particularly insisted that explorers should take formal possession in the name of the King of

---

[50] Miskoutenagachit in Albanel's journal (JR, 56: 186); the East Main River according to Crouse, *Geographical Contributions of the Canadian Jesuits*, 166.

[51] "Le Reverend Pere Albanel ... sçait en perfection la langue Montagneze." *Lettres de ... Marie de l'Incarnation*, 672.

[52] Cf. Albanel's journal, JR, 56: 188 ff.

[53] Neither in Albanel's journal nor in the declaration of Saint-Simon is there any mention of having found the arms of Great Britain set up at the mouth of the Rupert River. In January 1676, however, a petition of the stockholders of the Hudson's Bay Company to the King of England says that "there hath been of Late some attempts made from Canada to ye prejudice of yr Peticoners by a Father Jesuit one Charles Albanel ... [and] also in ye absence of yr Peticoners ships pulled downe yor Maes Ensignes wch were set up in Hudsons Bay" (Nute, *Caesars of the Wilderness*, 167); this was repeated in a letter of 1684 of Sir James Hayes. *Ibid.*, 153. No "prise de possession" at the mouth of the Rupert River is mentioned in Albanel's journal, but on the return journey, at "Nemiskau, nous arborâmes les armes du Roy sur la pointe de l'Isle, qui coupe ce lac le neufiesme de Juillet" (JR, 56: 206); and on July 19, "sur les deux heures aprés midy je plantay les armes de nostre puissant & invincible Monarque sur cette [Minahigouskat] riviere." *Ibid.*, 210.

[54] Enquete faite ..., November 2, 1688, AC, C 11A, 10: 98–98v.

France of all territories which they discovered,[55] because, as Callières wrote, by such acts the countries became the property of the sovereign in whose name possession was taken. In the case of Saint-Simon, however, this formality was quite useless, since, as Callières also said, in order to be valid the French should have reached the shores of Hudson Bay before the English. To say nothing of Button, Fox and James, Zachariah Gillam had taken formal possession of the Rupert River and of the adjacent territory in 1668, that is, four years before Saint-Simon arrived there; and on September 1, 1670 (O. S.), that is, two years before Saint-Simon's arrival, Bayly had taken "formal possession of 'all the Lands and Territoryes' of Port Nelson for his Matie and in token thereof, nayled up the Kings Armas in Brasse on a Small Tree there'."[56]

Albanel arrived at Tadoussac on August 1, 1672, whence he proceeded to Quebec and reported to those "who had employed me";[57] namely, to Father Dablon, who had returned from the West and who had been in office as superior of the Jesuit missions in New France since the preceding July, and to Talon who was soon to leave Canada.

Less than one month after Albanel's return, Frontenac landed at Quebec. In a long postscript to a letter of the following year, the governor wrote:

I forgot to inform you, my Lord, that upon learning that des Groseilliers was enticing all the Indians away from us and by making them presents was attracting them to Hudson Bay, where he has an establishment; I determined to make use of the zeal of Father Albanel, Jesuit, who wished to go and open a mission in that part of the coun-

---

55 Talon to Louis XIV, November 10, 1670, November 2, 1671, RAPQ, 1931, 121, 157 f; see especially Talon to Colbert, November 10, 1670, ibid., 137. "Le petit procès verbal cotté D. qu'ils [MM. Dollier and Galinée] ont dressé un peu à la haste et sans luy donner toute sa forme," which Talon mentions in this letter to Colbert is in AC, C 11A, 3: 56; printed in Margry, 1: 166.
56 Nute, op. cit., 136, quoting an affidavit of Nehemiah Walker of June 14, 1687.
57 JR, 56: 210.—A. C. Laut (The Conquest of the Great Northwest [2 vols., New York, 1908], 1: 130) writes that "the date of his journal, 1672, is wrong by two years." The date of Albanel's journal of his first voyage, 1671–1672, is quite correct; no journal of the second voyage, 1673–1674, if one was written (JR, 61: 150–152), has come down to us.

try. He will endeavor to dissuade the Indians, with whom he has
great influence, from going thither . . .

The said Father Albanel will sound out des Groseilliers, if he encounter him, and will try to win him over to our side.[58]

Having left Quebec too late in 1673, the missionary was
forced to spend the winter en route, and only reached the bay
at the beginning of September 1674.[59] What happened is
well known:—Bayly[60] shipped him to England the following
year.[61]

For the next seven years, writes Tyrrell, we know very little
about the movements of the English traders in the bay, but we are assured in a memorial prepared by the Hudson's Bay company in 1687
that it had had undisturbed possession of its trading-posts on the bay
up to 1682. In this time, in addition to the trading-post on the
Rupert river, trading-posts had also been built on the Moose and
Albany rivers.[62]

It is during the interval spoken of by Tyrrell that Jolliet
went to Hudson Bay.

2) JOLLIET'S ROUTE TO HUDSON BAY

The document translated below is in the Archives du Service Hydrographique, Paris, fifth *carton* (box or portfolio) and
is the fourth, but numbered *pièce* 3, of "six documents relative to Hudson Bay and to attempts made to discover the
northwest passage to the Sea of the South."[63]

In the upper left-hand corner of the first page a few can-
celled words are illegible; and just below, in pencil, are the
words: "Chercher la Carte." This map is referred to by the

[58] Frontenac to Colbert, November 13, 1673, RAPQ, 1927, 50.
[59] Cf. John Oldmixon, "The History of Hudson's-Bay," in *The
British Empire in America* (London, 1708), 382–412, reprinted by J.
B. Tyrrell, ed., in *Documents Relating to the Early History of Hudson Bay* (Toronto, 1931), 10, 393: "On the 30th of *August* [O. S.] a
canoo arriv'd at *Rupert's* River, with a Missionary Jesuit, a Frenchman born of English Parents." There is no authority for the last
clause.
[60] On Charles Bayly, cf. Rich, *Minutes of the Hudson's Bay Company*, li–liv and Appendix G, 209–213.
[61] Oldmixon in Tyrrell, *op. cit.*, 393–395; Rich, *op. cit.*, 212; Nute,
Caesars of the Wilderness, 152 f.
[62] Tyrrell, *op. cit.*, 10.
[63] ASH, 5: no. 4.

clerk who endorsed the document.[64] In the upper right-hand corner is the following note: "He [Jolliet] found the English established there [at the mouth of the Rupert River. He speaks of] the manner in which he was received and of their settlements."

After giving one of the several routes from Lake St. John to the mouth of the Rupert River which Jolliet may have taken, Gagnon goes on to say: "We shall now let M. Margry speak. He seems to have had in his hands the journal, now no longer to be found, which Jolliet kept during his exploration of 1679."[65] All that Margry saw is the document translated below. It is a report written by the explorer in Quebec, who made use of his field notes as a basis. As is expressly stated in the title it was abridged by some official, and as we learn from a note at the end of the document it was sent to Paris by Frontenac together with a map of Hudson Bay on November 8, 1679. In the third installment of his study on Jolliet, Margry "edited" this report, further abridged it, and, as was his wont, inserted in the text comments of his own, which, except for their silliness, are indistinguishable from the original report.[66]

Even with the help of Jolliet's map of 1679,[67] we are unable to determine which route he followed in his voyage to Hudson Bay. The title of the map says that this route is

---

[64] "Envoyé par M. de Frontenac le 8 no. 1679. auec la carte de lad. Baye." November 8, 1679, is also the date which Jolliet inscribed on his map. I have not seen this letter of Frontenac which is in ASH, 111-1: no. 5. In a document entitled "Memoire sur la domination des françois en Canada jusqu'en 1687" (AC, C 11A, 9: 281v), containing summaries and extracts from letters written by the governors and intendants of New France since 1669, it is said that, among other enclosures, Frontenac sent with his letters of November 6 and November 8, 1679, was "la relation et la carte du voyage que le Sr Joliet a fait a la baye d'hudson, et que les fermiers du Canada luy ont demandé; cette relation est datée du 27 octobre 1679 et signée Joliet"; therefore two days after the return of Jolliet to Quebec. This relation was probably the original which was abridged.

[65] Gagnon, Louis Jolliet, 191.

[66] P. Margry, "Louis Joliet," Revue Canadienne, 9 (1872): 123-127.

[67] Facsimile reproduction of the original in BN, Cartes, vol. 388 (153), in A.-L. Pinart, Recueil de Cartes, Plans et Vues relatifs aux États Unis et au Canada, New York, Boston, Montréal, Québec, Louisbourg (1651-1731) (Paris, 1893), pl. 23.

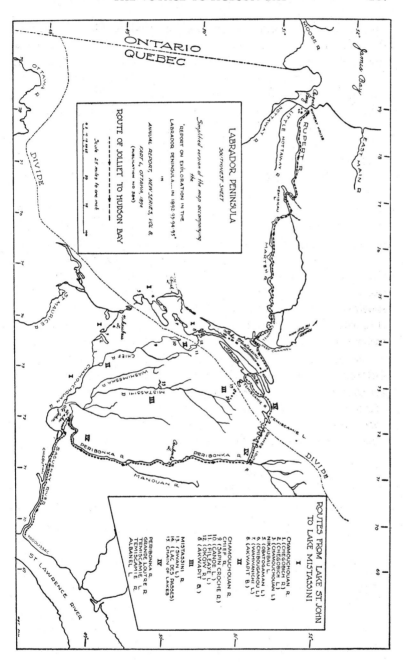

LABRADOR PENINSULA
30x7HN237 SHEET

Simplified version of the map accompanying the "REPORT ON EXPLORATION IN THE LABRADOR PENINSULA....IN 1892, 93, 94, 95"

IN

ANNUAL REPORT, NEW SERIES, VOL 8, PART L, OTTAWA, 1896 (PUBLICATION NO 384)

ROUTE OF JOLLIET TO HUDSON BAY

Scale 25 miles to one inch

ROUTES FROM LAKE ST. JOHN
TO LAKE MISTASSINI

I
CHAMOUCHOUAN R.
1. (CHEGOBICH R.)
2. (CHEGOBICH R.)
3. (CHAMOUCHOUAN L.)
4. NIKAUBAU L.
5. (BATOSKHAN L.)
6. (CHIBOUGAMOU L.)
7. (WAHWANICHI L.)
8. (AKWADIT B.)

II
CHAMOUCHOUAN R.
CHIEF R.
9. (SAPIN CROCHE R.)
10. (CANOE L.)
11. (FILEAYE L.)
12. (OKOW R.)
8. (AKWADIT B.)

III
MISTASSINI R.
13. (SWAN L.)
14. (LAC DES PASSES)

IV
PERIBONKA R.
GRANDE LOUTRE R.
TEMISCAMIE L.
TEMISCAMIE R.
ALBANEL L.

"marked in red," but on the black and white Pinart facsimile the red line cannot be made out. When I first studied this map, conditions precluded all access to the original, and to date it has been impossible to have it examined in Paris.[68] It should be observed, however, that there is uncertainty only with regard to that part of the route from Lake St. John to Lake Mistassini. There are several routes between these two lakes, anyone of which Jolliet may have taken, and he may have gone up one way and come back by another route.

Two of the three rivers shown on Jolliet's map of 1679 can be identified with certainty: the Peribonka is legended on the map "R. periboca" near its mouth, and "R. necouba" is the Ashwapmuchuan. The "R. Kakiga8sipi" very probably represents the Mistassini River with its tributary the Washimeska whose headwaters are a short distance from the Nestawkanow, the eastern branch of the Chief River. On leaving Lake Mistassini—oriented east-west on his map instead of northeast-southwest—Jolliet followed the Marten River down to where this tributary of the Rupert joins the main stream, about fifteen miles east of Lake Nemiskau.

A dotted line originating at Lake Nipissing follows the Ottawa, but the course of this river is not shown on the map; another dotted line begins at Fort Frontenac and meets that coming from Lake Nipissing at Montreal. These two routes are called "Chemin des Outaouas," and "chemin du fort frontenac," respectively. From Montreal the course of the St. Law-

---

68 While this book was being printed, I received from M. Jacques Rousseau, Director of the Montreal Botanical Garden, a thorough discussion of the various routes from Lake St. John to Lake Mistassini. With his permission I am printing his "Notes sur le voyage de Jolliet à la baie d'Hudson" in appendix A.

Since 1944, M. Rousseau has spent every summer exploring and surveying Lake Mistassini for the Canadian Government. His "Notes" testify to his thorough knowledge of the region.

It now remains to test M. Rousseau's conclusions by comparing the route marked on the map accompanying his "Notes" with the route marked in red on Jolliet's original. This comparison will be made this coming September. A friend of mine will examine Jolliet's original map in the Bibliothèque Nationale, Paris, and mark the red line on a tracing of the black and white facsimile in Pinart. Since this information cannot reach me on time to be inserted in this book, it will appear in the French edition of the *Life and Voyages of Louis Jolliet* to be published in Montreal.

rence through Three Rivers is represented by a dotted line; thereafter the river itself appears on the map.

Jolliet used his 1679 Hudson Bay draft to make the map of 1684.[69] In this latter, however, he began drawing the northern part too low, so that at the latitude of Quebec, he was at the end of his paper. In the lower left-hand corner he wrote: "Sault Ste Marie par 46," which is the latitude of this mission on the 1679 map. The frame of the 1684 map, drawn after the map was finished, cuts across the island [Baffin] bounded by David [Davis] and Hudson straits. On the earlier map, Baffin is represented as two islands separated by a "destroit qui est toujours plein de glace." This may have been intended to indicate Frobisher Bay or Cumberland Gulf, the northernmost part of which reaches the Arctic Circle. An unnamed bay, 125 miles deep, is shown on the map of 1684, and probably takes the place of the "strait which is always full of ice" mentioned on the map of 1679.

On both maps the Labrador coast from the Strait of Belle Isle to Cape Wolstenholme at latitude 63° is represented as a line running from the southeast to the northwest; the coast is unindented, and there is no indication of Ungava Bay. On both maps there is a difference varying from one to one and a half degrees between the position of identifiable landmarks and their true latitude. With regard to the legends inscribed on the two maps, the later one has more names along the banks of the St. Lawrence, while less rivers are shown or named than on the earlier one. For instance, he does not legend the Peribonka nor the Mistassini nor the Ashwapmuchuan.

Three routes to Hudson Bay not shown on the map of 1679 are on that of 1684. Two "chemins des sauuages a la baye" are indicated by dotted lines from "lac limibogon [Nipigon] par 51°"; the southern trail leads to the "R. Kechitchioüen" [Albany River], the northern one to the "R. Penatchichoüen" [Attawapiskat River?]. The third, "chemin des francois et des sauuages a la baye," is from the "R. Matoúan" [upper course of the Ottawa] to the "R. Monsonis" [Moose River].

---

[69] ASH, 123-8-1, reproduced in Gagnon, *Louis Jolliet*, between pp. 200-201.

To indicate that the English had trading posts at the mouth of these three rivers, there is a square legended "anglois."

Attention may be called to two descriptive legends. On the earlier map, south of Lake Mistassini near the discharge of Lake Albanel, Jolliet drew a square and wrote "francois"; inside the larger lake he inscribed the following legend: "Lac timigaming ou iay basti une maison." On the later map the wording of this inscription is simply "maison Jolliet." In view of these inscriptions, it is not improbable that in 1684 Jolliet was still using the building on Lake Mistassini as a warehouse or that he had agents there.

The second descriptive legend regards Anticosti Island. When he made the map of 1679 Jolliet had not yet been granted the Anticosti concession, but by 1684, he had spent several summers on the island. He called attention to his new domicile by inscribing "maison Jolliet" next to a square on the north shore of the island.[70]

3) THE VOYAGE OF JOLLIET TO HUDSON BAY

An abridged account of the voyage made by Louis Jolliet in 1679 as far as the Sea of the North, in a large inlet called Hudson Bay, where the English are carrying on at present the most lucrative trade of Canada.[71]

On May 13, 1679, I left Quebec with eight men[72] in order to visit all the rivers and lakes which are within the territory of the *Traite de Tadoussac*. I went into this territory by way

---

[70] On the location of this house, see *infra*, 189 f.

[71] The original French text will be found in "The Voyage of Louis Jolliet to Hudson Bay," *loc. cit.*, 245–250.

[72] "Ceste année [1679] Messrs de la Chesnay et Bo[i]sseau ont emploié Msr Jolliet—son frere Zacharie [,] Guill[aume] Bissot. Estienne Lesart—Louys le Mieux—pierre son frere [,] pierre Lesart —pierre Le grand—Denys—pour stablir la Traitte et la Mission de St François Xavier á Nemiskau par le p. Antoine Silvy [;] Le R. p. Claude Dablon estant Superieur de toutes les Missions [.] Conducteurs Jacq3 Kakachabeu et Sani8 [*or* Sari8]." Registre des baptêmes, mariages et sépultures des sauvages du Lac St. Jean, Chicoutimi, et Tadoussac de 1669 à 1692, fo. 61v. Archives of the Séminaire of Quebec (Laval University). The entry is in the handwriting of Father de Crépieul.—On this register, cf. A. Gosselin, "A Chicoutimi et au Lac St.–Jean à la fin du XVIIieme siècle. Notes tirées d'un ancien registre," in *Proceedings and Transactions* of the Royal Society of Canada, 3rd series, 11 (1917), section 1, 113–135.

of the Saguenay River, which originates near the great lake
called Timagaming [Lake Mistassini], the source of the Ne-
misco [Rupert] River, which empties into the Baye du Nord
[Hudson Bay]; on which I journeyed all the way to the sea.

After having traveled 343 leagues because of detours, although the distance is only 160 leagues in a straight line, and
after 127 portages, some long and some short, we came to a
cape of clay where tidal deposits made us think we were near
the bay itself. On rounding the cape we came upon the bay
all of a sudden, and had the pleasure at a time of lovely calm,
of viewing the sea and the English fort which was only a league
away from us.[73] The tidal current brought us imperceptibly
abreast of the fort, where no one was to be seen; so we fired a
shot in order to bring someone out, because we did not want to
surprise them by landing unannounced. We received a response at once, not from the fort, for there was nobody there,
but from the opposite bank of the river where three English-
men were hunting and where their boat was beached because
the tide was low.

They took us for foreigners who had come down to trade
with them, and shouted to us in some Indian language to come
over and take them to the fort. The river was very wide and
we were too far away to be recognized as Frenchmen, so we
went over toward them and they came walking along the shore
toward us. When the first of them, who was walking about
three hundred paces ahead of the others, saw that we were not
countrymen of theirs, he immediately doubled back to join his
companions, and the more I told him to come ahead and have
no fear, the more he hurried away. Then, as all three stood
and watched us, we landed and I spoke to them in French.
One of them, who understood French slightly, answered us and
asked who we were. When I shouted to him that I was a
Frenchman and that my name was Jolliet, he came toward us.

We treated them with great politeness, and they, on their
part, did not fail to reciprocate. The first man came aboard
with us, and the other three got into a bark canoe which we
had found six leagues farther up the [Rupert] River. The

---

[73] On the maps of 1679 and 1684, this fort is situated on the
south bank of the Rupert River, near present-day Rupert House.

man in this canoe had come back downstream to find out what was happening, for we had refused to tell him anything. He had joined us during the above-mentioned conversation, which he found very amusing, and which moved him to make fun of his compatriots for their timidity and inexperience.

Seeing that the man who was with us did not understand French, I spoke to him in Latin. He told me that he knew it better than our language.[74] From then on we had no trouble in making ourselves mutually understood. He showed me the peninsula where their governor was stationed,[75] three or four leagues away; anchored nearby was a ship of twelve guns and two small boats. They led us to the fort and received us very kindly; they gave the best of the food which they still had left, for the ship from London which brings their necessary provisions each year had not arrived yet.

My intention was to leave on the following day without waiting for the governor, but they pressed me so insistently to stay that I decided to remain. At daybreak a man set out in a bark canoe to inform the governor and I dispatched a letter to him which read as follows:

Sir:

Having been engaged by my Lord the Count de Frontenac, governor of all Canada, to visit the tribes and lands of the King's Domain in this part of the country,[76] I came down as far as Lake Nemiskau intending to return by way of Three Rivers.[77] When we reached Nemiskau our provisions were exhausted and we could find no game of any kind. The thought then came to me that in recent years, several Frenchmen who

---

[74] The identity of this English backwoodsman who knew Latin well enough to carry on a conversation in that language has not been ascertained.

[75] This governor was Charles Bayly. Cf. "The Voyage of Jolliet to Hudson Bay in 1679," MA, 26 (1944): 246, note 5.

[76] Jolliet was asked by Boisseau acting for the *Fermiers* to make the voyage (*supra*, note 64, and note 72); but he needed Frontenac's leave for a voyage of this kind.

[77] Neither in the document nor on the map of 1679 is there any indication that Jolliet returned to Quebec by way of the St. Maurice; a rough sketch of this river is shown on the map. For a description of this route, see Crouse, *Geographical Contributions of the Canadian Jesuits*, 145.

had visited you returned with nothing but praise for the hearty
welcome which you had accorded them,[78] and I thought that
you would be no less kind toward me than you had been toward
them, and that you would be willing to sell me some hardtack
and drink to facilitate my return. Your people give me hopes
that you will come here. I shall not leave until tomorrow. If
I am so fortunate as to see you, I shall be very glad to pay
you my respects and to assure you that I am etc.

He no sooner received my letter than he embarked with
fifteen men in a fifteen ton bark. Since the wind failed when
he was half way to the fort, he and five sailors made the rest
of the journey in a dory. I went by myself about one eighth
of a league along the shore to meet him, and hailed him from
afar. A sand bar prevented him from landing at the spot
where I was, and he said as he passed by: "Sir, I'll be with
you in a moment." Fifty paces farther on he was able to land
and came alone toward me. Meanwhile four of his men remained sitting in the dory and the fifth was standing on the
shore with a gun in his hand.

We exchanged polite greetings and tokens of good will.
His first words were: "You are welcome, Sir; you came here
with peaceful intentions and you have nothing to fear. Stay
as long as you like, and when you are ready to leave, I shall
give you all the help I can for your return journey. I heard
about you long ago, and I am delighted to have the opportunity of talking to you and of hearing what you have to say
about the great discovery of the river which the Indians call
Mississippi, which flows in the direction of Mexico. The English think highly of discoverers."

He then took my hand and said: "Come along, since you
have no intention of harming us, you have no reason to fear
that any harm will be done to you." He signaled his men to
be on their way, while the two of us went along the shore to
the fort, where he overwhelmed me with all possible kindness
and politeness. He was very glad to hear news from France
and from London. A year ago his ship had sailed away, and

----

78 Cf. the "Transactions" of 1687 in *Report on Canadian
Archives 1883*, 177, 178.

he was in daily expectation of it,[79] but as the season was already far advanced, he feared lest it had been blocked by the ice in the Strait. The rest of the day was spent in discussing miscellaneous topics. He told me that they had a ship of twelve guns to patrol the coast, which we saw riding at anchor off a point; that the ice of last spring's debacle had crushed a forty ton boat; that he had another one of the same tonnage and still another of fifteen tons as well as three launches. All these vessels, he said, were used for trading along the rivers of the Bay region down which the Indians come with their beaver pelts. He said that they had three forts at quite a distance from one another and that they were making ready to begin a fourth one in the coming spring.[80]

They are pushing more and more toward the west, toward the mouths of those rivers which have their headwaters near Lake Superior, where dwell tribes who used to trade with us. He also told me that they were sixty men in all.[81]

With regard to beaver pelts, he confirmed what I had learned from the Indians; that is, he is getting as many as he wants. This had been the case especially during the past year, ever since they began their push toward these other rivers. He added that there was also something better, which will make this colony still more important in the future, but he did not tell me what that was.

He asked me if I wished to become his associate, and offered me a lump sum of 10,000 francs and a salary of one thousand francs a year in this connection. I thanked him and told him that I was born a subject of the King of France and that I would glory in faithfully serving him during my whole life.

---

[79] The *John and Alexander* arrived shortly after the departure of Jolliet. Bayly returned on it to England and died in London on January 16, 1680 (N.S.).

[80] Besides the three English forts mentioned above, a fourth is indicated near the mouth of the "R. panachitchioüen" on the maps of 1679 and 1684.

[81] "Toward Hudson Bay... the English have some forts... in which, we are informed, are sixty men." Duchesneau to Colbert, November 14, 1679, in *Collection de Manuscrits... relatifs à la Nouvelle-France*, 1: 271. Duchesneau's source of information was Jolliet, who had returned to Quebec three weeks prior to the date of this letter.

He wanted me to explore the country beyond that of the Assiniboin and establish a post among these Indians, whom my Lord the Count has had coming to him for the past four years. He [Bayly] has sent presents to the Assiniboin this year to win them over so that he may trade with them, for their country is the only place where fine beaver and other pelts are to be found. There is no doubt that if the English remain in this bay, they will have control of all the commerce of Canada in ten years time.[82] Some of the Indians who used to come to Montreal went there this year and will go back again next spring. I mean the Temiscaming and Routin's band.[83]

Everybody knows that the Ottawa have no beaver pelts, and that they get them from the tribes around Green Bay or from the Indians who dwell on Lake Superior. It is likely, therefore, that when the Lake Superior Indians see that they are quite close to solidly established English posts well furnished with merchandise, those Indians will save their pelts for these posts as several have already begun to do.

When His Majesty decides on driving the English away from this bay and thus to become the master of the whole country and of the beaver pelt trade, it will be an easy thing to point out by what means this is to be done and to show how the plan is to be carried out.[84] At present their forts are forts

---

82 The same fear is expressed by Duchesneau in the letter quoted in the preceding note. Two years later, the intendant wrote: "They [English] are still in the north, in Hudson Bay, and do great damage to our fur trade. The revenue contractors feel it. The returns of their *Traite de Tadoussac* as well as those of the whole colony have fallen off, because the English entice the Ottawa to bring them their pelts. They do this damage by means of two forts, one situated in the Tadoussac region [the fort at the mouth of the Rupert River], the other at Cape Henrietta Maria [Port Nelson] in the country of the Assiniboin." Duchesneau to Seignelay, November 13, 1681. *Ibid.*, 286.

83 The Temiscaming were an Algonquian band whose habitat was in the vicinity of Timiskaming Lake, P. Q. The route from their habitat to the mouth of the Moose River was just as easy as, and shorter than the route to Montreal; moreover, the English paid two, three, and even four times more for their pelts than the French did.

84 The task was to be much more difficult than Jolliet thought. It took ten years and the daring and brilliance of Iberville to expel the English from Hudson Bay. See Frégault, *Iberville le Conquérant*, 89–127, 177–191, 236–263. In 1713, Louis XIV returned the bay to the English.

in name only: small square stockades which enclose their living quarters. The houses themselves are built to ward off the cold, but not the weapons of invading land forces. They make no provisions against an attack by land, thinking that they need protection only against attacks from the sea. Hence their ship in the Bay and the several thirty or forty ton boats, which can be used for voyages back to London. But it will be an easy matter, when His Majesty decides to give the order, to prevent from extending their posts farther; it will not be necessary to drive them out or to have an open break with them.[85]

After spending two days with him [Bayly] and finding out all that I wanted to know, I embarked in my canoe with the provisions he gave me: a bag of hardtack and a sack of flour, while he kept apologizing over and over again for not being able to give me more. I then set out for Quebec, arriving there on October 5, 1679.

L. Jolliet.

---

[85] "The only means to prevent [the English] from succeeding in that which is so prejudiciable to our trade would be to drive them out by armed force from that bay which belongs to us; or else, if this extreme measure is inadvisable, to build forts on the rivers leading into the lakes in order to stop the Indians at these points." Duchesneau to Seignelay, November 13, 1681, *Collection de Manuscrits . . . relatifs à la Nouvelle-France*, 1: 286 f.

CHAPTER IX

LAWSUITS. SURVEYING. FIRST LABRADOR VOYAGE

From the abridged report of the narrative of his voyage to the mouth of the Rupert River in 1679, one can see that Jolliet fully realized how detrimental the possession of Hudson Bay by the English would be to the trade of New France in general, and to the *Traite de Tadoussac* in particular. He was very much interested in the latter, for his concession was contiguous to the King's Domain, and his own trade would suffer if the pelts gathered by the Indians in that part of Canada were brought to the English on Hudson Bay instead of to the French on the St. Lawrence.

He was back in Quebec three weeks after the birth of his third son.[1] Two notarial acts dated February 4 and 19, respectively, show that he spent the winter of 1679–1680 in Quebec.[2] In the month of March 1680, Duchesneau granted to him in fief Anticosti Island "in consideration of his discovery of the Illinois country, . . . and of the voyage which he has just made to Hudson Bay in behalf and to the advantage of the Ferme du Roy in this colony."[3]

Sixty years later Charlevoix wrote that Anticosti Island was granted to Sieur Jolliet on his return from the discovery of the Mississippi. This was not a very valuable gift, for the island is worth absolutely nothing. It is thinly wooded,[4] the soil is sterile, and

---

[1] Tanguay, *Dictionnaire généalogique des familles canadiennes*, 1: 324, where Marie–Charlotte instead of Charles is given.

[2] Sale of a house "scituée sur la rue du Sault au matelot," to La Chesnaye, February 4, 1680, AJQ, Greffe Becquet, minute.—Dissolution of Jolliet's partnership with Gabriel Gosselin, February 19, 1680, *ibid.*, Greffe Duquet, cahier no. 16.

[3] *Inventaire de Pièces sur la côte de Labrador*, 1: 7 f.

[4] The author of the *Histoire chronologique* asserts that there was no wood on Anticosti (*supra*, 142, note 60), Champlain and Alfonce knew better. "Icelle [Anticosti] est couuerte de bois de pins, sapins, & bouleaux." C. H. Laverdière, ed., *Oeuvres de Champlain* (3 vols., Quebec, 1870), 3: 104.—"Et est l'isle de l'Ascension [Anticosti] une isle platte toute couverte d'arbres jusques au bort de la mer, assise sur roches blanches et albastres. Et y a toutes sortes d'arbres comme celles de France." J. Fonteneau *dit* Alfonce de Saintonge, *La Cosmographie avec l'Espère et le Régime du Soleil et du Nord*, G. Musset, ed., (Paris, 1904), 485.

there is not a single good harbor where a ship can safely anchor[5] . . .
The fishing along the coast is good enough, but I am persuaded that
Sieur Jolliet's heirs would willingly exchange their vast seigniory
for the smallest fief in France.[6]

This opinion of Charlevoix that Anticosti was a poor reward
granted to Jolliet for his explorations persisted until the nineteenth century. Of course, the size of the concession—over
two and a half million acres, half the area of the State of New
Jersey—would not of itself make it a princely domain, but its
products made it the most valuable concession in New France.
Then as now its stream abounded in fish and its forest was full
of game.[7] The legend that it was thinly wooded also persisted
until the nineteenth century. But the density of its forest was
not realized until the twentieth century, when expert foresters
estimated that it contained over two billion cubic feet of timber;
and they also found that with systematic cutting, the forest of
the island could be exploited indefinitely.[8] If Anticosti had
remained the possession of Jolliet's heirs, they would certainly
be unwilling today to exchange it even for the largest fief in
France. In July 1926, Gaston Menier, the owner of the island,
sold it to the Anticosti Corporation for 6,500,000 dollars.[9]

The concession in fief of Anticosti Island to Jolliet was objected to by Josias Boisseau who was then general manager in
Canada of the *Ferme du Domaine du Roy*.[10] On April 10,

---

[5] "There are but three bays called harbours: Fox Bay, Ellis
Bay and English Bay; but they are only safe in certain conditions
of the wind—and then for vessels of light draft." J. U. Gregory, *Anticosti. Its Shipwrecks* (Quebec, 1881), 15.—See however the "Lettre
du R. P. Adrien Pouliot" in the Quebec *Action Catholique* for September 15, 1945.

[6] Charlevoix, *Histoire et description generale de la Nouvelle-
France*, 3: 63.

[7] "Et y a, en la terre, forces bestes saulvaiges comme hours,
porcs espiz, cerf, biches et dains, et oyseaux de toutes sortes, et
foces poulles saulvaiges, lesquelles se tiennent ès boys." Alfonce, *op.
cit.*, 485. Cf. also Gregory, *op. cit.*, 14 f; J. Schmitt, *Monographie de
l'Ile d'Anticosti* (Paris, 1904), 11 f, 343 f.

[8] D. Potvin, *En Zigzag. Sur la Côte et dans l'Ile* (Quebec, 1929),
55–58. See V.-A. Huard, *Labrador et Anticosti* (Montreal, 1897),
221–258.

[9] Potvin, *op. cit.*, 77.

[10] Born in 1641, he seems to have come to Canada with his wife
in 1678. Frontenac was godfather of his eldest child who was baptized at Quebec on August 14, 1680. Tanguay, *Dictionnaire généalogique des familles canadiennes*, 1: 63.

1680, he had an act drawn by Romain Becquet, royal notary of the provostship of Quebec, wherein he stated that on the preceding March 14, he had petitioned Duchesneau to annul the concession made to Lalande and Jolliet,

because of the prejudice the said concession may cause to His Majesty's Domain of Tadoussac... The said Lord Intendant without adverting to the consequences and to the damage which the said concession of Anticosti as well as the trade which the said Lalande, Jolliet and other relatives of the said Sieur [Charles Aubert] de la Chesnaye carry on at Seven Islands and in the surrounding country, does to the Domain and to the *Ferme* of His Majesty, issued a ruling on the 29th of the same month of March [1680], which, among other privileges, allows the said Sieur Jolliet to go and settle on the said Island of Anticosti.[11]

This judgment, the petitioner repeated, cannot fail to be very prejudicial to the King's Domain; and he remarks that Anticosti is the key to Canada. Because of its strategic position, governors and intendants have always been unwilling to give the island as a concession. The importance of Anticosti has been recognized by His Majesty, "for when the king wished to entice Sieur Des groiseliers [Médard Chouart] from the English and have him return to this colony, he only granted the usufruct of the island for thirty years, and not the property thereof."[12]

These statements of Boisseau are somewhat confused. Anticosti Island was granted to Jolliet alone, in consideration of his services to the colony in general and to the shareholders of the *Ferme du Roy* in particular. What really alarmed the general manager was the trade which Jolliet, Lalande, and their associates ,were carrying on at Seven Islands, close to the King's Domain.[13] He repeated his protests again and again in Quebec, and his complaints are embodied in a memoir which reached Paris in the following year. We are not interested in the memorialist's accusations against all and sundry, but only in those against Jolliet. Before examining the indictment, however, we must place the document in its setting.

---

[11] 1680, April 10, AJQ, Greffe Becquet, minute; the pertinent passages are printed in Gagnon, *Louis Jolliet*, 323 f.

[12] The privilege was for twenty years. NYCD, 9: 974; *Jugements et délibérations du Conseil Souverain*, 2: 184 f.

[13] Cf. 1679, April 4, AJQ, Greffe Duquet, cahier no. 15; and 1680, October 2, *ibid.*, Greffe Becquet, minute.

By 1680 the question of the coureurs de bois had become very acute. From the very beginning of his term Frontenac had been ordered to rid the colony of these undesirables.[14] In 1674, he wrote to Colbert that only six were left;[15] but for reasons which do not concern us here, his zeal in carrying out the orders of the king soon abated, and the coureurs de bois so increased that before long they numbered 800;[16] mostly because, wrote Duchesneau in 1679, they were covertly protected by the governor.[17] Naturally, Frontenac claimed that it was the intendant who protected the coureurs, but the proofs sent by Duchesneau in 1679 were so decisive that they convinced even Colbert, who would have preferred to believe the worst of the intendant and to absolve the governor. The minister wrote to Frontenac that there was no doubt either in his own mind or in the mind of the king that Frontenac himself, and not Duchesneau, was guilty.[18]

In 1680, Duchesneau sent further proofs;[19] and we know from a letter of Louis XIV that Frontenac also sent his version of the affair. At least two of the governor's letters of this year have not come down to us; but we know from this letter of the king that Frontenac's account contained the same accusations against Jolliet as does the memoir here mentioned.

The memorialist begins by saying that the only reason why there are still coureurs de bois in New France, is because they are protected by Messrs. Duchesneau, Gaultier de Comporté, and Aubert de la Chesnaye. The first paragraphs of the document deal with the illicit trade in and around Montreal. Besides Duchesneau and La Chesnaye, Charles Le Moyne and Jacques Leber are singled out as the outstanding offenders in this

---

[14] Louis XIV to Frontenac, June 5, 1672, June 5, 1673; Colbert to Frontenac, June 13, 1673, in RAPQ, 1927, 3, 23, 24.

[15] Frontenac to Colbert, November 14, 1674, ibid., 57, 68. "In the first two years ... you [Frontenac] have entirely destroyed the coureurs de bois." C. Le Clercq, Premier Establissement de la Foy dans la Nouvelle France (2 vols., Paris, 1691), 1, dedicatory epistle.

[16] Louis XIV to Frontenac, April 30, 1681, in P. Clément, ed., Lettres, Instructions et Mémoires de Colbert (7 vols., Paris, 1861–1873), 3, part 2, 645; Duchesneau to Colbert, November 13, 1680, AC, C 11A, 5: 178; Louis XIV to Duchesneau, April 30, 1681, AC, B 8: 81.

[17] Duchesneau to Colbert, November 10, 1679, NYCD, 9: 131.

[18] Colbert to Frontenac, April 4, 1680, RAPQ, 1927, 113.

[19] Duchesneau to Seignelay, November 13, 1680, NYCD, 9: 143.

region. The memorialist then passes to what took place on the Lower St. Lawrence.

In 1679, he says, under the pretext of a fishing expedition, La Chesnaye sent a ship commanded by his nephew "to trade in forbidden places," *i. e.,* in the King's Domain; and what was worse, the pelts gathered during this expedition were brought to the English. All of this, he adds, is attested by unimpeachable, duly legalized testimonies.[20] When Duchesneau's attention was called to these violations of the trading laws, the intendant did not even listen to the accusations.

The men called Lalande and Jolliet, brother-in-law and nephew of La Chesnaye, respectively, having taken ship toward Tadoussac, under the pretext of their Anticosti fishing concession, were accused and convicted after their return [to Quebec] in the month of March of last year, 1680, of having enticed the Indians [to trade with them], and not only did they bring pelts to the English but they even traded with the governor of Hudson Bay, and received gifts from him.[21]

Jolliet did not go and could not have gone to Hudson Bay at this time as alleged. We know that he was in Quebec on November 9, 1679, and also on February 4, 1680,[22] and that it was impossible to make a round trip from Quebec to Hudson during the winter in the intervening time. The Anticosti concession was granted after the northern voyage, and it was given to Jolliet alone, as a reward for the discovery of the Illinois country and because of the information he had brought back to

---

20 These testimonies are first a declaration of Olivier Guillemot, a calker, on the *Sainte-Anne,* La Chesnaye's ship. He said that Maheu who was in charge traded below Seven Islands. The ship then went to Port Royal [Annapolis, N. S.] where Maheu boarded an English ketch and sailed to Boston. When he returned five weeks later, he was accompanied by "un jeune homme anglois de Baston appelé Israel." The merchandises brought from Boston were put on board the *Sainte–Anne* and delivered to La Chesnaye when the ship reached Quebec. Another declaration by Pierre Pilet confirms Guillemot's testimony. The third witness, Louis Fontaine, was the pilot of the *Sainte-Anne.* He specified that the trading took place "aux Isles Maingand au dessous des Sept Isles"; hence not in "forbidden territory" but in the Jolliet–Lalande concession. Fontaine's statement was confirmed by Antoine Goudreau.—The four documents (minutes) are in the AJQ, Greffe Becquet; the first two are dated September 16, 1680; the other two September 19 and October 15, 1680, respectively.

21 Mémoire et Preuve de la cause du désordre des coureurs de bois avec le moyen de les détruire. RAPQ, 1927, 121.

22 *Supra,* note 2.

Quebec from Hudson Bay in 1679. We also know that Lalande was not one of the eight who accompanied Jolliet in this
journey,[23] and that when the latter met Bayly at the mouth of
the Rupert River, he did not "trade" with the Englishman.
As for the presents, they consisted in "a sack of hardtack and
a sack of flour," which Bayly gave Jolliet and his men because
they had no provisions for the return journey.

It may perhaps not be out of place here to call attention to
the travesty of facts commonly indulged in by Frontenac's
protégés, partisans and hangers-on. Their letters, reports, and
books are the basis for most of the history of the governor's
first term. This "authentic" documentation has, on the whole,
been accepted uncritically by immature dissertation writers or
by self-styled impartial historians, who express pained surprise or stand ready to cry "prejudice" whenever one checks
the statements of their fustian heroes against independent evidence, especially if it so happens that these statements turn
out to be falsifications with malice aforethought.

The memorialist's accusations against Jolliet and Lalande
can only be explained on the ground that Boisseau and La
Chesnaye had some difference in the winter of 1679–1680. That
this difference—the nature of which we have not found—occurred at that time is deduced from the fact that in the spring
of 1679, La Chesnaye and Boisseau had financed Jolliet's expedition to Hudson Bay.[24] Another document showing that
previous to the winter of 1679–1680, Boisseau was friendly to
the Jolliets is a notarial act dated November 24, 1679, from
which we learn that before leaving with his brother for Hudson
Bay, Zacharie Jolliet had given Boisseau power of attorney.[25]
That Boisseau's main conflict was with La Chesnaye is clear
from a series of documents in the Judicial Archives of Quebec;[26] a conflict in which Duchesneau later became involved.[27]
As we shall see presently, the intendant sided with Jolliet and

---

  23 *Supra*, 170, note 72.
  24 *Supra*, *ibid.*
  25 1679, November 16, AJQ, Greffe Rageot, no. 2000.
  26 Cf. the documents in the AJQ, Greffe Becquet, under the following dates: 1680, March 3; April 10; June 27, 29; July 1, July 26,
August 12; etc.
  27 *Ibid.*, 1680, July 26, 29; August 11, 12; September 29; etc.

Lalande who were La Chesnaye's business partners. Thus Boisseau's attacks on Jolliet and Lalande were in reality directed against La Chesnaye and Duchesneau.

With the above accusations the memorialist of 1681 had only begun his indictment of Jolliet and Lalande. He went on to say that those guilty of the crime of "trading in forbidden territory" should have been fined 2,000 livres, their ship and cargo confiscated, and an exemplary punishment meted out to the culprits. Instead, on the 28th of the same month of March 1680,[28] "M. Duchesneau issued in his own house an ordinance signed by himself and by one of his secretaries, allowing the accused to leave for another fishing expedition merely forbidding them to trade with the Indians or to entice them to trade, under penalty of 2,000 livres fine and confiscation of the ship and cargo."

On the same day, the memorialist continues, Boisseau presented a second request, thinking that Duchesneau would modify the provisions of the above mentioned ordinance; but all that the intendant did was to issue a second ordinance similar to the first, in order to "save the accused who could not have been acquitted had the case been tried before the Sovereign Council." Boisseau protested loudly, and made it known that he would notify the *Fermiers,* his employers in France, of the glaring injustice of these two ordinances. To pacify him, Duchesneau issued a third ordinance, dated April 4, condemning "these Lalande and Jolliet fellows" to pay a fine of 500 livres fine, confiscating their ship and forbidding them to repeat the offense.[29]

The sequence of events, designedly confused by the memorialist can be re-established. While Jolliet went to Hudson Bay, two ships sailed for the Lower St. Lawrence; one, the *Sainte-Anne,* commanded by Maheu, stopped at Mingan, where Maheu did some trading;[30] the other ship was the ketch be-

---

[28] I did not find any of the ordinances mentioned in the "Mémoire et Preuve"; some notarial acts in the AJQ, refer to that of April 4.

[29] In the following year Jolliet sued the Fermiers for damages and was awarded 2,500 livres. 1681, August 23, AJQ, Greffe Becquet, two acts. Cf. 1685, September 9, *ibid.,* Greffe Rageot, no. 2981.

[30] *Supra,* note 20.

longing to Jolliet and Lalande which left Quebec on April 16,[31] with Lalande on board. By March 1680, Boisseau, who had had differences with La Chesnaye during the preceding winter, chose to accuse the relatives of the latter of having traded in "forbidden territory," although Mingan was well outside the limits of the King's Domain and in virtue of the concession granted to François Bissot, Jolliet and Lalande had the right to trade at Seven Islands. When Boisseau further learned that Jolliet had been given Anticosti Island in fief, he saw an opportunity for making La Chesnaye and Duchesneau appear in a very bad light before the minister, thus diverting the attention of the authorities in Paris from Frontenac's own violations of the king's ordinances.

If Sieur Boisseau thought that by the confiscation of Jolliet's ship all trade activities near the "forbidden territory" would be stopped he was soon undeceived.

And when, after Boisseau had seized the confiscated ship, the time to leave for trading drew near, La Chesnaye, an associate of those Lalande and Jolliet fellows, his brother-in-law and nephew, respectively, took all the men who were equipping the ships of the *Ferme* and set them hurriedly to refit his own ship, the *Sainte-Anne,* on which Jolliet and Lalande left during the first days of May, before any ship of the *Ferme* was ready to sail.

They returned to Quebec last September [1680] with their ship loaded with pelts and other merchandises.[32]

After this Boisseau complained more than ever. He accused Lalande and Jolliet of having enticed the Indians to Seven Islands, and of having traded within the limits of the King's Domain. He claimed that they had left men behind to winter in those parts, and said that by their trade they were ruining the *Traite de Tadoussac.*

Boisseau went to Duchesneau and asked that justice be done. All the redress which he obtained from the intendant consisted in the issuing of a private ordinance dated September 27, 1680, which permitted Lalande, Jolliet and their partners to unload their pelts, and forbade them from then on to trade within the limits of the King's Domain. As for La Chesnaye he was completely exonerated.

---

[31] 1679, April 4, AJQ, Greffe Duquet, cahier no. 15.
[32] Mémoire et Preuve, RAPQ, 1927, 122.

A note appended to the published memoir from which we have quoted says that the memoir "was dictated, if not written by M. de Frontenac himself."[33]   Although, as we shall see, the same accusations against Jolliet were also sent to Paris by Frontenac, we learn from a letter of M. Dudouyt to Bishop Laval that this memoir is not the governor's.   In this letter Dudouyt says that there had been much talk against Duchesneau in Paris.   It would have been desirable, he adds, to have someone who could have taken the defense of the intendant. "It was said (on a dit) that there was nothing so weak as his procès-verbaux," *i.e.*, Duchesneau's proofs that Frontenac was protecting the coureurs de bois; and it was also said that "the summary which Boisseau himself made of his own [procès-verbaux] was so well done that nothing could be better."[34]

By "on a dit" Dudouyt means that Frontenac's partisans in Paris had disparaged Duchesneau's procès-verbaux and had extolled Sieur Boisseau's memoir.   The king, however, took quite a different view of the matter.   To Duchesneau he simply wrote that the intendant had shown too great partiality toward La Chesnaye and that he had encroached upon the rights of the governor when he took it upon himself to allow "the man named Jolliet" to leave Quebec for the Lower St. Lawrence. The rest of the king's letter deals mostly with the coureurs de bois and with the absolute necessity of living on friendly terms with Frontenac.[35]

To the governor the king wrote in quite a different manner. He begins by saying that he has received Frontenac's letters of May 20 and of November 14, 1680.   These letters do not seem to be extant, but from what Louis XIV says it appears that Frontenac had asked His Majesty to distinguish between what had happened before he received the king's letters of 1680 and his conduct thereafter.   To this the king answered that he knew one thing: "You did not obey my orders concerning one of the most important points which regard my service," namely, the

---

[33] *Ibid.*, 124.

[34] Dudouyt to Laval, May 10, 1681, Archives of the Séminaire of Quebec (Laval University), *Lettres*, Carton N. no. 57.

[35] Louis XIV to Duchesneau, April 13, 1681, AC, C 11A, 5: 339; and April 30, 1681, AC, B 8: 20.

governor had not maintained friendly terms with Duchesneau. After adding that Frontenac's animosity against the intendant "appears in all your letters," he goes on to say:

You accuse the said intendant as well as Sieurs de la Chesnaye and de Comporté of carrying on trade and of profiting from the illicit trade of the coureurs de bois. In proof of your accusations, you mention what happened in the law-suit which the man Boisseau brought against Jolliet and others, because of their alleged trade at Seven Islands, to the prejudice of the *Traite de Tadoussac*. This has nothing to do with the coureurs de bois, since it is clear from the documents which you yourself have sent that you conceded the Mingan Islands to the said Jolliet, where he has begun an establishment, and that he only traded with the Indians who brought merchandise to his settlement. On this subject I shall repeat once more what I have said in my preceding letters; namely, everything which you write about the said intendant with regard to his trade and his support of the coureurs de bois appears to spring from a spirit of recrimination rather than being based on a real foundation.[36]

Frontenac was far too wise not to realize that he had made a mistake in supporting Sieur Boisseau and in sending a report which duplicated that of the general manager of the *Ferme du Roy*. In a letter to Colbert, he said that he had merely done his duty and obeyed orders.[37] To Louis XIV he wrote that he was unfortunate to have incurred His Majesty's displeasure for protecting the interests of the *Fermiers* of the King's Domain; adding that he had supported Boisseau only because of the king's own orders and only after the said Boisseau had shown him the secret instructions which he had received from his Paris employers. As a further justification, Frontenac enclosed copies of the letters which he himself had received from the *Fermiers* thanking him for the "protection extended to their agent in Quebec, and begging him to continue it."[38]

Judging from their actions, the *Fermiers* in France were not very much impressed by the wonderful summary, in the memoir, of Boisseau's procès-verbaux. They probably came to the conclusion that their interests would be better protected in the hands of a man of less uncontrollable temper. On one occa-

---

[36] Louis XIV to Frontenac, April 30, 1681, Clément, *Lettres, Instructions et Mémoires de Colbert*, 3, part 2, 644 f.

[37] Frontenac to Colbert, [1681], RAPQ, 1927, 118.

[38] Frontenac to Louis XIV, November 2, 1681, *ibid.*, 124.

sion, when a coureur de bois refused to change his testimony previously given under oath, Boisseau threatened to throw the man out of the window, then to lock him up in the cellar and let him starve there, and finally kicked him out of the house after slapping his face all the while "jurant horriblement contre Dieu Et comme un lyon."[39]   At another time, when a sheriff served on Boisseau two ordinances of the intendant, the general manager tore up the first, trampled on it and said: "B . . . . d'intendant sy ie [te] tenois Je ten ferois autant."   He then took the second ordinance and while promising to make a copy of it "auroit juré et Blasphemé le St nom de Dieu par plusieurs fois."[40]   What is certain is that by July 15, 1681, Boisseau had ceased to be general manager, for on this day he is referred to in the court records as "cy devant agent des sieurs interessez."[41] After November 1681, his name disappears from the records; he seems to have returned to France that same year.[42]

Duchesneau answered as follows the accusations in Boisseau's memoir:

Boisseau greatly maligned me by saying that I gave permission to the man named Jolliet to send out ships on a fishing expedition to the detriment of the authority and the right which M. the Governor has to grant these permissions.   In the suit which was tried before me, there never was any question of such permissions, but rather he [Boisseau] wanted me to forbid the said Jolliet from settling on his concessions and from fishing in those places, contending that this would be prejudicial to the Ferme du Roy.   Seeing that M. the Governor delayed granting these permissions [to leave for his concession] until I had issued my ordinances to that effect, I myself granted them but I was very careful to avoid attributing to myself powers which I do not have.   I simply decreed that, as far as I was concerned, I allowed the said Sieur Jolliet to settle and fish in those places which had been conceded to him with such precautions and defensive measures as were needed for the protetction of the Ferme.[43]

On May 29, 1680, the king ratified the Mingan conces-

---

39 *Jugements et délibérations du Conseil Souverain*, 2: 632.
40 1681, February 5, AJQ, Greffe Rageot, no. 2172.
41 *Jugements et délibérations du Conseil Souverain*, 2: 600.
42 His wife remained in Canada at least until the following year.   1682, October 26, AJQ, Greffe Rageot, no. 2479.
43 Duchesneau to Seignelay, November 13, 1681, AC, C 11A, 5: 294v.

sion,[44] and on October 24, 1680, that is, about the time when Boisseau was making his masterful summary, the royal decree was entered in the registers of the Sovereign Council.[45]

The document granting the Mignan concession to Jolliet and Lalande, the postscript containing the royal ratification and its registration with the Sovereign Council, are printed in Gagnon's book on Jolliet.[46] Farther down in his book, Gagnon writes: "The seignioral grant of the Island of Anticosti was ratified by Louis XIV on May 29, 1680, and the sovereign added a further favor by conferring on Louis Jolliet the title of 'hydrographe du roi'."[47] The Mingan concession, not the Anticosti, was ratified on May 29, 1680. I have found no document containing the ratification of the Anticosti fief; the undated endorsement on the original document merely means that the title was filed with the clerk of the Sovereign Council. Gagnon thus made the ratification of the Mingan concession serve for Anticosti as well; but a simple consideration of the dates involved clearly shows that the title granted by Duchesneau in March 1680, cannot have been ratified in Paris in May of the same year.

In a note appended to the above quotation, Gagnon warns us not to confuse the title of "hydrographe du roi" conferred in 1680, with that of "professeur d'hydrographie à Québec" which Jolliet received in 1697. Jolliet did not receive the title of "hydrographe du roi" in 1680. The first man who was officially appointed "hydrographe du Roi à Quebec" is Franquelin who received the title in 1686, with a salary of 400 livres per annum.[48] Since one of the obligations of the "hydrographe du roi" was to teach navigation at Quebec, he was also "maître d'hydrographie."[49] Thus there was no difference whatever be-

---

[44] *Inventaire de Pièces sur la côte de Labrador*, 1: 7.
[45] *Jugements et délibérations du Conseil Souverain*, 2: 424.
[46] Gagnon, *Louis Jolliet*, 187 f.
[47] *Ibid.*, 199.
[48] "Franquelin, Mapmaker," MA, (1943): 37.
[49] In 1687, Denonville and Champigny wrote to Seignelay asking that Franquelin be employed as mapmaker exclusively, and that the teaching of navigation be entrusted to the Jesuits (AC, C 11A, 9: 10v); but the authorities in Paris left things as they were. Nothing came of the same suggestion made three years later by Denonville after his return to France. *Ibid.*, 193.

tween the title "hydrographe du roi" and "maître d'hydrographie"; in the documents of the period the two expressions
are used indifferently to designate the same office.[50]

In the spring of 1681, the seignior of Anticosti seems to
have brought his family to the island. In the census of this
year, he is listed as residing there with his wife, four of his
children, five men-servants, and a maid. The census taker
noted that they had six guns, two heads of cattle, and that two
acres of land had been cleared.[51] His residence at Anticosti
was temporary, for, as we shall see, he had returned to Quebec
by the end of August 1681.

When discussing the original Jolliet settlement on Anticosti
Island, I said that some had thought that Jolliet's first house
was built on English Bay, while others, myself included, were
of the opinion that this house stood on Ellis Bay;[52] I also said
that the latter opinion proved to be untenable in view of the
following positive evidence.

On Franquelin's map of 1681,[53] a circle legended "Habitation du Sr Jolliet" is clearly meant to indicate a spot on the
north shore of the island, near a bay called on the map "Port
aux Ours" which approximately corresponds to present-day

---

[50] Franquelin, who was teaching navigation at Quebec, is called
"hydrographe du roy" in the following official documents in the
Jugements et délibérations du Conseil Souverain, 3: 416, 419, 669, 737,
782; and he is called once "maitre de géographie du roy." *Ibid.*, 579.—
After Jolliet had been officially appointed "maitre d'hydrographie,"
he is invariably called "hydrographe du roy" in documents posterior
to 1697: *Ibid.*, 4: 730, 942, 1015, 1079; BRH, 22 (1916): 336; *Inventaire de Pièces sur la côte de Labrador*, 1: 271. Note also that in
1695, Jolliet asked to be appointed "to the position of hydrographer
at Quebec, which was held by Sieur Franquelin." E. Richard, ed.,
Supplement to Dr. Brymner's Report on Canadian Archives 1899 (Ottawa, 1901), 27.

[51] Sulte, *Histoire des Canadiens-Français*, 5: 88. If the census
was correctly transcribed, there are several inexplicable errors in this
entry. The age of Jolliet is given as 42, he was 36 years old; his
wife's age is said to be 23, she was 25. The names of the children
and their ages are as follows: Louis, 5; Jean, 3; Anne, 2; and Claire,
1. With the exception of the oldest child, the ages of the other three
do not agree with their ages as given in the baptismal records. "1)
Jean who is apparently Jean-Baptiste was born in 1683; 2) Anne
was born in 1682; and Claire in 1685, that is, respectively, two, one,
and four years *after* the date of the census.

[52] "Louis Jolliet. The Middle Years," MA, 27 (1945): 90 f.

[53] In BSH, B 4040-3. On this map cf. "Franquelin, Mapmaker,"
MA, 25 (1943): 58 f.

MacCarthy Bay, the Grand Macastey of French maps. Again, Jolliet himself inscribed "maison Jolliet" next to a square at the same spot on his map of 1684.[54]   Finally, in the following year, Franquelin wrote "Maison de Mr Jolliet" at the same place as on his map of 1681, also specifying the place with a square.[55]   Now in the title of Franquelin's map of 1685, it is expressly stated that the map was made on the "memoirs and observations of Sieur Jolliet," and since we know from a letter of Denonville that Franquelin was given the sketches of Jolliet to draw this map, I concluded that Jolliet had apparently built his first house on MacCarthy Bay.

This opinion had also to be discarded as a result of the investigations of Father A. Pouliot, S.J., who went to Anticosti in the summer of 1945 and examined the terrain.   An account of his field work is published in the *Action Catholique* of Quebec for September 7, 14, 15, 1945.[56]   Father Pouliot's argument based on the map of 1684, namely, that east of the square inscribed on this map, Jolliet meant to indicate a river "by a short stroke of the pen," is invalid.   There is no stroke of the pen at this place as can be seen by examining the map itself which Father Pouliot reproduced between pp. 200 and 201 of the fourth reprint of Gagnon's book.   Much more convincing is the testimony of an old man who told Father Pouliot that, in his youth, he saw near the mouth of the Rivière à l'Huile distinct remnants of pile-work measuring 400 square feet, which was the size of Jolliet's house according to a document of 1725;[57] the same document says that near the house there was a clearing of eight or ten acres.   Father Pouliot himself saw near the spot unmistakable traces of a former clearing. It seems then that Jolliet's first house on Anticosti Island was

---

54 In ASH, 123–8–1.   On this map, cf. "The Voyage of Louis Jolliet to Hudson Bay in 1679," MA, 26 (1944): 241, note 82.

55 This is the house referred to by Lahontan: "Elle [Anticosti Island] appartient au Sieur *Joliet*, Canadien, qui y a fait faire un petit Magasin fortifié, afin que les marchandises & sa famille soient à l'abri des surprises des Eskimaux." *Nouveaux Voyages de Mr. Le Baron de Lahontan dans l'Amerique Septentrionale* (2 vols., La Haye, 1703), 2: 8.

56 A brief summary of these articles will be found in Gagnon, *Louis Jolliet*, 206, note 1.

57 In Gagnon, *op. cit.*, 320 f.

situated on the left bank and near the mouth of the Rivière à l'Huile.

For the next four years the documentation concerning the whereabouts of Jolliet is fragmentary. In the middle of July 1681, Jolliet had not yet returned to Quebec from his concessions,[58] but he was in this town by August 23, on which day he sued for damages suffered as a result of the confiscation of his ship by Duchesneau on April 4, 1680.[59] The court records prove that he was away during the summer months of 1682;[60] and these same court records attest his presence in Quebec in January and February 1683,[61] which shows that he had returned before winter set in. On October 10, 1683, he hired a manservant;[62] six weeks later he appeared before the Sovereign Council;[63] and on December 1, he signed a contract with Claude Baillif for building a house in Quebec.[64] On January 19, 1684, he signed a note in which he acknowledges having received 200 livres from Bishop Laval on that day.[65] At the beginning of March, he settled with his mother-in-law the accounts of his partnership with Lalande.[66]

From the Tadoussac register we know that he spent the summer of 1684 at Anticosti. By September 4, Jolliet was back in Quebec, for on that day he and Baillif went to Rageot and had the private contract of December 1, 1683, legalized.[67] Considering that on January 23, 1685, he was hiring a sailor for the "voyage de cette ville de Quebec a l'isle d'Anticosti" in the

---

[58] *Jugements et délibérations du Conseil Souverain*, 2: 593.

[59] 1681, August 23, AJQ, Greffe Becquet, two acts, minutes.

[60] *Judgements et délibérations du Conseil Souverain*, 2: 799, 807, 810, 813.

[61] *Ibid.*, 858, 867.

[62] Michel Desorcis jr. "acceptant de le [Jolliet] seruir pendant la navigation prochaine a compter du jour que lon commencera a Charger la barque dud. Sieur Jolliet, jusque enfin de la ditte navigation." 1683, October 10, AJQ, Greffe Duquet, cahier no. 23. Cf. also *Jugements et délibérations du Conseil Souverain*, 2: 904.

[63] *Jugements et délibérations du Conseil Souverain*, 2: 911.

[64] Chicago Historical Society Library, Gunther Collection; printed in *Le Canada Français*, 2nd series, 33 (1945) : 70–72.

[65] 1684, January 19, AJQ, Greffe Duquet, cahier no. 23.

[66] 1684, March 9, *ibid.*, Greffe Genaple. The account itself is a Jolliet holograph.

[67] The notarial act is appended to the private contract. *Supra*, note 64.

coming spring,[68] it is clear that he spent the winter of 1684–1685 in town, and it is also clear that Margry was imagining things when he wrote that by 1685, Jolliet "had already spent two winters at Anticosti."[69]　On March 2, 1685, he signed in Quebec a lease entitling him to exploit Lalande's share of the Mingan concession.[70]　Two documents dated June 14 and July 12, 1685, respectively, show that he was then absent from Quebec;[71] but another document dated September 9, proves that he had returned by that date.[72]

Only one conclusion can be drawn from the dates of the documentation cited in the two preceding paragraphs:—during these years Jolliet spent the winters in Quebec and the summers in his concessions on the Lower St. Lawrence.

On November 10, 1685, he wrote from Quebec the earliest autograph letter which has come down to us.[73]

To My Lord,

My Lord the Marquis de Seignelay,

Minister and Secretary of State.

My Lord:

It is not without reason that from the very beginning ship captains coming to New France have always been apprehensive of the entrance of the Gulf of St. Lawrence [Cabot Strait] and of the navigation from Anticosti to Quebec,[74] a distance of more than one hundred and thirty leagues.

It is known, my Lord, that several ships sent by His Majes-

---

[68] 1685, January 23, AJQ, Greffe Auber, no. 483.

[69] Margry, "Louis Joliet," *Revue Canadienne*, 9 (1872) : 131.

[70] 1685, March 2, AJQ, Greffe Rageot, no. 2905; printed in *Inventaire de Pièces sur la côte de Labrador*, 1: 252–254.

[71] 1685, June 14, AJQ, Greffe Duquet, cahier no. 26; 1685, July 12, *ibid.*, Greffe Rageot, no. 2958.

[72] 1685, September 9, *ibid.*, Greffe Rageot, no. 2981.

[73] A clerk in Paris wrote on the first page: "Le Sr Jolliet 10 9bre 1685 envoye une Carte du Golphe et fleuve St Laurent quil dit tres bonne." The same clerk wrote on fo. 134v, "Observations de la navigation du fleuve de St Laurens sur lesquelles La Carte envoyée à Monseigneur par Mr de Denonville a esté dessinée."

[74] "J'aymerais mieulx aller de France à l'Acadie que de monter de là le fleuve Sainct Laurens jusques à Quebec à cause des grands risques qu'il y a à monter ce fleuve." Mémoire sur l'Acadie, [1683], *Collection de Manuscrits . . . relatifs à la Nouvelle–France*, 1: 292.

ty as well as by merchants, have been shipwrecked in the said river, for lack of accurate and reliable navigation maps.

Since I completed my studies in philosophy and mathematics eighteen years ago, I have acquired much experience during the voyages I made to the Mississippi River, the Illinois country, the Lake of the Pouteouatami [Green Bay], the country of the Ouenibegons [Winnebago], Lake Superior in the Ottawa country, Baye du Nord [Hudson Bay], Anticosti, Percée Island, Belle Isle and Newfoundland, always with dividers or compass in hand, noting every cape and spit, as well as the bearings from one to the other. This experience emboldens me, my Lord, to present to you this map which is [the result of] my work during the past six years. You will see marked on it all the coves, islands and islets, all the coasts and sand bars from Quebec to Newfoundland. The pilots of the ships of His Majesty and of other ships have nothing to fear if they use this map and navigate by it.

I do not hesitate to say that this map is complete, for I inserted in the final draught the information and the noteworthy details observed during forty-six voyages on a bark and three in a canoe. Coves and anchorages, good and bad, as well as the bearings, are faithfully entered.

I am not adding the map of the Illinois country, of the Mississippi, or that of the overland route to Hudson Bay, because the maps of these regions which have been sent to His Majesty these past years were all based on my memoirs, and those very enterprises which are now in progress in Canada are the result of the information which I brought back.

[Hence] it only remained, my Lord, to give you a map of the St. Lawrence River, as accurate and as trustworthy as possible for the navigation of barks and vessels, made by a man with several years of experience. He begs you to accept it as coming from one who considers himself, with all possible respects, my Lord,

Your most humble and most obedient servant,

Jolliet.[75]

---

75 Jolliet to Seignelay, November 10, 1685, AC, C 11E, 13: 135–136. The letter is printed with slight changes in G. Marcel, *Cartographie de la Nouvelle France* (Paris 1885), 14 f; also in BRH, 51 (1945) : 182.

Eighteen years back brings us to 1667, the year when Jolliet left the seminary, and six years back, when he began the survey of the St. Lawrence, would be in 1679, the year when Duchesneau granted the Mingan concession. The journeys he speaks of were made during the spring and the summer months; for he evidently does not mean that in five years' time, he made forty-nine journeys from Quebec to the mouth of the St. Lawrence, but rather that whenever he sailed he noted down all that would be useful to pilots and all that helped to make the navigation on the river safer.

Father Steck sees in the second paragraph of this letter an attempt on the part of Jolliet "to counteract the influence of what Thevenot put out as Marquette's narrative." After quoting Jolliet's reason for not sending maps of the Illinois country, of the Mississippi and of Hudson Bay, Father Steck goes on to say: "The circumstance that this was written four years after the appearance of Thevenot's volume and that no allusion is made to Marquette in connection with the Illinois and the Mississippi is very significant, especially since Thevenot had a map of the Mississippi region."[76]

The significance of this "circumstance" is not at all striking for anyone who has some knowledge of the cartographical output in New France between 1675 and 1684, and who is not preoccupied with looking for *midi à quatorze heures*. First of all, it is plain that Jolliet does not especially single out the map of the Illinois country or that of the Mississippi, but lumps these together with his two maps of the Labrador peninsula which were sent to Paris in 1679 and in 1684. Secondly, he clearly wished to remind the minister that the Randin map of 1675 and that of Franquelin of 1678 were based on his memoirs or on his sketches. Finally, if, as is quite probable, Thévenot's *Recueil* published in 1681, had by this time found its way to Canada, Jolliet knew that the map published by Thévenot was not Marquette's map, for he would immediately recognize it as a variant of the map which he drew from memory after his return to Quebec in 1674.[77]

---

[76] Steck, *The Jolliet–Marquette Expedition*, 238.
[77] "The Jolliet Lost Map of the Mississippi," MA, 28 (1946): 81–87, 114 f.

What Jolliet says about "those very enterprises which are now in progress in Canada" refers to an important expedition in preparation. In October 1685, the shareholders of the *Compagnie du Nord*, having learned of the latest treason of Radisson which, they claimed, cost them more than 400,000 livres, prevailed upon Denonville to send an expedition to Hudson Bay to expel the English.[78] The information which Jolliet brought back is contained in his report of 1679 translated in Chapter Eight of this book.[79]

From the wording of the letter it is clear that the map of the St. Lawrence River was an autograph map. Marcel prefaced his publication of the original text by saying: "We have not been able to find out . . . to which map the following letter of Jolliet refers."[80] The reason why Marcel was unable to identify this map, which Harrisse had listed fifteen years earlier,[81] is because he had apparently not seen a letter of Denonville in which the following passage occurs:

I have had Sieur Franquelin make drawings of Sieur Jolliet's sketches.[82] The latter is seriously interested in his work and has made a thorough study of the river. He has had a great share in many of the discoveries made in this country. He is a good man who could teach navigation and form pilots in this country, if you were kind enough, my Lord, to give him a subsidy each year.

The said Jolliet, my Lord, is hoping that his work of the past several years which I have the honor of sending to you, will be rewarded with some pecuniary bounty. He has a fishery at Anticosti, an island which has been granted to him. I am sending in his name a memoir on sedentary fishing to M. Morel, who will speak to you about it. It would be well to employ our Canadians in this occupation. You

---

78 Caron, ed., *Journal de l'expédition du Chevalier de Troyes à la Baye d'Hudson*, 2–5; Frégault, *Iberville le Conquérant*, 80–84.
79 Cf. De Meulles to Seignelay, [November 4, 1683], *Collection de Manuscrits . . . relatifs à la Nouvelle–France*, 1: 318.
80 Marcel, *Cartographie de la Nouvelle France*, 14.
81 Harrisse, *Notes pour servir*, 205, no. 209.
82 Carte ‖ du Fleuve St. Laurent ‖ dressée sur les Mémoires et ‖ observations du Sr. Jolliet en 46 Voyages. ‖ Par J. B. Louis Franquelin. 1685. ‖ in ASH, 126–1–3; photograph in the Karpinski Series of Reproductions. The map represents the St. Lawrence from Quebec to a "Riv. par 51d 15m dou le Sr Jolliet est retourné," that is, to beyond the mouth of present-day St. Augustin River.—I have not seen the map said by Harrisse to be in ASH, 126–1–1; from his description of it, I judge that it is a larger and a later state of the one mentioned above.

will see on the map, my Lord, how many settlements there are on both sides of the lower course [of the St. Lawrence River].[83]

Denonville was so impressed by the work of Jolliet that, besides the above passage in the general despatch, he sent a special letter to the minister in behalf of the explorer. The governor begins by expressing the hope that the minister will be pleased with the work of Jolliet who, as a reward, is asking to be allowed to teach navigation at Quebec.

He is also asking, my Lord, for some bonus for the map which I am sending you.[84] It is the result of forty-nine voyages[85] which he made in order to acquire a thorough knowledge of this river, [the navigation of] which is very difficult in several places, especially for those who are not accustomed to sail it. As soon as the ice melts, Sieur Deshayes[86] will verify the accuracy of this map.[87] However, he tells me, my Lord, that he cannot do this with a launch, and that he needs a bark and a canoe.[88] He is sending you his reasons.[89]

---

[83] Denonville to Seignelay, November 13, 1685, AC, C 11A, 7: 104.

[84] Jolliet received 300 livres for his map. AC, F 1A, 2: 417.

[85] As can be seen, Denonville added the three journeys made by canoe which Jolliet mentions in his letter to the forty-six in a bark.

[86] On Jean Deshayes, cf. J.-E. Roy, "La cartographie et l'arpentage sous le régime français," BRH, 1 (1895): 36; [P.-G. Roy], "Jean Deshayes, hydrographe du Roi," ibid., 22 (1916): 128–138; 38 (1932): 281.

[87] Deshayes' detailed survey of the St. Lawrence (Archives of the Séminaire of Quebec [Laval University], Polygraphie, Carton 2, no. 24) will be discussed in a forthcoming study.

[88] The punctuation of this passage in Gagnon (Louis Jolliet, 209) is faulty, and the identification of "il" as Jolliet contradicts what Denonville says in the next paragraph. The passage should read as follows: "... surtout à ceux qui ne sont pas accoutumez d'y venir. Sitost que les glasses seront [not "sont"] passées, le sieur des Hayes verifiera si cette carte est juste. Mais, Monseigneur, il [Deshayes, not Jolliet] me dit ... "

[89] "Mr le Marquis de Denonuille dans ce temps là Gouuerneur de la Nouuelle france eut un peu de difficulté a resoudre quel batiment et quel equipage il me donneroit pour ce voyage, parceque Mr. l'intendant estoit absent et que Mgr le Marquis de Seignelay n'auoit ordonné de me donner qu'une chaloupe. Mais je demanday une barque en ayant preueu les consequences pour giter et pour viure pendant cinq ou six mois, et ayant deja assez vu l'etat du pays. De sorte que joint a un auis qu'on en demanda au Sieur Joliet et qui le donna par ecrit [two words deleted, illegible] J'eus une barque, son bateau et un canot d'ecorce, et sept hommes d'equipage.
Extrait de l'auis du Sr Joliet Canadien En Chaloupe il faut la mesme somme qu'en barque pour les hommes et leur viures, le batiment ne coutera pas tant pour le fret mais les hommes et les viures seroient en risque a cause du mauuais temps qui souuent surprend

Our need of maps is most imperative in order to obtain a better knowledge of the Gulf of St. Lawrence than we have now. If a bark is necessary [to survey the Gulf] it would be a good idea to have this survey thoroughly made. Had I dared, I would have sent back to France the said Sieur Deshayes, because I believe that Sieur Jolliet would have done the work well. However, since you gave orders that Deshayes should come here, I did not think that I should interpret them. Be kind enough, my Lord, to let me know your decision on this matter, and whether [for the survey of the Gulf] you wish to employ Jolliet who owns a bark. He gave me a memoir on a fishery project in which he could be successful if you were kind enough to help him.[90]

I am sending an estimate of the expense necessary to equip the bark of Sieur Deshayes, so that you may judge and give the necessary orders.[91]

In the general despatch from which we have quoted above, besides Jolliet, Denonville had also proposed Franquelin as teacher of navigation in Quebec; the latter was appointed royal hydrographer in the following year.[92]

Jolliet was in Quebec on April 6, 1686, when he waived his rights to the Lauzon seignioral grant,[93] and he was ready to leave on May 3.[94] He was in Quebec during the winters of 1686–1687,[95] 1687–1688,[96] and 1688–1689.[97] The text in the *Histoire chronologique* quoted above[98] leads me to think that

---

des gens dans les lieux hors et eloignez des hauures qu'ils cherchent et ne connoissent pas.

Le Sr Joliet auoit un establissement deuers Anticosti ou il alloit tous les ans en barque de Quebec, et il auoit fait une carte de la Riuiere a sa mode et pour sa propre satisfaction."—Riuiere de St Laurens. Deshayes, in Archives of the Séminaire of Quebec (Laval University), *Polygraphie*, Carton 2, no. 24, fo. 7.

[90] I did not find this memoir of Jolliet. It may be that the three paragraphs in Margry, "Louis Joliet," *Revue Canadienne*, 9 (1872): 131, are a résumé of the project referred to by Denonville.

[91] Denonville to Seignelay, November 13, 1685, AC, C 11A, 7: 117–117v. The letter is printed in Gagnon, *Louis Jolliet*, 209 f.

[92] Franquelin to [Seignelay], November 15, 1686, BN, Clairambault, 879: 285 f.

[93] 1686, April 6, AJQ, Greffe Auber.

[94] P.-G. Roy, ed., *Inventaire des insinuations de la Prévôté de Québec* (3 vols., Quebec, 1936), 3: 247.

[95] He signed a receipt on February 25, 1685, AJQ, Greffe Rageot, no. 3234.

[96] November 5, 1687, *ibid.*, Greffe Rageot, no. 3353; 1687, December 20, *ibid.*, Greffe Genaple.

[97] 1688, September 3, *ibid.*, Greffe Genaple; 1688, September 7, *ibid.*, Greffe Rageot, no. 3579.

[98] *Supra*, 142, note 60.

he made his first voyage of exploration of the Labrador coast in 1689. While we know that his wife and his mother-in-law were taken prisoners by the English in October 1690,[99] we do not know where Jolliet himself was during these stirring days. He did not leave Quebec in the summer of 1691,[100] and from an answer of Frontenac and Champigny to a letter of Louis XIV, it appears that he was also there in 1692.[101] Apart from these bare mentions in legal documents and in official despatches, we have no knowledge of his whereabouts during these six years.

The letter translated below shows that at some time previous to its date, Jolliet had made a voyage to the Labrador coast and also that he was in Quebec on November 2, 1693. It is an autograph letter addressed to Lagny and is in the same archival depot and in the same box as a copy of Dablon's narrative of the discovery of the Mississippi and the abridged narrative of Jolliet's voyage to Hudson Bay in 1679. The same clerk who wrote the note on the fly-leaf of the account of the discovery of the Mississippi comments on Jolliet's letter as fol-

---

[99] Lahontan (*Nouveaux Voyages*, 1: 210 and 216) is the only one to say that Jolliet was taken prisoner by the English. He wrote: "Le Sieur *Joliet* qui étoit dans sa Barque avec sa femme & sa belle-mere fut pris par cete Flote sur le Fleuve St. Laurent"; and again, "Il [Phips] envoya demander à Mr. de Frontenac quelques prisoniers anglois, en échange du Sieur *Joliet*, de sa femme, de sa mere & de quelques matelots, ce qui fut executé sur le champ." These statements appear in every edition of the *Nouveaux voyages* until that published at Amsterdam in 1725, re-issued at La Haye in the following year. In these later editions the text of this letter was recast. In the other accounts of the siege of Quebec, Marie Couillard is mentioned as the intermediary between the English and the French for the exchange of prisoners: Frontenac to Seignelay, November 12, 1690, RAPQ, 1928, 41; La Potherie, *Voyage de l'Amerique*, 3: 121. Marie Couillard and Claire Bissot—not Jolliet—are named among those who were captured by the English between Tadoussac and Anticosti. Cf. Janclot's narrative in *Collection de Manuscrits ... relatifs à la Nouvelle France*, 2: 23; the account of Mother Jeanne-Françoise de St. Ignace in E. Myrand, ed., *Sir William Phips devant Québec* (Quebec, 1893), 86; Frontenac's letter to Lagny, October 25, 1693, BN, Clairambault, 879: 335v. Frontenac knew the facts better than anyone else.

[100] He was in Quebec on June 9, 1691, AJQ, Greffe Genaple; on June 19, *ibid.*, Greffe Rageot, no. 4275; and on September 11, *ibid.*, no. 4369.

[101] Frontenac and Champigny to Pontchartrain, September 15, 1692, RAPQ, 1928, 108 f.

lows: "Jolliet is saying almost nothing at all about the [Labrador] coast and about the Eskimo. He is asking for help if we wish to know them better and be of service to them." It is quite true that Jolliet gives little information about the coast and about the Eskimo, for his primary purpose was not to send a detailed account of a previous voyage to the Labrador coast, but, as he himself states, to comply with Lagny's request for one of his maps.

From Quebec in Canada
November 2, 1693.

Sir:

As soon as I heard that you wished to have one of my maps,[102] I set to work with all possible zeal and diligence to satisfy your wish. In the past eighteten years, I have navigated the whole of the [St. Lawrence] River several times; I have noted the bearings from one point to another, and have taken and kept a record of latitudes of many landmarks. [The drawing] of Hudson Strait [on this map] is based on very accurate memoirs which M. d'Iberville gave me.[103] You will not find on my map the "passage de Canceau"[104] nor is Placentia inscribed on it, because I was never there, and I prefer for the present to send you an incomplete rather than a defective map.

I only went within five or six days' sailing of that sea which I call "Unknown," at latitude 57° 30'.[105] However, the Indians whom I met on the way assured me that it is a large sea, that the water extends indefinitely toward the north.

---

102 From what Jolliet says in this paragraph, the map represented, with added nomenclature, the same area as shown on his maps of 1679 and 1684. Frontenac mentions this map in his letter of October 5, 1693, to Lagny, BN, Clairambault, 879: 335v; and he probably refers to the same map in 1695; cf. Richard, ed., *Supplement to Dr. Brymner's Report on Canadian Archives 1899*, 27.

103 Iberville had made two voyages to Hudson Bay *via* Hudson Strait by this time.

104 The "passage de Canceau" is the narrow strait joining George Bay and Chedabucto Bay, the strait that separates Cape Breton Island from Nova Scotia.

105 This is five minutes of arc south of Okkak. Jolliet may be referring to Ungava Bay.

This makes me think that the whole coast line that borders on Hudson Strait is just a series of islands, and that other passages by which to enter the bay could be found which are not so far north, and consequently off the route of our enemies [*i. e.,* the English].

The Indians who live on the shores of this "Unknown Sea" have never seen a Frenchman. They wear caribou skins; they eat caribou and beaver flesh, sometimes salmon, trout or seals. Seal oil is used by them both as butter and vinegar. Their canoes are quite different from ours.

Eskimo are numerous along the Labrador coast. When they have no means of making fire, they eat raw meat and raw fish. They are tall, their faces and bodies are white, and their hair is curly. Each one has several wives. The women are very white and shapely, with hair so long that it touches the ground. They sew very well, and dress in sealskins like the men, and manifest great skill in all sorts of things.

Had it not been for the two serious losses[106] inflicted on me by the English, I would have followed up this discovery, but unless the Court gives me some assistance, it is useless for me to think of it. You are all powerful, Sir, and I have no doubt that if the king wishes this discovery to be followed up, you will one day experience the joy of having been the first to make known to those barbarians the light of the Gospel and the knowledge of His Majesty's magnificence. We might be able to carry on a rather heavy trade with them in seal and whale oil, and defray part of the expenses by catching codfish on the way to their country.

If I am considered able to accomplish any enterprise, I will continually hold myself in readiness to undertake it promptly and to be faithful in my service.

---

[106] "He sustained a serious loss three years ago when the English came to attack us. They seized his bark, his wife, his mother-in-law, and goods worth more than ten or twelve thousand francs. Last year, two English ships consummated his ruin:—all the buildings at Mingan and at Seven Islands were burnt down, and all that was left to him carried away." Frontenac to Lagny, October 25, 1693, BN, Clairambault, 879: 335v.

With all humility I beg of you, Sir, to present my petition to my Lord de Pontchartrain, and to remember what M. the Count de Frontenac is writing to you in my behalf.[107] I will be infinitely obliged for these favors, yet they will not make me to be more completely than I now am, Sir,

Your most humble and most obedient servant,

Jolliet.[108]

---

[107] "[Jolliet] takes the liberty of sending a petition. He is clever, intelligent, and able to acquit himself successfully of any undertaking entrusted to him." Frontenac to Lagny, October 25, 1693, *ibid.*, 335.

[108] ASH, 5: no. 15, 3a–5a. The French original is printed in Gagnon, *Louis Jolliet*, 220–222, and in RAPQ, 1944, 168–170.

CHAPTER X.

SECOND VOYAGE TO LABRADOR

Between November 2, 1693, the date of his letter to Lagny translated in the preceding chapter, and April 28, 1694, when he left for another voyage to the Labrador coast, Jolliet remained in Quebec.[1]

As in the case of the voyage to Hudson Bay, we shall briefly recall the voyages to the Labrador coast previous to the survey of 1694.

From his journal translated below, it is clear that Jolliet calls "Labrador" the sea coast north of Cape St. Charles. Generally speaking, however, the northern shore of the St. Lawrence River east of Pointe-des-Monts was also in Labrador, and was called "Côte du Nord"[2] in the eighteenth century. From the wording of documents of this latter period, the western limit of Labrador at this time seems to have been the St. John River, some fifteen miles west of Mingan. As is well known, this river was the first of the boundaries assigned to Labrador by the English government in the numerous transfers of jurisdiction over this peninsula which time and again shuttled back and forth between Canada and Newfoundland.

The history of the discovery of the Atlantic coast of Labrador has been thoroughly discussed by those writers who attempted to determine the landfall of John Cabot, and also by those who studied the voyages of the Corte Reals. As for the Laurentian Labrador, the writings of Jacques Cartier tell the story of its discovery and of its early exploration.

During the seventeenth century the Gulf of St. Lawrence and the river itself were surveyed and mapped as far as Quebec by engineers and hydrographers, among whom Jolliet figures

---

[1] *Judgements et délibérations du Conseil Souverain*, 3: 824, 850.

[2] Today's *Côte Nord* which is bounded in the west by the Portneuf River, and in the east by the Nataskwan River; the Canadian Labrador extends from the latter river to Blanc Sablon. Locally, people call *Petit Nord* the shore line from Pointe-des-Monts to the Natshkwan, and *Grand Nord*, from the Kegashka to Blanc Sablon.— E. Rouillard, *La Côte Nord du Saint-Laurent et le Labrador Canadien* (Quebec, 1908), 11 f.

prominently.[3]   In the eighteenth century, because of the numerous concessions granted from Cape Whittle to Red Bay, that
stretch of the Laurentian Labrador was more thoroughly surveyed and mapped than other sections of the Côte du Nord.

The exploration, survey, and mapping of the Atlantic Labrador, however, lagged far behind, as a glance at the available
maps of the eastern coast makes immediately apparent.[4] In the
eighteenth century, the French were familiar with the eastern
coast as far as Eskimo Bay, above latitude 54°; but for reasons
given in the preceding chapter, the exact status of their knowledge cannot be ascertained at present.

Before 1694, there is no record of exploration of the 350
miles of coast between Cape St. Charles and present-day Zoar.[5]
This does not mean that other explorers had not previously
sailed along the coast; for we know that English and French
navigators had done so long before the date of Jolliet's journal.

Thus in August 1586, John Davis wrote that "we arrived
in a very fayre harbor in the latitude of 56 degrees, and sailed
ten leagues into the same, being two leagues broad, with very
fayre woods on both sides."[6]   Davis was some fifteen miles
below the highest latitude reached by Jolliet in 1694. "I landed, and went six miles by ghesse into the country . . . The third
day [of September] being calme, at noone we strooke saile,. . .
being in latitude 54 degrees 30 minuts." This is the latitude
of Aviktok or Eskimo Bay, the entrance of Hamilton Inlet.[7]

It was here that Davis sent five of his men "a shore to an
Island to fetch certaine fish which we purposed to weather,

<hr>

3 *Supra*, p. 195, n. 82.

4 References to available maps will be found in "Last Voyages
and Death of Louis Jolliet," RAPQ, 1944, 162.

5 A. P. Coleman, *La partie nord-est du Labrador et le Nouveau
Québec* (Ottawa, 1922), 3.

6 A. H. Markham, ed., *The Voyages and Works of John Davis*
(Hakluyt Society Publications, first series, no. 59, London 1880),
28 f.—"The 'very fayre harbor' in latitude 56° cannot be identified.
as deep fiords are numerous on that part of the coast. Sandwich
Bay is no doubt the locality where he harboured." W. G. Gosling,
Labrador: its Discovery, Exploration and Development (London,
1910), 120.—Latitude 56° is ten miles below Zoar; Sandwich Bay is
more than two degrees farther south.

7 Cf. Gosling, *op. cit.*, 120. The Strait of Belle Isle, an alternative
suggested by Markham (*op. cit.*, 29) is out of the question.

and therefore left it all night upon the Isle: the brutish people of this countrey lay secretly lurking in the wood, and upon the sudden assaulted our men." A volley of musket fire put the attackers to flight; "notwithstanding to our very great griefe, two of our men were slaine with their arrowes, and two grievously wounded, of whom, at this present, we stand in very great doubt; onely one escaped by swimming, with an arrowe shot thorow his arme. These wicked miscreants never offered parly or speech, but presently executed they cursed fury."

In 1602, George Waymouth also explored an inlet at latitude 56°, and four years later, on June 13, 1606, John Knight sighted land

in latitude 57° 25', but was caught in the ice and drifted south to latitude 56° 48'. Finding his ship badly damaged, he decided to put into a small cove to effect repairs if possible. While exploring the neighbourhood, looking for a suitable place to careen his vessel, he [John Knight], his brother, Edward Gorrill the mate, and another man were set upon by the savage Eskimos and slain. The rest of the ship's company were left in a sore plight, with their ship almost in a sinking condition, short handed and continually attacked by the Eskimos, whom they described as "little people, tawney coloured, thick-haired, little or no beard, flat nosed, and are man eaters."[8]

These and other explorers of the sixteenth and seventeenth century were mostly interested in the Labrador coast because they hoped to find—especially in the high latitudes—an entrance to the Northwest passage. When Davis was at Eskimo Bay, for instance, he noted that eight leagues from his anchorage, "we had a perfect hope of the passage finding a mighty sea passing between two lands West." As for the French explorers in the seventeenth century, they were mainly concerned to find a short cut to Hudson Bay by sailing along the same coast.[9]

The earliest of these voyages from Canada is that of Jean Bourdon, who, in 1657, reached latitude 55°, the latitude of Cape Harrison. Like John Davis' expedition seventy years earlier, the French suffered an unprovoked attack on the part of the Eskimo, which resulted in the killing of a Huron, the

---

8 Gosling, op. cit., 123.
9 Supra, p. 200.

wounding of a Frenchman and of another Huron who later died of his wounds.[10]

Twenty-five years elapsed before another Canadian expedition attempted to reach Hudson Bay by sea. In 1682, Médard Chouart and Pierre-Esprit Radisson sailed up the Labrador coast, with Pierre Allemand as pilot. They landed above latitude 57° 30′, in the vicinity of present-day Okkak, and remained two days to trade with Eskimo whom they met there. On their return journey from Hudson Bay in the following year, they sought refuge "in the most favorable harbor in the world, in which fifty ships could have remained in safety without cables or anchors during the fiercest storms."[11] In his narrative of the expedition, however, Radisson does not give any indication of the position of this harbor.

The special importance of this voyage of 1682 consists in the christening of Atlantic coastal landmarks. Until this date, the maps of this part of New France which were made in Canada have no nomenclature at all, or indicate only a "Baye Sauuage" at the latitude of Eskimo Bay.[12] As for the mapmakers in France, they took the nomenclature of the coast from Dutch maps . But beginning with Pierre Allemand's map of 1687, a new nomenclature appeared.[13] The map of Delisle of 1700, and especially that of 1703, made it known all over Europe. Combined with a few place-names from Dutch maps, this nomenclature lasted until well into the second half of the eighteenth century, as is evidenced by the d'Anville map of 1746, and the famous Mitchell map of 1755. It must be added, however, that the latitudes of these landmarks vary from one map to another.

Reading from south to north this new nomenclature is as follows: 1) Cap Chouard; 2) Grande baye des Esquimaux; 3) Ance Ste Anne; 4) Havre St. Pierre; 5) Cap Enchanté. One

---

[10] *Supra,* 159.

[11] "Relation du voiage du sieur Perre Esprit Radisson," in D. Brymner, ed., *Report on Canadian Archives 1895* (Ottawa 1896), Note A, 50.

[12] See Franquelin's map of 1681 in BSH, B 4040–3. This legend is derived from Champlain's *Carte geographique de la Nouvelle France* of 1612.

[13] Carte des Costes de l'Amerique Septentrionalle ... par Pierre Alemand ..., in ASH, 124–1–1.

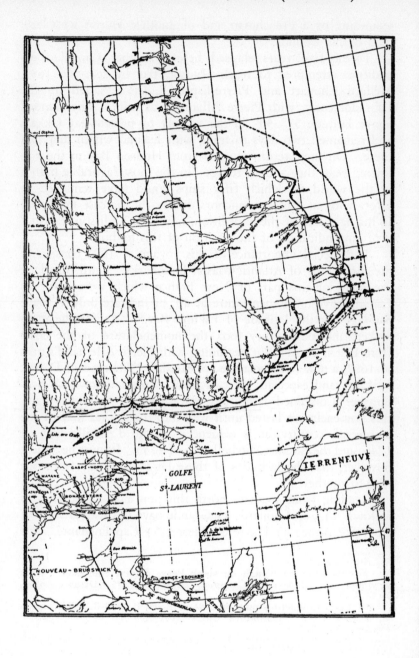

name on Allemand's map, "ance des holandois," below "C.
Chouard," disappeared altogether; and on later maps new
names described the "Escueils des monts pointus," at latitude 59° 30′, three degrees above "Cap Enchanté."

Beside the fact that these names do not appear before 1683,
there are several reasons for saying that they were given at the
time of the Chouart-Radisson expedition. First, with the exception of "Cap Chouard," they are found on Franquelin's map
of 1684;[14] second, one legend, "Havre St. Pierre," is found in
Father Silvy's journal of 1684; and third, "Cap Chouard" is
evidently named after one of the leaders of the expedition,
and the names of the two ships were the *Sainte-Anne* and the
Saint-Pierre.

The journal of Father Silvy mentioned above is the earliest
detailed record of navigation along the coast.[15] The sailing
directions and the latitudes were clearly supplied by Pierre
Allemand, the same pilot who had gone with Chouart and
Radisson in 1682. For all its details, however, this document
does not supplant the later journal of Jolliet. For as soon as
these explorers had passed Belle Isle, they "sailed on the open
sea to steer clear of the islands that fringe the Labrador coast."
Their first landing was at latitude 56° 3′, that is not far south
of present-day Zoar, some ten miles below the highest latitude recorded in Jolliet's journal, at almost the same place
where Davis had landed a century earlier. They anchored
"among denuded rocky islands," at latitude 56° 43′, between
Nain and Port Manvers; and on August 4, 1684, they were
"at latitude 54° 6′ [*i. e.,* 57° 6′] opposite to Havre St. Pierre,
which we had been looking for during the past few days to
take in water and wood. We entered the harbor about noon

---

[14] Carte de la Louisiane..., reproduced in JR, 63, frontispiece.
No nomenclature at all is inscribed along the Labrador Coast on
the tracing in the d'Anville collection, BN, Ge DD, 2987. No. 8782.
On these two maps, see "Franquelin, Mapmaker," MA, 25 (1943):
59–62.

[15] Printed from BN, Clairambault, 1016: 613–622, by C. de
Rochemonteix, ed., in *Relations par lettres de l'Amerique Septentri-*
onalle (années 1709 et 1710) (Paris, 1904), xxxiii–lxiii; reprinted by
Tyrrell, ed., *Documents Relating to the History of Hudson Bay*, 81–
101, and translated into English *ibid.*, 37–80.

time." It seems then that Havre St. Pierre was the bay at Port Manvers, which lies in latitude 57° 4'.[16]

It is unlikely that the journals of voyages between Canada and Hudson Bay during the next ten years were very different from that of Father Silvy. Once past Belle Isle or out of Hudson Strait, the ships very probably sailed the open sea making only an occasional landing to take in wood and water.

Jolliet's journal of his voyage to Labrador is in the same archival depot and in the same box as his letter to Lagny of November 2, 1693. It is preceded by the following letter whose addressee is very probably the same Lagny.

From Quebec in Canada
October 28, 1694.

Sir:

I have just returned from my exploration of Labrador, the country of the Eskimo. My journal is ready,[17] but the map is not ready yet.[18] I will take the liberty of sending both by the last ships [sailing for France].[19] My voyage lasted five and a half months.[20] I wrote down all that is noteworthy concerning the country, the navigation, the Indians, their customs, habits, modes of government and other things unknown up to the present. When you receive my work, Sir, you will realize, first,

---

[16] For all these identifications as well as those mentioned in Jolliet's journal below, we suppose that the positions were correctly calculated. There may have been an error of one degree or even more, but except when a definite, identifiable landmark is given, we have no means of verifying the accuracy of the explorer's computations.

[17] Besides what Jolliet is saying here, it is clear from several passages of the journal, that he re-wrote it after his return to Quebec.

[18] The general map of that part of the Labrador coast which he explored in 1694 has not come down to us. In the journal each sketch represents a section of the coast. There is no mention of a general map in the king's letter: "Le sieur Jolliet... a envoyé les cartes de ses découvertes des costes du Labrador de l'année dernière." Louis XIV to Frontenac and Champigny, June 14, 1695, RAPQ, 1929, 261.

[19] In 1694, the last ships left Quebec between November 3 and November 15. Jugements et délibérations du Conseil Souverain, 3: 938.

[20] He had therefore been in Quebec two weeks when he wrote this letter.

how great is my zeal for the glory of God and the service of the king, and then, with how much respect I am, Sir,

Your most humble and most obedient servant.

Jolliet.[21]

The same clerk who wrote the note on the flyleaf of Jolliet's letter to Lagny of November 2, 1693, says of the journal of the voyage to Labrador:

The account of this voyage of Jolliet is purely historical. The interesting part of it is the little he has to say about the habits and customs of the Eskimo; all that these have to sell is seal oil.

His sketches of the coast line do not inspire confidence any more than his latitudes, which he took with an astrolabe.

It would be interesting to know the anonymous annotator's reasons for saying that the sketches "inspire no confidence," and what other sketches he might have considered more trustworthy than those of Jolliet. It would be still more interesting to know why the latitudes in the journal "inspire no confidence." Is it because Jolliet was using an astrolabe thirty years before Thomas Godfrey of Philadelphia invented the sextant? We do not know whether Jolliet's declination tables were for 1694, nor do we know whether in his calculations he took account of the difference in longitude between the standard meridian—probably that of Paris—for which the tables were computed, and the meridian of the place where he took the latitude. Very likely, his astrolabe was no better than the one used by Deshayes,[22] who succeeded Jolliet as royal hydrographer in Quebec. Still, as can be seen from the notes added to the text of his journal, in spite of the limited means at his disposal, Jolliet's latitudes are remarkably accurate.

Besides being the earliest extant detailed survey of the Labrador coast from the Strait of Belle Isle to present-day Zoar, this voyage of Jolliet is the only one of which we have the journal; and what is more, this journal is in his own handwriting.

---

21 ASH, 5: no. 15, 7a f.

22 Deshayes' astrolabe is described in a letter of Father de Bonnécamps to Joseph-Nicolas Delisle, cited by Aug. Gosselin in "Encore le P. de Bonnécamps (1707–1790)," *Proceedings and Transactions* of the Royal Society of Canada, 2d series, 3 (1898), section 1, 98.

The whole journal was published in the original French in the *Rapport de l'Archiviste de la Province de Québec pour 1943-1944*. The sixteen original sketches illustrating the route were reproduced in the same publication.[23]   In the following translation we have omitted the sailing directions and have abridged several passages containing details which are not strictly relevant to the journey itself; the passages which contain references to the sketches are indicated by dots.

Journal of Louis Jolliet's Exploration of Labrador, the Country of the Eskimo

—— 1 6 9 4 ——

Under the Orders of My Lord the Count de Frontenac, Governor and General Lieutenant of the King in the whole of Septentrional France

On April 28, 1694, at about three in the afternoon I embarked on a ship armed with six *pierriers*[24] and fourteen guns. The crew numbered eighteen persons including a Recollect Father[25] and three cadets.

I shall not give the details of my route [from Quebec] to Mingan, having taken many times previously all the bearings, noted all the harbors, islands and shoals of the river.   These details have all been entered in the maps which I drew as carefully as possible and which I sent to the Court.[26]

I shall content myself with saying that on May 1, we sailed past Matane[27] where there usually is a tricky northwest wind. On the 3rd we anchored off Egg Island.[28]   During the four

---

23 RAPQ, 1944, 171-206.

24 That is, guns whose cannon balls were of stone.

25 Contrary to what Gagnon thought (*Louis Jolliet*, 227, note 1), Jolliet does not give the name of this Recollect in his journal.   The text of Le Tac mentioned by Gagnon in the same note will be found *supra*, 0000, note 62.

26 From what Jolliet says here it would seem that he made more maps of the Lower St. Lawrence than are now known.

27 Present-day Matane, on the south bank of the St. Lawrence.

28 The west side of this island provided an excellent shelter against these winds. Cf. Huard, *Labrador et Anticosti*, 106; United States Hydrographic Office (US. H. O.), *Sailing Directions for the Gulf and River St. Lawrence* (6th ed., Washington, D. C., 1934), 309.

days which we spent there, the wind shifted from the northeast to the east and then to the south; we weathered an extraordinarily fierce driving snowstorm. When we weighed anchor in calm weather, the sheet cable broke, and as we had no buoy rope, we lost the anchor.

A favorable wind brought us to Mingan (May 11), where I put my children and my wife ashore. She found her mother and three Frenchmen who had spent the winter there.

We remained at Mingan during the rest of the month of May, trading with the Indians and rebuilding our post[29] which the English destroyed by fire.[30]

On June 9, we set sail. My wife, her mother, three of my children,[31] four men and a man-servant remained at Mingan. That evening we passed Oüebitchoüen[32] twelve leagues to the east-southeast.

. . . .

I forgot to say that as soon as we reached Mingan, we de-

---

[29] The buildings were situated west of the mouth of the Mingan River.

[30] *Supra*, p. 200, note 106.

[31] His wife, Claire Bissot, had seven children, four boys and three girls. Tanguay, *Dictionnaire générale des familles canadiennes*, 1: 324. It is probable that the three children whom he left at Mingan were Jean-Baptiste, Marie-Geneviève, and Claire, and that the older three who accompanied him in this voyage were: 1) Louis, who had left the seminary in the preceding March (A. Gosselin, "Jean Jolliet et ses enfants," *Proceedings and Transactions* of the Royal Society of Canada, 3rd series, 14 [1920], section 1, 71); 2) Charles, not Marie-Charlotte as in Tanguay, known later as Jolliet d'Anticosti; and 3) François, known later as Jolliet d'Abancourt.

[32] Bechewun. This and many other place-names on the north shore of the St. Lawrence which are mentioned in the journal, appear on the 1685 Franquelin map of Jolliet's voyages (*supra*, p. 195, note 82). They are also found—sometimes in a slightly different spelling —on Franquelin's subsequent maps; for instance on BSH, B 4040-9 and 10. Unless otherwise specified the references are to Franquelin's earlier map. About twelve leagues east of Mingan, on Boishébert's Carte de la Coste de Labrador depuis les Isles de Maingan Iusqu'au detroit de Belisle, there is a "H[avr]e Ouabedchiaoüan." This map, a contemporary copy, is among the "Cartes marines" in the E. E. Ayer Collection of the Newberry Library, Chicago, which are catalogued in C. A. Smith, *List of Manuscript Maps in the Edward E. Ayer Collection* (planographed, Chicago, 1927). On Bellin's *Carte de la Partie Orientale de la Nouvelle France ou du Canada* (in Charlevoix, *Histoire et description generale de la Nouvelle-France*, 3, between pp. 438–439), Boishébert's "Houabedchiouan Isle," an island near the entrance of the harbor of that name, is called "les Betchouen."

bated whether it would be advisable to send to Quebec for a sheet cable and an anchor. Opinions were divided. We finally decided that we should risk the voyage with the other two anchors, the sheet anchor and two very poor cables. The ship belonged to M. Pachot[33] who had spared no expense to equip it, but he had been cheated. Cables rot away more quickly in an attic than on the high sea.

On June 10, they sought shelter amid the islands at the mouth of the "Napesipi" River,[34] and reached the mouth of the "Noutascoüan" on the following day. "The latter river," notes Jolliet, "is wide but its entrance is dangerous on account of sand shoals and a jutting spit."[35] They entered the Kegashka River on June 12, at dawn.

There we found a few Indians and some Frenchmen who had come to trade. When they had transacted their business, I ordered the French to return to Mingan, and the Indians left for a spot ten leagues farther down the St. Lawrence where we usually make seal oil.

Contrary winds delayed them at Kegashka until June 18. On that day, "after Mass, and after having said the customary prayers for the king, for the ship owner and his associates, and for the success of our voyage," Jolliet weighed anchor and headed for "Natasti-goüa,"[36] where he arrived in the evening. Trade and bad weather kept him there until June 26.

On June 23rd, I went ashore to measure the height of the sun above the horizon and found it to be 62° 50'; hence the north

---

[33] Francois Vienney or Vianney Pachot. Cf. P.-G. Roy, *La Famille Vianney Pachot* (Lévis, 1915).

[34] "Napesipi," Franquelin; "R. Napisipi," Bellin. The Nabesipi River; the name is Montagnais, "napeushipi," and means "man's river"; the "R. des Hommes" on Beauvilliers' map of 1715. Smith, *List of Manuscript Maps*, no. 100, [99].

[35] "Noutascouan," Franquelin; "Grande R. Natachquoin," Bellin; the Natashkwan River; from the Montagnais "Natashkuan," meaning "where we hunt bears." This is also the Montagnais name of Anticosti Island. On Boishébert's map five leagues west of the "Re de Noutasquan," there is a "R. de Lours."—The Natashkwan River is "d'après M. de Puyjalon, une rivière riche en saumons et en truites ... L'ours y est en grande quantité." Rouillard, *La Côte Nord du Saint-Laurent*, 113.

[36] From the distances given in the journal and from the aspect of the shore east of the Olomanoshibo River, "Natastigoüa" seems to be Coacoacho Bay.

pole's altitude was 50° 40′,[37] which is the latitude of the place. The variation of the magnetic needle was 22° 29′ 16″ west of north.[38]

On June 27, they left the harbor near the mouth of the "Natasti-goüa" River and passed by an island on which Jolliet had formerly erected a cross. Until noon contrary winds prevented them from making much headway. At noon, on June 28, they reached St. Mary Islands where they found shelter and good anchorage. Because of rain and fog, their progress was slow; to avoid the reefs along the coast, they kept well offshore. When they were ten leagues out, they "steered for land and entered Mekattina which lies in latitude 51°, Master Moore,[39] an Englishman, found it to be 50° 55′."

As soon as we had dropped anchor at Mekattina (July 1), some Indians caught sight of us and sent up smoke signals. Their chief was Missinabano, a man over seventy years old, connected with our Mingan Indians. He never came to Mingan in our time, although we have been there for twenty years. He is well-built, very tall, and very gentle. The one thing he likes is wine, and even this he is not very fond of. He has three wives, one very young, and a very pretty daughter one year old.

They told us that several Eskimo had wintered in this place. These Eskimo had built three wooden houses coated with mud, one of which was still intact. They had no fire inside, but had a special place for it in the open. In the autumn they store up seals and game for the winter; and when the snow permits it they hunt caribou.

Our Mingan Indians found four Eskimo here last spring and defeated them. It is probable that the others had fled, for they have no firearms, although they are expert bowmen.

These are the very first facts which we learned about this nation.

---

[37] Latitude 50° 40′ is the latitude of the mouth of the Mekattina River. Whether "Natastigoüa" is Coacoacho Bay or some other harbor on the north shore of the St. Lawrence between the Olomano-shibo River, the latitude is twenty-five minutes too high.

[38] On Halley's chart of 1701, the isogonic line of 22° west of north declination follows the north shore of the St. Lawrence from Cape St. Charles to Mingan.

[39] This is probably Thomas Moore. On this pilot, cf. P.-G. Roy, "Le sieur Thomas Moore," *Les petites choses de notre histoire,* sixième série (Lévis, 1931), 116–119; *id.,* "La flibuste du sieur Le Neuf de Beaubassin en 1707," in RAPQ, 1923, 348–355.

Missinabano left in a canoe (July 2) for the "Pegoüasiou" River,[40] ten leagues farther down. He did not want to come with us in our ship, because he wished to pick up some seal skins which he had cached. Two canoe-loads of his men came on board and we sailed for the mouth of the above mentioned river where we had agreed to meet Missinabano and the rest of his men. There the ship at anchor would be protected from all winds during the small bit of trading which we realized we could do with them.

We spent some time there waiting for Missinabano and other Indians who were due to arrive.

This river is beautiful, wide and deep. In it are several kinds of fish, such as trout and salmon,[41] and much codfish in the open sea. There are also bustards and seals. Caribou and beavers are found in the interior, but no moose and very few otters.

The altitude of the sun above the horizon measure with the astrolabe was found to be 62° 30′; hence the latitude of this place is 51° 20′.[42]

. . . .

We remained with the Indians until the morning of the 6th (of July), when we weighed anchor. But owing to calms and shifting winds caused by thunderstorms, we were able to make only five leagues east-by-northeast and east to St. Jacques Islands[43] opposite a bay which the Indians of these parts call Missina.[44] From here in clear weather one begins to see the coastline of Newfoundland twelve or fifteen leagues to the south-by-southeast. Here we erected a cross on an island.

---

[40] The St. Augustin River.

[41] The St. Augustin River "fourmille de saumons et de truites d'une grosseur prodigieuse. C'est l'un des plus beaux et des plus importants cours d'eau du Labrador inférieur. Son estuaire qui a un mille de largeur est parsemé d'îles bien boisées." Huard, *Labrador et Anticosti*, 459.—"Les seuls poissons qui fréquentent cette rivière et le saumon. Seulement on les trouve en grande abondance, surtout sur le tributaire appelé rivière à Saumon." Rouillard, *La Côte Nord du Saint-Laurent*, 139.

[42] The latitude of the mouth of the St. Augustin River is 50° 10′. Bellin marked it at latitude 51°.

[43] Bellin marked "I. S. Jacques" five leagues east of the mouth of the "R. des Esquimaux."

[44] Napetepee or Manistoque Bay? A "R. Missina" is marked on Bellin's map.

There is much codfish here, but very small and fit only to be dried.

. . . .

Leaving the cross (July 7), we gained the open sea and made two leagues east-southeast, leaving islands and channels and large bays to our left. Soon afterwards we entered a cove of the Eskimo River.[45] This river is thus called because the Eskimo used to live here. They left because of the fights they had with the St. Malo fishermen. We estimated the distance from here to the cross on one of the St. Jacques Islands as three leagues.

The sun was 61° 10′ above the horizon, hence our latitude was 51° 27′.[46]

Note. While I was on the large island at the mouth of the Eskimo River, I could see land to the westward in the direction of Pegoüachiou and eight leagues away toward the east southeast, I could see "Balsamon" (Belles Amours) which marks the beginning of the Strait of Belle Isle. The shore line is circular between these two points.

The Eskimo River abound in salmon and trout;[47] at its mouth there are two islands, one large, the other small two leagues apart.[48] The chain of islands which begins at the "Oüiatessaou" River[49] ends a little beyond the Eskimo River.[50]

Two Indians who had fled from Mingan when they heard that the English were besieging Quebec came aboard with their beaver pelts. This forced us to remain here a while, although the wind was favorable.

. . . .

[45] This river is sometimes called the St. Paul River.
[46] The latitude of the mouth of the Eskimo River is 51° 30′.
[47] "Ce cours d'eau [Eskimo River] est à peu près sans rival dans le bas Labrador pour ... la prodigieuse abondance du saumon qu'on y trouve." Huard, Labrador et Anticosti, 461.
[48] "The Esquimaux River at its eastern entrance is but a few rods wide." A. S. Packard, The Labrador Coast (New York, 1891), 74.—"The eastern entrance to Eskimo Bay is a very narrow channel between the island and the mainland to the eastward." US. H. O. Sailing Directions for the ... St. Lawrence, 257.
[49] On Bellin's map, a large "R. Ouiatessaou" is shown emptying into the St. Lawrence west of the "R. Missina."
[50] "Au delà de la baie de Shécatica, la chaine des îles qui bordent la côte est interrompue durant quelques lieues." Huard, op. cit., 460.

On July 8, wind and fog and rain delayed our departure. Although it was still foggy we left on the 9th at noon. In the morning, the Indians embarked for the Pegoüachiou River, where others were awaiting them so that they could take to the woods together as they do every year, to look for food and suitable winter quarters. That evening we reached Belles Amours Islands.[51]

At this point there is a seventy-five mile gap in the description of the northern coast. Jolliet passes from Belles Amours to Chateau Bay without mentioning any landmarks. Judging from the sketch of this part of the voyage in his journal and from a few lines in the July 11 entry, he seems to have covered the distance on the preceding day.[52]

The July 10 entry contains only sailing directions. At the end of the Strait of Belle Isle, he mentions the "Baye de la Citadelle" (Chateau Bay), "Port St. Paul" (Niger Sound?), "Cap Charles" (Cape St. Charles), which some call "Pointe du destour."[53] On this same day, they saw several castle-like icebergs, which notes Jolliet, are very dangerous at night or in foggy weather.

The "Citadelle" is an island so called because it is a steep, perpendicular rock thirty feet high, which cannot be ascended. It forms a triangle whose perimeter is more than fifteen arpents; all around it are natural moats and parade grounds strewn with gravel and pebbles.

At about 3 o'clock in the afternoon (July 11), we rounded the "Pointe du destour" and entered Labrador. Just ahead of us we saw a cove full of islands. There is an island in the open sea in the northeast, three leagues away. For reasons to be given later on, we named the headland opposite this island "Pointe au caribou."[54]

Although the south-southeast wind was favorable for our voyage, we cast anchor among these first islands, because we

---

51 "Belles Amours" is a corruption of "Belsamont" or "Balsa-mon"; both names are found on seventeenth and eighteenth century maps.

52 "The next day [August 26, 1864] ... our good ship made a fine run [from Belles Amours] to Henley Harbor; time from 6 A. M. to 3:30 P. M." Packard, The Labrador Coast, 115.

53 The Delisle maps of 1700 and 1703 have "C. Charles"; one of the drafts of these maps (AN, JJ, 75–129) has "Cap Charles ou Pointe du Detour." Bellin has "Pte du Detour ou Cap Charles."

54 The island and the cape still bear this name today.

were afraid of being caught in bad weather past these islands without shelter or anchorage.

We computed our latitude on that day (July 12), and estimated that Belle Isle was at 52° 9′ N. latitude and that its longitude was 330° 30′,[55] considering that the longitude of Quebec is 314° and its latitude 46° 45′.

In the morning we thought we heard two cannon shots. With two men I went out in a canoe to investigate. We found out that some icebergs were breaking up, and this is the sort of noise they make when they fall apart.[56]

Landing near a point, we caught sight of an Eskimo house in a little cove with three hills around it. We found that it looked exactly as our Indians had described it to us. It had a room and an anteroom built of logs eight, twelve and fifteen feet in length, fastened to a beam supported by posts. These logs were set alongside one another, with turf on top and a foot of mud covering them. There was one door to the anteroom on the south end, and two large windows for the room, slanting skyward,[57] which served as chimneys in fine weather

---

55 The northernmost point of Belle Isle lies in latitude 52° 2′; the longitude is four degrees too far west.

56 "With a report like the discharge of a park of artillery, [the iceberg] burst into a thousand pieces." Packard, *The Labrador Coast*, 136. Cf. C. W. Townsend, *Along the Labrador Coast* (Boston, 1907), 146.

57 For purposes of comparison we are giving the French text: "Il y auoit chambre et antichambre c'estoit plusieurs pieces de bois rond, de 8. 12. et 15 pieds de long, posées sur un feste, soustenû de poteaux; ces bois estoient ioints l'un contre l'autre, et par dessus des tourbes et un pied de terre pour couuerture. Une porte a l'antichambre au midy, et deux grandes fenestres a la chambre regardant le ciel..." The Eskimo house is described as follows in Rochemonteix, ed., *Relation par lettres*, 51: "Ils [Eskimo] y font une grande chambre qu'ils forment avec plusieurs pieces de bois jointes les unes contre les autres de 12 à 15 pieds de long posées sur un feste, soutenües par des poteaux; ils couvrent ce feste de tourbes et d'un pied de terre et y font deux fenestres auxquelles ils mettent deux peaux passées en parchemin."
Even if the author of these "letters" had not mentioned Jolliet as one of his sources for the specific details regarding the Eskimo, the dependence of the above and of other passages on Jolliet's journal is obvious . The last letter on these Indians begins thus: "Je vous ay escrit dans mes precedentes tout ce que iai pû apprendre des Esquimaux; personne en ce pays [Canada] n'a eu commerce avec ces peuples que le sieur Joliet et Constantin qui ont été avec eux chacun une fois; ils sont venus aussy une fois au fort que le sieur Courtemanche a étably dans la Coste de Labrador." *Relation par lettres*, 58.

and apparently as doors too, besides the small door three feet high which was the entrance from the anteroom.

They had made a fire, but just a small one, although the household apparently consisted of more than twenty persons and many dogs. They seemed to have spent several winters here. Outside the house chunks of fat of recently killed seals could be seen on all sides; inside, in both rooms, there were many bones, heads of foxes, hares, martens, bears, caribou, seagulls and ravens. All around the house and in the harbor there were chips of wood and shavings. The remnants of plankings of their biscayner ships[58] showed that they had fashioned them with care and skill. Near the house we saw bricks, tiles, and charcoal, and four or five staves of barrels which had contained lamp-oil. We also found a piece of twill sewn on linen cloth as well as a small fishing net. Inside as well

---

By 1709, the alleged date of this letter, Jolliet had gone at least twice to the Eskimo country, in 1689 and in 1694; and Pierre Constantin also had had twice "commerce avec ces peuples." See Roy, ed., *Inventaire de Pièces sur la côte de Labrador*, 1: 273–275.

I have shown (*Frontenac and the Jesuits*, 65, note 44) that Rochemonteix' attribution of authorship to Father Silvy is erroneous. The arguments in the preface to these letters tending to establish Silvy's authorship on the basis of the information contained in the letters concerning the Eskimo will not stand examination. Rochemonteix failed to see that the manuscript which was formerly among those of the Collège Louis-le-Grand is the copy utilized by Charlevoix to write his *Journal historique*. There was no need of going to Berlin for permission to publish these letters, for the manuscript from which this copy was made was at that time in Paris; it had been listed in Brymner's *Report on Canadian Archives 1887* (Ottawa, 1888), ccxxvi, and in the very year when this *Report* appeared, Margry published six of these letters—46 to 51—in the last volume of his *Découvertes et Établissements des Français*, 6: 7–16. In his text Margry entitled these letters: "Notes ... extraites des lettres d'Antoine-[Denis] Raudot."

Beside the contemporary note on the manuscript saying, "Cecy est fait par Mr Raudot le fils," internal evidence shows conclusively that the letters were not written by a Jesuit. There are eighty-nine letters in the *Relation*, but in only three paragraphs of the last one is there any mention of the missions. Nobody who has read the *Relations de la Nouvelle France* will believe that Father Silvy who had done missionary work among the Indians for nearly forty years, would give so little prominence to what in his eyes was far more important than any of the other matters mentioned in these "letters."

[58] See the description of the "biscayenne" in "Relation du detroit et de la Baie de Hudson par Monsieur Jeremie," in J. F. Bernard, ed., *Relations de la Louisiane et du Fleuve Mississipi*, (Amsterdam, 1720), 5.

as outside the house, there were iron and wooden nails, some of which were serviceable. The Eskimo had left this place not long ago and all these things led us to believe that they were trading with Europeans.

As we were embarking, a caribou came along to make us a present of its hide and meat. If our men had not been in such a hurry we would have had both, as well as its fine, large antlers.

On this day (July 12) we weighed anchor and sailed into the bay which we christened "Baye St. Loüis" (St. Lewis Bay). We sent up smoke signals and fired a cannon shot to attract attention and make people come to us.

On the following day, contrary winds forced us to prolong our stay. We repaired the ship and sent up smoke signals from different places. I went to an island two leagues from the entrance of the bay. From a hill I could see that the bay extended at least ten leagues toward the northwest, and by the gaps in the mountains, I judged that it extended still farther. In the bay there are several small rocky islands; the other islands and the mountains around the bay are covered with great forests of sloes, aspens, and birches. Only the islands near the sea are treeless and covered with moss. Note that most of the islands rise high above the sea and the middle of each looks like the mountains on the mainland.

The sun rose 59° 20′ above the horizon, which means that the latitude of this place [St. Lewis Bay] is 52° 30′.[59]

We can see Belle Isle about seven leagues away.

That evening a violent wind blew from the west-southwest. We needed two anchors although we were in a harbor and there was a good anchorage of twenty fathoms. The day ended and the sun went down without satisfaction of our earnest desires to see some Eskimo.

As the same wind continued to blow, we remained here another day (July 14). It would have been bad for us if we

---

[59] The middle of the entrance of St. Lewis Bay lies in latitude 52° 23′.

had been under way, for the storm would have driven us far out to sea.[60]

. . . .

On July 15, the wind became a little more favorable, and we set sail. On leaving St. Lewis Bay, we saw a biscayner boat on its way to Newfoundland. We thought at first that it had come from a ship, because it reversed its course. But two hours later, we had some Eskimo with us.[61] Only two came, each in one of their seal-skin canoes bringing a few pelts to exchange. They refused to come on board, but shouted incessantly *Ahé, Ahé, thou, tcharacou.* We understood clearly that they were beckoning to us. I took three men with me in the ship's launch and some knives for trading. They were easy to approach.

One of them, an old man with a black beard a quarter of an inch long, was called Capitena [Ms?] Ioannis; the other was beardless, and his name was Kamicterineac. They were both large men, fat, white and tall. We were half a league from the shore, but did not see the others nor the biscayner ship. They invited us to come and anchor in a nearby cove. We could do our trading there, they said, and all bivouac together; they would provide girls to entertain us during the night. This was their way of letting us know that *tcharacou, i. e.,* peace prevailed everywhere. We let it go at that.

Each of the two men wore a well tanned and well sown seal-skin coat to which was attached a hood like the cowl of a Recollect, with a tail sewn to the tip. Each wore fur trousers and seal-skin boots, all well made and well sewn.[62] In the hope of trading with them and of learning something about this place, we resolved to enter the harbor which was christened

---

[60] Cf. Packard, *The Labrador Coast*, 65; W. T. Grenfell, *A Labrador Doctor* (Boston and New York, 1922), 314; W. T. Grenfell and Others, *Labrador: the Country and the People* (New York, 1910), 42.

[61] The various etymologies of the word are discussed by K. Birket-Smith, *The Caribou Eskimos* (2 parts, Copenhagen, 1929), part 1: 58 f.—"They speak of themselves as 'Innuit,' that is 'men,' in distinction to the rest of the world, whom they call 'Kablunaet,' meaning 'sons of dogs'." Gosling, *Labrador*, 156.

[62] Cf. *Relation par lettres*, 49.

"St. François" after the ship,[63] and in honor of Sieur François Pachot who had provided everything for this undertaking.

At this point Jolliet's journal contains detailed sailing directions from Cape St. Charles to St. Lewis Bay; he says that the subjoined sketch should make these directions clearer.

We kept good watch during the night. At about 8 o'clock in the morning (July 16) the two same men appeared on a hill crying *Ahé, Ahé*. Seeing that they would not come aboard, I ordered four men to row me ashore. As they approached us, they were continually crying *Ahé, Ahé, thou, tcharacou* in a loud voice,[64] often repeating the last two words which mean "lay down the arms, no treachery." They had their bows and arrows and a gun, which they laid on the ground quite a distance away, and signaled us to do the same. Both they and we crying *tcharacou*, they came near to where we were waving seal-skins. As we were still in the boat near the reefs, I landed alone with the intention of going to them all by myself. They looked quite astonished and immediately retreated, signalling that I return to the boat, which I did. On seeing this, they said *catchia*, "that's good," and their faces showed gladness and joy.

Finally they came and traded with us. One of them, however, always stood by their bows and arrows while the other bartered, and they always came up one at a time, saying *tcharacou*, that is, "peace! no treachery!" I wrote down several words of their language which they gave me with manifest signs of joy.

They gave us to understand that we should return to our ship and they would join their people who had left this harbor not long ago. We counted eleven huts built for the spring. They had made canoes and repaired a few biscayner ships. We parted without having seen anyone except these two men.

On the following day (July 17) we put to sea, but the wind was slack and the strong south-southeast current[65] carried us toward Belle Isle.

---

[63] St. Francis Bay and Sound.
[64] Cf. Fornel's Relation in *Inventaire de Pièces sur la côte* de *Labrador*, 2: 209.
[65] The Labrador current.

The entries for the rest of July 17 and the next four days contain the distances between various landmarks of the coast as well as sailing directions.   Although Jolliet does not explicitly say so, we learn from the entry of July 17 and from his sketch of this section of the coast that he erected a cross in St. Francis Harbor situated behind a cape at the entrance of St. Francis Bay.   Among the identifiable landmarks are the following: Occasional Harbor, Cape St. Michael, and St. Michael Bay.   From the wording of his journal, Jolliet seems to have christened this last bay on his previous voyage to the Labrador coast.   Beyond St. Michael Bay, they sighted at the entrance of another bay a group of islands which they named St. Thomas, the group of which Spotted Island and the Island of Ponds are the largest, or else the bay is Partrige Bay and the islands are the Seal Islands group.   Beyond the St. Thomas Islands,

I landed on an island and climbed a hill with two men. From the top we could see very far in all directions, but there were no Eskimo in sight. On our way up we saw an old hut, but we could not build a fire or send up smoke signals, for there was neither wood nor peat.

On the morrow (July 22), as the wind was still coming from the south-southwest, we left our anchorage. We were all hoping that we would meet someone during the day. So it happened. We were sailing toward the north-northeast and were still three leagues from the end of the cluster of islands, when we sighted to the north-northwest a large bay of which we could not see the end.[67] We immediately thought that this might be the river we were looking for and that there ought to be Eskimo there, or at least that we would find a short cut through the islands. After examining all the surroundings from the deck of the ship and from the top of the masts, I decided to enter this bay.

. . . .

After sailing about one league and while we were passing close by an island filled with sea-gulls, we heard voices on another and we saw a group of Eskimo as well as two masted-biscayner ships. They sailed away as fast as they could to an island, then waving seal-skins and shouting *Ahé, Ahé,* like the

---

66 See RAPQ, 1944, 191, fig. 12.
67 Either Table Bay whose entrance lies in latitude 53° 43′, or Sandwich Bay whose entrance lies in latitude 53° 50′.

other Eskimo we had previously met, six of them in so many canoes (only one man can fit into a canoe)[68] came to the ship. After trading a few seal-skins, they told us by signs to sail into the bay which lay before us, that they would follow us in their biscayner ships, and lead the way to their village where we would find better trading. (Everything hinges on the word "trade," yet thus far, this "trade" does not amount to much). We trusted them and soon saw them following us. We clewed up our sails and waited for them. Two canoes showed us the way and went back to their ship. We let them take the lead and after sailing four leagues through a channel in a north-northwest direction, we arrived at their village.[69]

. . . .

The height of the sun above the horizon, one league from the entrance of this channell was 56° 30'. I estimated that the latitude was 53° 44'.[70]

At about 2 o'clock in the afternoon we anchored off their village. We counted nine lodges, three biscayner ships and a *charoüet* [?], all in good order and well kept. Nine men came to us signaling and haranguing in the usual way; they traded with us and went back very happy.

From the top of a hill they sent up smoke signals to warn the others who were in the bay. Two canoes came; in one of them was a chief by the name of Quignac. He wanted to come straight to the ship, but his men called him back. Then ten other canoes all in a line came with him, all saying in unison *tcharacou,* "peace to all, peace everywhere, lay down arms, no treachery, good captains."

The meeting took place in the boat alongside the ship. We embraced, showed mutual marks of affection, and traded. As

---

[68] Jolliet is speaking of the kayak. Father Silvy wrote in his journal of 1684: "Des que nous fumes pres de terre nous apperçumes venir à nous entre 2 eaux comme des anguilles une douzaine de canots d'esquimaux avec un homme seul dans chacun, aussi n'en peuvent-ils porter davantage, n'aiant qu'un trou rond au milieu pour l'y recevoir." *Relation par lettres,* xxxiv. Cf. also *Relations de la Louisiane et du Fleuve Mississipi,* 5; E. W. Hawkes, *The Labrador Eskimo* (Ottawa, 1916), 71.

[69] See the sketch showing the location of this village, RAPQ, 1944, 193, fig. 13.

[70] Cartwright is at latitude 53° 45'.

they went away they gave us to understand that they would come back on the following day.

The following are the articles they exchanged with us: a new white shirt, a colored linen handkerchief, a sack in which were a few leaves from a Spanish book that had some passages from the Acts of the Apostles written in the margin; they also had remnants of linen belts and bags. From all these and also from the fact that they had biscayner ships, we concluded that they had despoiled fishermen or had traded with them.

They came back the following morning (July 23) and everything went on as on the preceding day. I wrote down several words of their language which seems rather easy to learn. They were always cheerful, affable, and inclined to laugh;[71] they invited us to their huts several times.

That evening they came back once more. I do not know what they noticed when they came on board, but they did not dare to remain. In order to get away, they gave as a pretext that they wanted to fetch something on shore. They kept watch the whole night long. As soon as it was light, we saw a high column of smoke. Amidst shouts of joy, protestations of peace, and promises of trade they invited us to go to their village. Their womenfolk, whose voices are sweet and pleasing,[72] were ordered to sing. When a long dance accompanied by their melodious song was over, I shouted to them to have no fear but to come and trade with us and I enumerated in their own tongue all our wares.

After listening attentively to what I said, eleven canoes came. The trading over, we made a kind of alliance and a pact of peace, and as a token [of our good faith] I gave the

---

71 Cf. *Inventaire de Pièces sur la côte de Labrador,* 2: 252; Townsend, *Along the Labrador Coast,* 183.—"They have an innate sense of humour, which turns the most trifling circumstance into a joke... They say that they dislike a 'sour face'... It is remarkable how cheerful their outlook is on life which at best is a cold and hard one." Hawkes, *The Labrador Eskimo,* 118.—"The features of native life which appealed most to us were the universal optimism, the laughing good-nature and contentment." Grenfell, *A Labrador Doctor,* 129.

72 Cf. Townsend, *Along the Labrador Coast,* 182; Hawkes, *The Labrador Eskimo,* 122 f.

chief a small present which he accepted with marks of joy satisfaction and happiness.[73]

In our turn, we gave them a demonstration of French chant. The Reverend Recollect Father intoned the *Sub tuum* [*praesidium confugimus*] and the *Domine salvum* [*fac regem*]. They listened and then departed with shouts of joy and thanks.[74]

This took place at about 8 o'clock in the morning. After dinner, the Reverend Recollect Father, one of my children and five men went ashore to visit them. Everything went off well. Chief Quignac came to meet them in his canoe and showed them the best landing place, a gun shot from where the huts were. Showing great delight, he took the Father by the hand and led him to the village. The men remained under arms in the launch, where they were visited by young people. The women remained ashore, watching. Not a word was spoken except *catchia, catchia,* "that's good," which they repeated in a soft tone, all the while smiling and rubbing their arms and chests.

The Father was led straight to the chief's cabin. The latter's wife entered first, then the Father and lastly the chief. He showed him his whole establishment, and later the other huts, holding the Father's hand all the time. In each hut he was given seal meat and seal oil; this was the best food they had. After these visits, the chief brought back the Father to the launch, embraced him and returned to the village saying *tcharacou,* "peace everywhere," *catchia,* "that's good."

On the following day (July 25) with eight armed men, I took the launch and ordered the canoe to follow us. Captain Quignac was just as civil as yesterday. He came toward us alone in his canoe, harangued us and showed us where to land. He reached the shore before we did and came to the launch as we landed. He embraced me and took my right hand, while another old man took my left, and another chief took the hand of M. [Denis-Joseph Juchereau] de la Ferté. All the young men whom we met along the way gave signs of great friend-

---

[73] See Silvy's journal in *Relation par lettres*, xxxv.

[74] "Of the 'white man's songs,' they like best the old-style hymns." Hawkes, *The Labrador Eskimo*, 124.

ship, embraced us, complimented us in their language; from their gestures we easily understood what they were saying.

I went into the chief's cabin. He introduced me to his elderly wife. She took my hand and embraced me in the French fashion, so did his married daughter, who had a ten month old child, well-formed, fat, and very white. The chief's son-in-law indicated that the woman was his wife and the child his son. Remembering how the grandmother had greeted me, I embraced all three, for I judged that it was a token of friendship and politeness among them. (In passing I may observe that there is nothing unpleasant in these manifestations). They led us by the hand to the other cabins, and we were received with the same courtesy everywhere.

I then told them that I would like to hear them sing and see them dance. Immediately sixteen women formed in line and the second chief danced in their midst while the women sang. Their dance is somewhat like that of our Indians, but their singing is more melodious, for their voices are more pleasing.[75]

The men are well dressed, each wears a jerkin made of seal skin, trousers made of dog skin, of fox skin, or bear skin, and boots. All their clothes are well tanned, well made, and well sewn. Their hair is black, and cut below their ears; their beard is also black, and nearly all of them shave.[76] Chief Quignac had only a great mustache which was twirled up in Spanish style. Their complexion is not as swarthy as that of our Indians. They like to laugh; in wit and in way of acting, they are altogether like the French, not at all like the Indians.[77]

The women are well formed, except that most of them are snub-nosed. Their complexion is white, they are tall, stout and fat. They wear boots which so increase in width that the top which reaches their waist is more than a foot wide. Inside

---

[75] The author of the *Relation par lettres*, 47 f, embodied the above three paragraphs in letter XVIIth.

[76] See how differently this is described in the *Relations de la Louisiane et du Fleuve Mississipi*, 6; this version was adopted by Charlevoix, *Histoire et description generale de la Nouvelle France*, 3: 179.

[77] Cf. *Relation par lettres*, 47.

these large boots are smaller ones which reach their knee. Both kinds are made of well tanned seal skin.

From the navel down they wear the skin of an otter or caribou or some other animal; this garment reaches the abdomen and passes between their legs to hide what should not be seen.

The upper part of their bodies is covered by a seal-skin jerkin which reaches their waist; it has leaves like our coats, and a cowl similar to that of the Recollects, which they sometimes put over their heads.[78] They make it large for they carry their children in it.[79]

Their breasts are always covered; and although they nurse their own babies, their breasts are never seen.[80] In this particular they are more reserved than our Frenchwomen, who display them ostentatiously, especially during the first years of their marriage.

I had forgotten to say that fastened to their jerkin is a long tail more than half a foot wide which almost touches the ground.[81]

As for their hair, the young women make a bun which covers each ear, the rest is braided and wound in a spiral on the top of the head, making it appear like a rose in full bloom. This hair-do, along with their sweet fair faces and soothing voices, is by no means disagreeable.

Polygamy is allowed among them. The women do the

---

[78] See Hawkes, *The Labrador Eskimo*, 38.

[79] Cf. S. K. Hutton, *Among the Eskimos of Labrador* (London, 1912), 81 f; Birket-Smith, *The Caribou Eskimos*, part 1: 214–223; pt. 2: 79–82.

[80] The author of the *Relation par lettres*, 50 f, lifted these paragraphs out of Jolliet's journal.

[81] The following passage shows how the Eskimo dress impressed Jean Fonteneau *dit* Alphonce: "Ceste terre tient à la terre du Labrador; et y en a auculnes desdictes terres qui ont gens qui ont queuhes et visaiges de porceaulx, et le reste d'homme, et sont les plus prochaines à la Terre Neufve et à la terre du Labrador; et font leurs maisons dessoubz la terre et les doublent de tables de sappins et d'autres choses." *La Cosmographie auec l'Espère et le Régime du Soleil et du Nord*, 179. Again, "Passee la terre de Labrador, tourne la coste au Nortnortoest, & Nortoest plus de deux cens cinquante lieues iusques a septante dix degrez, & puys vire a l'Oest plus de cent lieues. Tous les gens de ceste terre ont queue. Ils sont vestuz de peaux, & font leurs maisons soubs terre." *Les Voyages auantureux dv capitaine Ian Alfonce, Sainctongeois* (2d ed., Poitiers, 1559), 27v.

household work while the men go hunting; families live in great harmony.[82]

I saw in their cabins three large caldrons in which they were cooking meat. They have few caldrons,[83] for they have no regular commercial relations with anybody; only accidentally do they trade with Newfoundland fishermen.

Water is kept in leather buckets. M. de la Ferté who was with me wished to know whether the water was sweet— we had been told that they drank salt-water—took some with his hand. The chief immediately ordered to give him one of their wooden cups. The water was sweet[84] and the chief's politeness worthy of note.

Their beds are one foot above the ground; the blankets are pelts of caribou, seals, bears and of other animals. Their cabins are neat and clean. In the summer they are circular in form and covered with seal hide, really tents.[85] But in the winter their houses are such as I have described above. They also make earthenware pots large and small, in which they refine oil and cook food. I never saw any roast meat, which is common among our Indians.

The three biscayner ships and the *charoüet* at anchor in the roads were a pleasant sight. All these ships were new, with grapnels fore and aft, masts, sails, and oars; there was a keg of nails of various kinds, a barrel of black colophony, an empty barrel and a trunk. On one of the barrels the following inscription was written in large letters *I.H.S. Maria Joseph.* I had occasion to look into only one barrel, and do not know what was in the others. But everything looked new, well painted and in good shape. We were unable to learn where, and how they had obtained all these things, or what they had given in exchange for them.[86]

As there was a circular cove between the village and the place where the launch was, I hailed our canoe in order to

---

[82] Cf. Hawkes, *The Labrador Eskimo*, 116 f.

[83] *Id., ibid.,* 88–92.

[84] Nevertheless, the author of the *Relation par lettres*, 48, wrote: "Ces Esquimaux boivent l'eau salée comme l'eau douce."

[85] The "tu. pik" or skin tent; cf. Hawkes, *The Labrador Eskimo*, 63.

[86] See *Relations de la Louisiane et du Fleuve Mississipi*, 5.

shorten the way. The two chiefs embarked with us, while the women and the men came to the launch on foot. I exchanged some merchandise for seal oil. We then separated after embracing one another and giving the usual manifestations of friendship.

Rain, heavy fog and high wind marked St. Ann's day (July 26). We did nothing. The following night was nasty: it rained and the wind shifted from the southwest to the north, then to the northwest; the weather was very cold.

At 7 o'clock in the morning (July 27), a northwest wind lifted the fog; by noontime the weather had cleared, and the wind had shifted to the southwest. Our Eskimo came on board with some seal fat. The two chiefs boarded the ship, one at a time (they had not dared to do this previously). We gave each one a present which made them very happy.

They gave us to understand that after five days' sailing, we would meet an Eskimo captain by the name of Ipillac and his men; that they themselves would leave in their boats at the same time as we, and that in ten days they would be back here waiting for us. This was our last farewell. We embraced and parted after giving the marks of courtesy and friendship which are customary in such circumstances.

They sailed off that evening and spent the night some little distance away. We thought that they wished to seek shelter from the wind or to cache their dried meat, of which they had several pack-loads; dried meat is a part of their winter provisions.

The *Saint-François* left the anchorage near the Eskimo village on the morning of July 28. Jolliet notes in his journal that from this anchorage he could see a river which he believed was the "Quichesaquiou."[87] He describes the coast and gives sailing directions for

87 "Ketsicagouesse," a variant of "Quichesaquiou," was first applied to the country lying between Bradore Bay and Cape St. Charles, as can be seen on Franquelin's map of 1678, (ASH, 125-1-1) and on that of 1681 (BSH, B 4040-3). In a document of 1689 (*Inventaire de Pièces sur la côte de Labrador*, 1: 10), this section of the north shore of the St. Lawrence is called "coste des Esquimaux." In the first decade of the eighteenth century (*ibid.*, 1: 16, 21, 27, 38), "Kesesakion" and "Quitzezaqui" were the names of a river on the northern shore of the St. Lawrence. From what Jolliet says in his journal, the name began to be used at the end of the seventeenth century to designate Hamilton Inlet. The "Kessessakioüi R." emptying

the next ten leagues. At this point he reached a strait which he estimated lay in latitude 54°.

Our Eskimo were following us in their four biscayner ships. They entered the bay beyond latitude 54°; a shift of wind forced us to enter it too. About three leagues to westward, we found shelter against all winds and a good anchorage in nine fathoms. This bay is more than fifteen leagues deep in is studded with islands.[88] At the end of it can be seen a huge, high mountain and a river seems to have its mouth there, for in the morning we saw driftwood floating down. If the other river is not the "Quichesaquiou," this must be it. We spent the night here. We killed three ducks, but found no codfish. Note that the mountains, valleys and coves are all covered with trees. We had not seen so many trees since coming to Labrador.

This part of Jolliet's journal contains sailing directions from the strait at latitude 54° to latitude 55° 15'.[89]

North of Eskimo Bay, Jolliet's route can be followed easily enough on the sketch maps which he inserted in his journal, but except when he gives latitudes it is next to impossible to identify the landmarks, bays, groups of islands, capes, headlands and points, which he mentions. Above Cape Harrison, the Labrador coast is still more indented by bays and fjords, and at their entrance hundreds of islands extend far out to sea. The next latitude which Jolliet mentions is 55° 34', about ten miles north of present-day Hopedale. Three leagues beyond this latitude

We entered Pachot Bay (August 4). No sooner had we christened it than we heard voices of Eskimo. We found an anchorage and remained there three days, partly because of them and partly on account of bad weather.

The name of the Eskimo chief was Alienak. They were in three biscayner ships and fourteen canoes. All of them,

---

into the Grande Baye des Esquimaux" [Eskimo Bay] first appears on the drafts of Claude Delisle's map of 1703, v. g. on that of 1702 in the Archives des Affaires Étrangères and on AN, JJ, 75–174. On the map made to illustrate the "Novuelle Decovuerte Faite par Constantin" (Smith, *List of Manuscript Maps*, no. 99 [102]), there is a "Riuiere de Cheche8esquiou," and farther north, a "grande riuiere de Quessesakiou." The latter is clearly intended to designate Hamilton Inlet, and is the river referred to as "Rivière des Esquimaux" in a document of 1701. *Inventaire de Pièces sur la côte de Labrador*, 1: 273 f.

[88] Aviktok or Eskimo Bay.
[89] This is the latitude of Kaipokok Bay.

men, women and children, came to our ship in several groups, going through the same ceremonies and showing the same marks of politeness as the others whom we had previously met. They had a sailor's cap, and showed us a pair of socks for a very young child and a few Spanish knives. We noticed that the sails of their boats were repaired with red and white cloth.

On Sunday (August 8) they were grounded between two islands, but when the tide set the ship afloat, they made for the open sea. On August 9, Jolliet went ashore to measure the altitude of the sun; he found it to be 50 degrees and estimated that the latitude was 55° 45′, five minutes of arc below Cape Harrigan. He also found that the declination of the magnetic needle was 26 degrees west of north.[90]

Across from the place where I computed this last latitude, is a great bay whose end cannot be seen, any more than one can see the end of Pachot Bay. I do not know where these bays may lead, but they are from twenty to thirty leagues deep and it would take several voyages to explore them. There are doubtless Indians living on the shores. Thus far I have not seen any indication that great profits can be expected from this country. The soil seems barren of everything.

A sea wind prevented their departure until August 11. On the 10th they were visited by Eskimo who said that they would bring seal fat. Jolliet was weighing anchor, August 11, when

Three canoes commanded by Captain Alienak came to the ship. He told us that Indians with their chief Amaillouk were in the bay opposite to us, that he had sent word to them, and that they would come without fail the next day before noon. He repeatedly told us by signs to drop the anchor, and even got angry when he saw that we were unfurling the sails, so we decided to wait.

Hardly had we dropped anchor, when we sighted eight canoes and four biscayner ships. Only the canoes came to our ship on that day. They did only a little trading, and then went ashore for the night.

As soon as it was daylight (August 12) we saw twenty-two

---

[90] On Halley's chart of 1701, the isogonic line of 25° west of north declination—the highest line shown on the chart—meets the Labrador coast one degree below the latitude given by Jolliet in his journal.

canoes and three biscayner ships coming toward us. They were full of women, girls and boys of all ages and sizes, young and old, tall and short.

They traded the few seals which they had and sang their songs as usual, showing that they were glad to see us and to be able to barter for the few things they needed.

The Reverend Recollect Father went on board one of their biscayner ships and made a few presents to the women and children. He was very well received, especially by the women. Some embraced him from both sides at once, and a few old women kissed him and acted as though they wanted to bite him,—this was only their way of showing friendship. The Father having told them several times with feeling in his voice *Tcharacou*, which means "peace everywhere," was very glad to get off their boat as fast as he could and come back to our ship. Thereafter he showed no desire to go back with more presents.—They are very fond of jesting.

I invited Amaillouk to come on board, and he did so accompanied by a young man who on arriving showed how clever they are at stealing. While in my room, he very neatly stole my compass as I was talking with the old man. On returning to his canoe he gave the compass to his wife who was in one of their boats, and someone saw her hiding it inside her boot. I sent for it, and as she refused to give it back, I ordered that she be searched. She tried to hide it in a place which I would rather not mention, but the searcher's hand was quicker than her own and seized the compass, which because of its make cost more than two *louis*. I would have lost more than she would have gained. The episode ended in a general laugh.[91]

---

[91] Stealing is very rare among Eskimo of one community, but stealing from members of other groups or tribes, and especially from white people is common enough. See A. N. Gilbertson, *Some Ethical Phases of Eskimo Culture*, 57-61; a reprint from articles in the *Journal of Religious Psychology*, 6 (1913): 321-374, and 7 (1914): 45-74. "The actions of the thieves when detected throw light on their feelings about the matter." Some have no feeling of shame, others blush, and "others appear to regard the matter as a good joke. Beechey relates that when thefts were detected, the goods were immediately returned 'with a hearty laugh in addition'." *Ibid.*, 59.— "Ce sont d'insignes voleurs Et des pirates a redouter Le Long de la Coste plusieurs fois en s'approchant de nous pour nous donner des marque d'amitié ils ont par Subtilité mis les mains dans nos poches

When the harangues and ceremonies were over we left them. We named the bay Bay Sainte-Caire, because it was her feast day. The wind fell just as we were ready to go, and in spite of ourselves we had to cast anchor once more. We did not make so much as one league on that day.

It should be noted that there is no codfish in these parts, in fact, although we often tried, we have not caught any since latitude 52° 30′. The Eskimo had a few but they were small. We are approaching latitude 56°.

While they were waiting for favorable weather, some Eskimo brought them a few slices of porpoise meat.

On the following day (August 14), some other Eskimo came in a biscayner ship, bringing what was left of their porpoise fat. They traded and sang as usual, made merry and entertained us. They held out hope of greater success in some later year, and mentioned several chiefs who were too far away for us to reach them because of the advanced season and because our anchors were too weak and the only cables we had left were worn-out.

For explorations of this kind, sailing a ship through islands, islets and reefs, over the shoals of bays ten, fifteen and twenty leagues wide, whose end cannot be seen, one must have plenty of time, much experience, good judgment, and uncommon prudence. And after a successful voyage, the only thing to say, in all honesty, is

Soli Deo honor et gloria.

Seeing, then, that we were practically without anchors and cables that would hold in heavy autumn weather; since we could not be sure of finding good, safe anchorages; since summer was already far advanced, and we were in a country where it is always cold, where icebergs are found the whole year round,[92] and where the hills, valleys and the top of the moun-

pour nous voler. nos françois qui les ont surpris en flagrant delit ne Leur ont point épargné la bastonade, ni Les coups de poing pour leur faire rendre ce qu'ils avoient volé, jusqu'aux ustensiles de navires qu'ils voulaient emporter." Remarks added to Fornel's account of his 1743 voyage to the Labrador Coast. *Inventaire de Pièces sur la côte de Labrador,* 2: 225.

[92] Compare what Jolliet says here with the remarks in Grenfell and Others, *Labrador: the Country and the People,* 41 f.

tains are always covered with snow;[93] since we were compelled to use our salt for codfish which we had to find elsewhere, and we were 106 leagues away from Belle Isle in a straight line, and at the most fifteen or twenty leagues from Havre St. Pierre;[94] since, moreover, we saw no immediate prospect of meeting Indians with whom we could do enough trade to defray the cost of each day's sailing—we unanimously resolved to find a harbor where we could condition the ship for the return journey to Quebec.

On that day (August 14) we were certainly lucky. For we came upon a very fine harbor fifteen and eighteen fathoms deep, sheltered by mountains on all sides, opposite a beautiful wood with pleasant creeks and a fine beach oriented to the northeast. And that evening, while we were taking supper— which was scanty as usual— we sighted two caribou, a female and her young. The launch and the canoe were soon out and we had the good fortune of catching them. This was truly a fatted calf given to us by Divine Providence, and we surely needed it, for I have already said that there was no codfish, and game is very scarce in this country of rocks and snow.

The following day, the feast of the Assumption (August 15), was spent in prayer.

At noon, in clear weather, I measure the height of the sun above the horizon with the astrolable, and found 47° 45', which means that we were at latitude 56° 11'.[95]

Whence may it please God to bring us back from here with the same good fortune which we have had on our journey thus far.

---

[93] Cf. W. B. Cabot, *Labrador* (Boston, 1920), 35.

[94] Hence Havre St. Pierre was shown on his map at latitude 57°, at the latitude computed by Allemand in 1684. Father Silvy describes this landmark as follows: "C'est un bassin de plus d'une lieüe ½ de diametre entouré de grandes montagnes de roche pelée au pied desquelles neanmoins on trouve quelque peu de bois; entre ces montagnes on voit une assez belle riviere qui se decharge dans le bassin dans lequel on est a couvert des vents, et il passeroit en Europe pour un port tres seur et tres beau." *Relation par lettres*, xxxv. See also Radisson's description in Brymner, *Report on Canadian Archives 1895*, Note A, 50.

[95] This is a few miles above present-day Zoar, which lies in latitude 56° 8'.

We do not know anything about the return journey. But since it took Jolliet more than two months to go by slow stages from Mingan to latitude 56° 11′, and since he was in Quebec by the middle of October, and, as he says in his journal, would have been obliged to catch codfish to defray a part of the expenses, it seems quite probable that he sailed the open sea to the Strait of Belle Isle, then up the St. Lawrence to Quebec, with a stopover at Mingan, where he had left his wife and three of his children in the preceding June.[96]

---

[96] The whole journey is graphically shown on the modern map inserted in Gagnon, *Louis Jolliet,* between pp. 258–259. See *Supra,* p. 206.

CHAPTER XI

LAST YEARS AND DEATH

We saw in the preceding chapter that Jolliet was back in Quebec from his voyage to Labrador by the middle of October 1694. Later in that month or in the first days of November, besides sending the journal of his voyage to Lagny [?], he also wrote to Pontchartrain, the minister of the colonies. Of this letter the following extract is all that is extant.

Sieur Jolliet.
Has sent the journal of his discoveries. In consideration of these discoveries which he hopes to pursue and of which he will send accurate maps and relations, he is asking to be given for twenty years the exclusive privilege of trading with the Indians of the country to which he has gone. He also begs to be given the same gratuity as in 1691, in compensation for the losses which he incurred when the English attacked Quebec as well as a garde-marine commission for one of his four sons, two of whom are actually in service.[1]

As we have seen, the mapping of the Gulf of St. Lawrence and of the lower course of the river as far as Quebec had long been a matter of concern with the authorities in Paris, a concern which was heightened by the shipwreck of the *Corossol* off Seven Islands in November 1693.[2] In the following May, Pontchartrain urged Frontenac and Champigny to do everything in their power to assure the safe navigation of the river by having it surveyed anew. The governor and the intendant suspecting that Franquelin who was then in France had given an unfavorable report to the minister, had refused to consider the

---

[1] Demandes des officiers et des particuliers du Canada, [1694], AC, C 11A, 13: 43.
[2] On this shipwreck cf. Frontenac to Pontchartrain, November 4, 1694, Frontenac and Champigny to Pontchartrain, November 5, 1694, RAPQ, 1928, 189, 209; BRH, 25 (1919): 280 f, 32 (1926): 434; *Inventaire de Pièces sur la côte de Labrador*, 1: 254–256; *Jugements et délibérations du Conseil Souverain*, 3: 1008.

mapmaker's memoir which, they thought, dealt with the navigation of the St. Lawrence.[3] In their answer to Pontchartrain's expostulations they said:

Nobody is better equipped to make the necessary study than the ship captains who come to this country. Sieur de Champigny knows that Sieur d'Iberville has particularly devoted himself to this task. His journals will be very useful to perfect the maps of the river, for he took care to record all the points of the compass which must be held when sailing it.

If His Majesty would kindly take care of the necessary expenses, we could certainly find here a man who could acquire a thorough knowledge of the river, if he were to devote his full attention to this during one summer. This would be more useful than all that has been done thus far. However, we shall do our best to have Sieur Jolliet and others who sail this river, make a full report of all they know about it.[4]

The answer to this letter is found in a memoir which the king sent to the governor and the intendant in the month of June of the following year.

His Majesty has always given orders to the officers of his ships that are sent to far off countries, to keep a journal of what they notice along the coasts as well as of other observations which may be useful for the safety of navigation. They are particularly instructed to do so with regard to Canada and its dependencies, and above all with regard to the approaches, islands, coasts and entrances of the St. Lawrence River. They [Frontenac and Champigny] should none the less urge those in the colony who have a greater experience to pool their knowledge, to redraw the maps and have them sent to Paris, so that those maps which are already here may be corrected and completed. Sieur Jolliet, whom they recommended for this work on account of his services and of the losses which he claims to have incurred, has already sent the maps of his discoveries of last year on the coast of Labrador. His Majesty is returning the petition presented in his behalf so that they may report on what reasonable provision can be made regarding this matter. To encourage him His Majesty is willing if they think proper, to give him some bonus from [the funds set aside for] the war budget.[5]

---

    3 "Franquelin, Mapmaker," MA, 25 (1943) : 48 f.
    4 Frontenac and Champigny to Pontchartrain, November 9 [i. e., 5], 1694, RAPQ, 1928, 208 f.
    5 Louis XIV to Frontenac and Champigny, June 14, 1695, ibid., 1929, 261.

In their joint dispatch of November 10, 1695, Frontenac and Champigny notified the minister that Jolliet would be paid 400 livres "as a reward for what he has done in the past."[6] They promised to employ him in mapping the St. Lawrence, because, besides being the man best equipped in Canada for the work, he has the opportunity of doing it, they said, while going to and coming from his Anticosti concession.[7]

What confidence Frontenac and Champigny had in Jolliet's ability is shown by an important assignment given to him during the same month of November. The *Charente* had arrived late at Quebec this year. The advanced season made the captain apprehensive about the safety of his ship on its way to the open ocean. "He represented to M. the Intendant and to me [Frontenac] that he had no pilot who was well enough acquainted with the river and with the coast at the entrance of the Gulf of St. Lawrence." This reasonable request could not be refused, and "we could not give him a better pilot than Sieur Jolliet who is perhaps the only one in this country capable of acquitting himself well of this task. I am very much pleased that he should have the opportunity of presenting his maps to you in person, and of telling you of his discoveries; and I shall be very much pleased if you will do him all the favors you can."[8]

Since this assignment "will force him to go to France," wrote Frontenac and Champigny to Pontchartrain a week later, "we did not think that we could give him less than 600 livres, seeing that he leaves his family and abandons his trade and his enterprises. We believe, my Lord, that you will approve of what we have done."[9]

In the list of military and civil officials made by Frontenac in the same year, the governor recalls that it is Jolliet who first discovered the Mississippi; that he has since prepared a map of the St. Lawrence River and of the Labrador coast; that he has

---

6 Jolliet received 675 livres. AC, F 1, 9: 43.
7 Frontenac and Champigny to Pontchartrain, November 10, 1695, RAPQ, 1929, 293.
8 Frontenac to Lagny, November 2, 1695, *ibid.*, 270 f.
9 Frontenac and Champigny to Pontchartrain, November 10, 1695, *ibid.*, 295.

left the colony to take the *Charente* down the river,[10] and that Jolliet "begs to be appointed to the position of hydrographer at Quebec, which was held by Sieur Franquelin."[11]

From what Frontenac wrote to Lagny, it seems that Jolliet went to Paris at this time. We know nothing else about where he went while in France. He left France for Canada in the spring of 1696,[12] for on June 13 of this year he stood godfather at the baptism of an Indian at Seven Islands,[13] and from a receipt of November 7, 1696,[14] we know that he had returned by this date, bringing to Frontenac the only cheering news of that year. The royal order forbidding the granting of *congés* had thoroughly dispirited the governor.[15] In a long letter to Lagny in which he inveighs against the revenue contractors, against some members of the Sovereign Council, against Champigny, and against many others, he says: "We are living in a time so little propitious for obtaining favors that it is much that Jolliet should have obtained the position of professor of hydrography."[16]

Since there is no reference to this appointment in the official correspondence of that year, Jolliet must have been told

---

[10] He left after November 9, 1695, on which day he signed a contract in Quebec. The document is in the Chicago Historical Society Library, Gunther Collection.

[11] Richard, ed., *Supplement to Dr. Brymner's Report on Canadian Archives 1899*, 27.

[12] "1696. Un tonneau de fret fut accordé, par le Roy, au Sieur Joliet avec son passage sur ses vaisseaux qui passeront en Canada." *Collection de Manuscrits ... relatifs à la Nouvelle France*, 2: 223.

[13] "Une autre quittance de Monsieur de Villeray agent pour MM. de la Compagnie pour le cens de l'emplacement size en cette dt. ville de Quebecq en date du sept novembre mil six cens quatre vingt seize." This receipt is mentioned in the copy dated December 17, 1710, of the "Inventaire des biens, meubles, papiers, argent monnaye et non monnaye dependants de la succession de Claire Bissot, veuve de Louis Jolliet." Archives de la Province de Québec, Collection Pierre-Georges Roy, *Carton* Louis Jolliet.

[14] "[1696] Junii 13°. Item ⌊scl. baptizavit], ibidem [scl. juxta Septem Insulas Vulgó le Ka8i], idem [Pater de Crespieul] 2 juvenes, Adolescentes Barbaros 13 circ. ann. orphan. quorum lus 8tati8abanat 2us La Montagne.—lum Ludovicum 2um v[er]o Renatum app[ella-verunt] DD. Ludovicus Jolliet, et Renatus le Dauphin galli."—Quebec Archiepiscopal Archives, "Liber miscellaneorum," f. 172.

[15] Cf. "Antoine Laumet, *alias* Cadillac, Commandant at Michilimackinac: 1694–1697," MA, 27 (1945): 233 ff.

[16] Frontenac to Lagny, October 25, 1696, BN, Clairambault, 874: 29v.

in Paris that henceforth he would be royal hydrographer at Quebec.[17] The commission itself is dated April 30, 1697.[18] By a curious coincidence, on this very day, Frontenac and Champigny were granting him in fief a small property on the Etchemin River.[19]

Until his death three years later, Jolliet's name rarely appears in the extant documents. A map which he drew of Anticosti and of the Gulf of St. Lawrence, intended for pilots entering the gulf through Cabot Strait, is dated 1698.[20] This map was very likely made in Quebec during the winter of 1698–1699, for the professor of hydrography taught there during this season of the year when all travel and sailing on the river virtually stopped; hence he must have been in Quebec when Frontenac died, on November 28, 1698.

The Quebec court records of August 26, 1699, contain Jolliet's name, but from the wording of the document it is not clear whether he was present on this date.[21] The dedication of one of his maps shows that he was in Quebec on October 23, 1699.[22] Three documents attest his presence in Quebec during the month of March, 1700,[23] and he was still there on May 4. On this day, he signed the cathedral register as one of the witnesses of the marriage of Jérôme Corda and Anne Normand.[24]

This is his last known signature. He very likely left Quebec for Anticosti and his other establishments on the Lower St.

---

[17] In the budget for 1696, we find the following entry: "Au Sr Joliet a la place du S. franquelin pour 1696 ... 400 livres." AC, F 1, 9: 130.

[18] AC, B 19: 262, printed in Gagnon, Louis Jolliet, 330.

[19] Gagnon, op. cit., 288–288. The petition for royal ratification signed by Champigny is dated October 20, 1697. BN, Clairambault, 849: 342.

[20] Reduced facsimile reproduction in Schmitt, Monographie de l'Ile d'Anticosti, facing p. 26; described in Gagnon, op. cit., 203 f.

[21] Jugements et délibérations du Conseil Souverain, 4: 343.

[22] ASH, 123-8-5. Title in Harrisse, Notes pour servir, 213, no. 255.

[23] A receipt of March 9 and a servant's contract of March 16. Copies in the Archives de la Province de Québec, Collection Pierre-Georges Roy, Carton Louis Jolliet.—On March 15, he was assigned to appear before the Sovereign Council. Jugements et délibérations du Conseil Souverain, 4: 401.

[24] He signed thus "Jolliet hydrographe du Roy." Registre des baptêmes, marriages et sépultures de la paroisse de Notre-Dame de Québec pour l'année janvier 1681 à janvier 1703, fo. 199v.

Lawrence during the month of May, 1700, and he had been dead for some time by Septetmber 15.

Until 1914, the earliest date by which he was known to have been dead was October 18, 1700, the date of a letter of Callières and Champigny to Pontchartrain, in which they notified the minister that the Jesuits of Quebec had offered to take over the class of hydrography left without a teacher since the death of Sieur Jolliet.[25] In 1914, however, a memorandum book was found in Quebec in which the parish priests of the cathedral recorded the days on which burial services were to take place, or on which Requiem masses were to be sung. This memorandum book has an entry which says: "On September 15, a mass [to be said for the repose of the soul] of the late M. Jolliet in grateful acknowledgment for his having played the organ at the cathedral and parish church [of Quebec] during many years. No fee."[26] Father Charland, who unearthed this evidence, comments as follows: "The solution of this question has thus been advanced one step further; namely, Louis Jolliet died before September 15, 1700. It is certain that the Mass was said shortly after the news of his death became known, but how long did it take for it to reach Quebec?"

While we have some indication as to the date of Jolliet's death there is none whatever as to where he died. Eighty years ago Ferland said: "It is probable that he died on Anticosti Island, where he used to go each year for the purpose of trading and of seal hunting."[27] Ten years later, however, Margry wrote in the last of a series of articles on Jolliet: "My honorable friend, the late Abbé Ferland, supposed that he died on the island of Anticosti. A document enables me to say that he was buried in one of the Mingan Islands, the one situated across from Gros-Mecatina."[28]

In 1873, that is, in the year following the publication of

---

[25] Callières and Champigny to Pontchartrain, October 18, 1700, AC, C 11A 18: 12.

[26] P.-V. Charland, "La date de la mort de Louis Joliet," BRH, 20 (1914) : 267.

[27] Ferland, *Notes sur les registres de Notre-Dame de Québec*, 54.

[28] "Louis Joliet," *Revue Canadienne*, 9 (1872) : 218. Harrisse (*Notes pour servir*, 139, note 2) repeats Margry's statement with regard to the place of burial.

this article, Tanguay wrote to Margry in order to show him that Jolliet died between May 4 and October 18, 1700. Since his death occurred in "one of the Mingan Islands, the one situated across from Gros-Mecatina," it must have taken place, Tanguay argued, "considerably before October 18, and shortly after May 4, 1700, in order that MM. de Callières and de Champigny could have known about it in the middle of October."[29] His argument is all the stronger since Father Charland's discovery of the memorandum book showing conclusively that the death of Jolliet was known in Quebec before September 15, 1700; that is, one month earlier than was formerly thought.

Tanguay, however, missed the point. Margry was not contradicting Ferland with regard to the date, but with regard to the place where Jolliet was buried. Tanguay should rather have inquired about the "document" vaguely mentioned by Margry.

In 1902, Gagnon took Margry to task about his reference to this same document. His criticism, however, came too late, for Margry had been dead eight years by this time. "What is this document?" asked Gagnon. "Why did not M. Margry produce it?" After recalling Margry's mania for affecting secrecy, and his habit of preventing investigators from making full use of the public archives of which he was merely the guardian, Gagnon goes on to say: "Gros Mécatina is more than one hunddred miles east of the Mingan Island. We believe, however, that Jolliet had established a fishery on the island facing this mountain, and we know that his heirs unwarrantably considered this island as one of the Mingan islands and islets."[30]

---

29 *A travers les Registres*, 87.
30 Gagnon, *Louis Jolliet*, 254.—In a note appended to this passage, Father Pouliot, the editor of the fourth reprint of Gagnon's book, calls attention to a document of April 18, 1725 (printed in Appendix F, *ibid.*, 320–322), in which the heirs of Jolliet declare that in their Mingan fief there were two establishments, each consisting of a house and a clearing. The first was on "one of the islands of the said fief, in the said river [St. Lawrence]"; and the second "on another island of the said fief, in the bay [Gulf of St. Lawrence], situated across from the place called Mekattina." Father Pouliot then asks: "Is this the document alluded to by Pierre Margry?" It is not, for this declaration never left Quebec. As for the establishment on the island opposite Cape Mekattina, there is no evidence whatever that it was founded by Jolliet. Father Pouliot then tells us that there is, in the Taché family, a tradition according to which

The distance between Mingan and Cape Mekattina is actually about 200 miles. What evidence Gagnon had for believing that Jolliet had a fishing establishment on the island facing Cape Mekattina, he does not say, any more than Margry explained what his "document" was.

Today, the islands in the vicinity of Cape Mekattina are not considered as belonging to the Mingan group, but in the days of Jolliet and until the middle of the eighteenth century, all the islands that fringe the northern shore of the St. Lawrence from Egg Island to Bradore Bay belonged to Jolliet and his partners, and afterwards to their heirs, as part and parcel of the Mingan fief.[31] This is clear from the concession granted to François Bissot in 1661,[32] from the grant to Jacques de Lalande and Louis Jolliet in 1679,[33] from the lease of Marie Couillard to Louis Jolliet in 1679,[34] and from the donation of François Brissonet to Jacques Pichot in 1722.[35] In 1733, Jolliet's heirs lost their fishing and hunting privileges from Cape Cormorant to Egg Island ,as well as their seignioral right to this island,[36] but they remained in possession of their original rights from Cape Cormorant to Bradore Bay. It was therefore not unwarranted on their part to consider the islands above and below Cape Mekattina as belonging to the Mingan concession.

Among the many documents which could be quoted to prove this point, we are selecting one of 1742, because it clearly shows what was still meant by "Mingan Islands" even at this

Louis Jolliet—one of their ancestors—was buried on one of the Mingan islands, that which is nearest to the Mingan harbor. But we are not told anything about the origin and the transmission of this tradition, nor are we told why this tradition is not found in the families of the descendants of the other two children of Louis Jolliet, Charles and Jean-Baptiste. As for the line in the letter of Vaudreuil: "Le Sieur Jolliet fit son établissement à mingan et il y mourut quelques années après"; we must observe first, that the reference is very vague; secondly, that Jolliet did not die "quelques années" but twenty-one years after receiving the Mingan concession; and finally, that this earliest mention of the place of Jolliet's death is in a letter written more than forty years after the event.

[31] Today the Mingan seigniory extends from Cape Cormorant to the Goynish River. Rouillard, *La Côte Nord du Saint-Laurent*, 139.
[32] *Inventaire de Pièces sur la côte de Labrador*, 1: 3 f.
[33] *Ibid.*, 5–7.
[34] *Ibid.*, 252–254.
[35] *Ibid.*, 282 ff.
[36] *Ibid.*, 141 ff.

date, and also because it shows that the rights of Jolliet's heirs were upheld by the French government.

It must first be noted that the concessions made in the eighteenth century along the northern shore of the St. Lawrence were mainland grants, and did not include the islands. If any grantee judged that the islands facing his concession were useful or even indispensable to his trade, fishing and hunting, he had to pay the owner for their use, provided the latter had no fixed establishment on these islands.[37] Owing to the vast size of the original concession, the owners of these islands in nearly every case were themselves Jolliet's heirs.

In 1738, the governor and the intendant granted to Jean-Baptiste Pommereau a tract of land extending five leagues to the northeast from the "pointe du gros Mecatina [Cape Mekattina]."[38] In September 1739, Beauharnois and Hocquart issued an ordinance regulating the payment which Pommereau was to make to Jolliet's heirs as compensation for their rights to the islands opposite Pommereau's mainland concession. The repeated protests of the heirs against the small amount of this compensation finally determined Beauharnois and Hocquart to put the case to the minister in Paris. Maurepas answered that there was no difficulty about granting to Pommereau a concession "on the mainland which is across from the *Isles de Mingan,*" since this mainland had thus far not been conceded to anyone. But, he added, no matter how necessary it may be for Pommereau to have also the islands lying in front of his mainland concession, "it would not be just to deprive the owners of these islands without a suitable compensation. The dues of one and a half per cent of the fishing products, which you propose to give to Jolliet's heirs to whom these islands belong in virtue of the grant of 1679, originally made to Sieurs de Lalande and Jolliet, appear sufficient."[39]

---

37 Cf. Président du Conseil de Marine to Beauharnois and Hocquart, April 21, 1739, AC, B 68: 32-33.

38 *Inventaire de Pièces sur la côte de Labrador,* 1: 64 f.

39 Maurepas to Beauharnois and Hocquart, April 12, 1742, AC, B 74: 31-31v. The letter is printed in *Inventaire de Pièces,* 2: 197-199. See also *ibid.,* 1: 193-195, the ordinance of Beauharnois and Hocquart dated October 4, 1743, which embodies the minister's decision.

The foregoing letter of Maurepas to Beauharnois and Hocquart is perhaps the "document" which enabled Margry to say
"that Jolliet was buried on one of the Mingan Islands, the one
situated across from Gros-Mecatina." If so, Margry may have
re-read the document when he received Tanguay's letter, and
then even he would have seen that there was no question of
Jolliet's being buried there. This would explain why, as
Tanguay noted in 1883, "the document was never published."[40]

---

[40] *A travers les Registres,* 87.

EPILOGUE

Since there is no indication whatever with regard to the place where Jolliet died or where he was buried, the hypothesis that he was the victim of an accident at sea, or that he was washed overboard is not unreasonable. In the latter case, certain verses of *Oceano Nox* would aptly apply to his passing and to its sequel:

Oh! combien de marins, combien de capitaines
Qui sont partis joyeux pour des courses lointaines,
Dans ce morne horizon se sont évanouis!
Combien ont disparu, dure et triste fortune!
Dans une mer sans fond, par une nuit sans lune,
Sous l'aveugle océan à jamais enfouis!
. . . .
Nul ne sait votre sort, pauvres têtes perdues!
Vous roulez à travers les sombres étendues,
Heurtant de vos fronts morts des écueils inconnus.

In the last page of his book, Gagnon speaks of "the mystery which shrouds the end of Jolliet's life." After all he was no ordinary adventurer. As late as 1695, Frontenac recalled that it was he who had discovered the Mississippi; he was seignior of the most prominently situated concession in Canada, Anticosti Island, which every ship coming from or going to France had to pass; he held an official position in Quebec, and until the last years of his life, his name often occurs in the official correspondence. One day this man leaves Quebec and dies somewhere in the Lower St. Lawrence in circumstances unknown to us, but hardly unknown to his wife, to his children, to the colonial officials, or to the people of Quebec. Yet so far as we know, mention was never made of the date of his death, the place where he died, or the circumstances of his passing.

On s'entretient de vous parfois dans les veillées.

Beginning with the year 1700, the year of his death, whenever his name appears in official or legal document, he is simply referred to as "the late Louis Jolliet, in life royal hydrographer in this colony."[1]

Bientôt des yeux de tous votre ombre est disparue.

. . . .

Seules,
Vos veuves aux fronts blancs,
Parlent encor de vous en remuant la cendre
        De leur foyer et de leur coeur!

We do not know whether Claire Bissot had white hair when her husband died—she was only forty-four—but we know that she soon found herself in very difficult circumstances. Charles Aubert de la Chesnaye, who for the past twenty-five years had always come to the help of Jolliet, gave strict orders, before sailing for France in November 1700, to his agent in Quebec, not to furnish Jolliet's widow with the merchandise necessary to keep her late husband's business going at Mingan and at Anticosti. From the fact that she transferred all her rights to her three sons,[2] it would seem that for some unknown reason La Chesnaye objected to her personally.

Jolliet who opened the way to an empire died poor. So poor that in 1702, Claire Bissot petitioned the Sovereign Council to have the inventory of the estate sent to her, so that she could decide whether it would not be more profitable to waive all claims as her husband's heir.[3] She herself died destitute. The writer who published the inventory of the poor belongings found in her house after her death comments as follows: "One cannot help feel a profound sadness when reading the description of [the furniture in] the poor lodging in which the widow of the discoverer of the Mississippi ended her days."[4]

---

[1] *Inventaire de Pièces sur la côte de Labrador,* 1: 271; *Jugements et délibérations du Conseil Souverain,* 4: 730, 942, 1015, 1079; BRH, 22 (1916): 336.

[2] *Inventaire de Pièces,* 1: 271–273.

[3] *Jugements et délibérations du Conseil Souverain,* 4: 730.

[4] J.-B. Caouette, "Documents inédits sur Claire-Françoise Bissot, veuve de Louis Jolliet," BRH, 22 (1916): 338.

Et quand la tombe enfin a fermé leur paupière,
Rien ne sait plus vos noms, pas même une humble pierre
Dans l'étroit cimetière où l'écho nous répond.

Jolliet's grave is not only unmarked, it is unknown; his name, however, has not been forgotten. After translating the short notice on Jolliet published by Shea in 1852,[5] Ferland exclaims: "Here is another of the most remarkable men of Canada rescued from oblivion by a foreigner! How many among educated Canadians know of Sieur Jolliet? They have some vague idea that, in company with a Jesuit, a man of that name discovered the Mississippi, and that thereby some honor redounds to Canada. That is all."[6]

Jolliet may not have been well known in Canada during the first half of the nineteenth century, but this was not due to any lack of available evidence about his achievements, for in the seventeenth and eighteenth centuries writers had been careful to record the part played by him in the epochal voyage of discovery of the Mississippi.

Jolliet's name became known in Europe as early as 1681, owing to the publication by Thévenot of Dablon's narrative of this discovery, for it appears in the preface of Thévenot's *Recueil* and four times in the narrative itself. Furthermore, this narrative has been the basic account utilized by all writers who have since then concerned themselves with the discovery of the Mississippi. The very first sentence of this narrative clearly identifies Jolliet as the leader of the expedition: "Je [Marquette] m'embarquay avec *le sieur Jolliet qui avoit esté choisi pour conduire cette entreprise.*"[7]

In 1683, Hennepin's *Description de la Louisiane* appeared. For reasons which do not concern us here, the author claims that, although Jolliet was on the Mississippi before La Salle, he did not go below the mouth of the Illinois River.[8] As is well known, this book was published six times between 1683

---

[5] Shea, *Discovery and Exploration of the Mississippi Valley,* lxxix–lxxx.
[6] Ferland, *Notes sur les Registres,* 50.
[7] M. Thévenot, ed., *Recueil de voyages de Mr Thevenot,* (Paris, 1681), 1.
[8] L. Hennepin, *Description de la Louisiane* (Paris, 1683), 13 f.

and 1689:—three printings in the original French, and three translations, in Italian, in Dutch, and in German, respectively.

The *Premier Etablissement de la Foy dans la Nouvelle France* was published in 1691, under the name of Chrestien Le Clercq. In this book as in that of Hennepin, the length of the voyage is misrepresented, but whoever wrote Chapter Twenty-Five of Le Clercq's second volume, was more generous than Hennepin had been with regard to the terminus of the expedition; for we are told that Jolliet went as far as Cap Saint-Antoine, thirty or forty leagues below the mouth of the Illinois River.[9]

In 1697, Hennepin published his *Nouvelle Decouverte*. To make his account of the voyage of 1673 more plausible or for other reasons, he claimed to have been told by Jolliet himself that the explorer did not go as far as the Arkansas villages, nor even as far as where the "monsters" were, namely, not even as far as the petroglyphs between the Illinois and the Missouri rivers.[10] The *Nouvelle Decouverte* was even more popular than the *Description*. Bibliographers know of eight French editions, four translations in Dutch, three in English, and two in German.

It should be noted that these four books agree in declaring that Jolliet was on the Mississippi before La Salle; the only difference between them concerns the length of the voyage of 1673. Finally, Thévenot's book and the two books of Hennepin were re-issued many times before 1700, before the death of Jolliet.

In view of all this it can hardly be said that Jolliet's name had been forgotten, and that it had to be rescued from oblivion by a foreigner. There is no Canadian in the seventeenth or eighteenth century whose name was better known than that of Jolliet, not only in France, but in the whole of Western Europe.

---

[9] C. Le Clercq, *Premier Etablissement de la Foy dans la Nouvelle France* (2 vols., Paris, 1691), 2: 364–366. On this passage cf. "The Jolliet Lost Map of the Mississippi," MA, 28 (1946): 118 f.

[10] L. Hennepin, *Nouvelle Decouverte d'un tres grand Pays Situé dans l'Amerique* (Utrecht, 1897), 283 f. On this passage cf. "The Jolliet Lost Map," *loc. cit.*, 120, and "Hennepin's Voyage to the Gulf of Mexico 1680," *ibid.*, 21 (1939): 66 f.

The historians of the eighteenth century were no less careful than Jolliet's contemporaries to keep his name before the public. La Potherie in 1722,[11] Barcia in 1723,[12] and Lafitau in 1724,[13] based their accounts of the discovery of the Mississippi on Thévenot's book. Twenty years later Charlevoix published his history of New France and a journal of his voyage in America. Though Charlevoix seems to suggest that Marquette was the leader of the expedition, the fact remains that Jolliet's name appears prominently in the chronological tables of the history,[14] as well as in the chapter in which the discovery of the Mississippi is narrated.[15] In his *Journal historique*, Charlevoix again refers to Jolliet, but is mistaken in saying that the latter received in seigniory the Island of Anticosti "à son retour de la Découverte du Micissipi."[16]

Ferland noted that Jolliet's "Christian name is not even given by Mr. Shea, nor even by Charlevoix."[17] This omission is not at all surprising. In the official correspondence which Charlevoix saw and in the books which he used to write his history, Louis Jolliet is invariably referred to as "le sieur Jolliet." The explorer himself, whether from an early acquired habit or because of a realization that he was *the* Jolliet, practically always signed his name "Jolliet." It is perhaps just as well that Charlevoix made no attempt to mention Jolliet's Christian name seeing that the well known name of Jacques Marquette—who besides was a fellow Jesuit of Charlevoix'—underwent two transformations in his hands. The missionary is called Pierre Marquette in the chronological tables of Char-

[11] La Potherie, *Voyage de l'Amerique*, 2: 130 f. Another edition appeared in 1753.
[12] Barcia Carbillado y Zunigo, A. G. de, *Ensayo cronologico para la Historia general de la Florida* (Madrid, 1723), 229. Barcia's mistake making Jolliet a Jesuit does not affect the question. Anyone wishing to learn about Jolliet could have done so by looking up Thévenot's book to which Barcia specifically refers. "Los PP. Marquete y San Joliet, de la Compañia de Jesus...," in which "San" is clearly a misreading of "sieur" in Thévenot.
[13] J. F. Lafitau, *Moeurs des sauvages ameriquains comparées aux moeurs des premiers temps* (2 vols., Paris, 1724), 2: 314 f.
[14] Charlevoix, *Histoire et description generale de la Nouvelle France*, 1: liij.
[15] *Ibid.*, 4: 45 ff.
[16] *Ibid.*, 3: 63.
[17] Ferland, *Notes sur les Registres*, 50.

levoix' history, and appears as Joseph Marquette in the *Journal
historique.*

Today, owing to the systematic exploitation of the archives
of France and of Canada, and also through the use of better
methods of historical criticism, we know more about Jolliet
than was known in the eighteenth century, or at the time when
Shea and Ferland were pioneering in the field of early Canadian history. Nevertheless, the above references show that Jolliet's name was by no means forgotten, that for nearly one
hundred years one writer after another recalled that he took
a prominent part in the discovery of the Mississippi.

APPENDIX A

VOYAGE DE JOLLIET A LA BAIE D'HUDSON[1]

I. Les Traversées du Lac Mistassini
vers la Rivière Rupert

1. Le voyageur qui se trouve au sud-ouest du lac Mistassini (par exemple celui venu du lac Saint-Jean par la rivière Ashouapmouchouan [*alias* Chamouchouan and Ashwapmuchuan]) traverse le lac, à la sortie de la baie Abatagouche, en passant entre l'île Manitounouk et l'île Marie-Victorin, suivant ainsi la direction nord-ouest. Parvenu à l'autre rive, il longe le bord vers le nord-est et s'engage dans la baie Duhamel du Monceau, où il double l'île de la Grosse Roche, ainsi nommée d'après un gros boulder granitique d'une dizaine de pieds de haut, au pied duquel les Indiens Mistassini avant la traversée du lac offrent du tabac aux esprits pour se les rendre favorables (quand ils procèdent en sens inverse du trajet présentement décrit). Le las Mistassini doit son nom à cette grosse roche (*mista*, grosse, *assini*, roche). Tout près de ce lieu de sacrifice, au fond d'une petite anse, un court portage permet d'atteindre les eaux de la Rupert en franchissant l'isthme étroit qui relie à la terre ferme la presqu'île Louis-Jolliet[2] (généralement représentée comme une île sur les cartes). Ce portage raccourcit le trajet d'une quinzaine de milles.

2. Le voyageur qui vient de l'est du lac (celui, par exemple, venu du lac Saint-Jean par la rivière Mistassini ou la rivière Péribonca), s'engage au contraire directement dans la rivière Rupert, à la décharge même du lac, nommée Akopitoun par les naturels. Celui qui fait ce trajet peut donc ignorer entièrement l'existence de la grande baie Duhamel du Monceau, non représentée d'ailleurs sur les cartes de Jolliet. Pour traverser le lac dans la partie nord-est, le voyageur passe dans le détroit (le "Grand Percé" du père Laure),[3] situé entre l'île Tchapahipan et la péninsule Washimmiskow, pour rejoindre la rive opposée, à l'est de la rivière Mikoassass, à l'endroit ou une grande pointe rétrécit le lac de façon appréciable.

3. Pour la traversée du lac Mistassini, les Indiens utilisent les

---

[1] Plusieurs noms géographiques cités dans ces notes sont encore inédits. Ils doivent être soumis incessamment à la commission de géographie du Canada et faire l'objet d'un mémoire.

[2] J'avais appellé d'abord temporairement cette presqu'île "Presqu'Ile du Portage." C'est une des plus importantes du lac Mistassini comme étape des voyages. Je la dédie maintenant à Louis Jolliet.

[3] On his map of 1732, reproduced in Rochemonteix, *Les Jésuites et la Nouvelle-France au XVIIe siècle*, end of volume 3.—J. D.

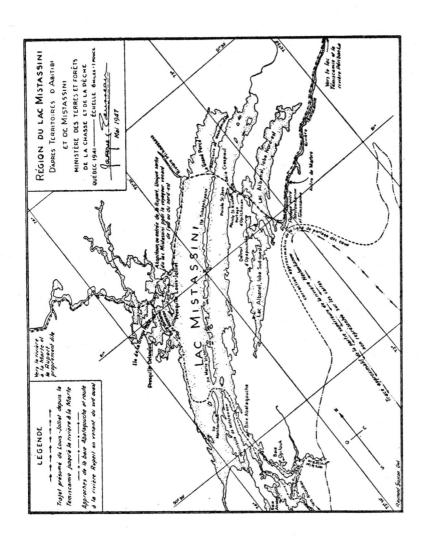

points les plus étroits afin de rester le moins longtemps à distance de la terre ferme et s'y réfugier rapidement en cas de tempête, toujours à craindre sur ce lac. Pour toutes fins pratiques, les naturels traversent aux deux endroits décrits.

4. La rivière Rupert, près de sa source, se divise en deux bras, la Rupert proprement dite et la rivière à la Marte. Les deux bras se rejoignent plus loin. Il semble qu'autrefois l'on suivait davantage la rivière à la Marte lorsqu'on se dirigeait vers la baie d'Hudson. C'est du moins le trajet des Indiens à la fin du siècle dernier lorsqu'ils voyageaient dans de gros canots de trente à trente-six pieds pour transporter leurs fourrures du lac Mistassini à Rupert House, sur la baie James, ou faisaient le trajet inverse pour apporter des provisions au lac Mistassini. C'est aussi le seul trajet que décrit l'explorateur Peter-Albert Low, lors de son voyage de 1885.

II. COMPARAISON SOMMAIRE DES DEUX CARTES DE JOLLIET.

1. Les cartes de Jolliet de 1679 et de 1684 sont presque superposables. Le contour des lacs et le tracé des rivières, de Tadoussac à l'embouchure de la Rupert, sont les mêmes dans les grandes lignes; mais sur la carte de 1684 se rencontrent des imprécisions qu'il y a lieu de souligner: a) au milieu du parcours de la Péribonca on remarque le dessin d'un lac immense à l'endroit oú devrait se trouver le triangle de terre borné par la rivière Saint-Onge et la Péribonca proprement dite. D'autre part le lac Onistagan n'apparait pas sur cette carte et il semble que le cartographe, lors d'une copie hâtive d'un relevé, ait confondu avec ce lac le triangle précité. (Sur la carte de 1679, le lac Onistagan porte le nom de *mistassiny*). b) La rivière Shipshaw, se jetant dans le Saguenay, près de Chicoutimi, est une décharge de la Péribonca sur la carte de 1684, mais s'en distingue nettement sur celle de 1679. c) Sur la carte de 1684, la rivière Mistassini (nommée Kakiga8sipi) coule du lac Albanel au lac Saint-Jean.

2. La carte de 1684, d'autre part, renferme des détails qui ne se trouvent pas sur celle de 1679: a) La baie Crespieul (pour emplacement voir ma carte) est mieux dessinée. b) La décharge du lac Albanel n'est plus un détroit, entre deux lacs, comme l'indique la carte de 1679 et la plupart des cartes anciennes mais une rivière marquée par un trait de plume. c) Au sud de la Témiscamie (coulant de l'est à l'ouest au sud du lac Albanel), se trouve un étrange dessin rappelant vaguement un oméga dans lequel se trouve un cercle en pointillé. Je crois que le symbole représente l'Antre de Marbre dont parle le père Laure [JR, 68: 48] et qu'il mentionne sur ses cartes de 1731, retouchées en 1732. (Cette caverne est au mauvais endroit sur la carte de Laure du 23 août 1731). Sur celle de 1684 le dessin décrit plus haut se trouve presque au site de la caverne.

3. Tous ces faits laissent croire que les deux cartes de 1679 et de 1684 ont de copies hâtives d'une carte plus parfaite que devait conserver Jolliet.[4]

III. Le Trajet de Jolliet
de Chicoutimi au Lac Mistassini.

1. Six routes de canot relativement pratiques pouvaient conduire les Blancs au lac Mistassini: la rivière Rupert (qui se ramène à deux routes différentes sur une partie du parcours: la Rupert proprement dite et la rivière à la Marte), allant du lac Mistassini à la baie James et que Jolliet utilise dans la deuxième partie de son voyage; la route actuelle d'Oskelaneo-Chibougamou-Mistassini, qu'auraient pu emprunter les voyageurs venant directement des Trois-Rivières; enfin les quatre routes du lac Saint-Jean (le seules qui nous intéressent ici): a) Ashouapmouchouan via Nicaubau; b) Ashouapmouchouan via rivière du Chef; c) rivière Mistassini; d) rivière Péribonca, depuis le lac Saint-Jean, ou depuis Chicoutimi en passant d'abord par la rivière Shipshaw. Notons aussi que Jolliet a pu faire le voyage aller et retour par le même chemin ou deux différents.[5]

2. *Jolliet n'est pas passé par l'Ashouapmouchouan* (qu'il nomme Necouba). La précision qu'il met à tracer la Péribonca, la rivière Saint-Onge, les lacs entre la tête de la Péribonca et la Témiscamie, témoignent de son habileté de cartographe. S'il avait emprunté l'une ou l'autre des routes de l'Ashouapmouchouan, il aurait mis plus d'exactitude, disons simplement plus de vérité, dans son tracé. S'il avait avironné sur le lac Nicaubau, grand centre de ralliement pour les Indiens et les traiteurs, sa carte en ferait certainement mention: de même l'immense lac Chibougamou, méritait d'être relevé; le trajet du lac Waconichi, de la baie du Poste et de la baie Abatagouche ne serait pas représenté par une simple rivière (carte de 1679), ni même par une rivière finissant en une baie (carte de 1684); mais comprendrait une série de lacs, comme il y en a à la tête de la Péribonca. Si, après avoir parcouru la partie inférieure de l'Ashouapmouchouan, il était passé, non pas par le lac Nicaubau, mais par la rivière du Chef et le lac File-axe (ou lac à la Meule), il n'aurait pas manqué également de dessiner une chaîne de lacs. Il est évident que Louis Jolliet ne connait que par ouï-dire l'une des deux routes empruntant l'Ashouapmouchouan.

3. *Jolliet n'est pas passé par la rivière Mistassini*. Autrement, sur la carte de 1679, il aurait dessiné une chaîne de lacs (lac des Cygnes, lac des Iles, lac Long, etc.) entre la rivière Mistassini (R. Kakiga8sipi) et la partie supérieure de la Nestowkanow. Les anciens voyageurs français ignoraient que cette dernière se dirige d'abord vers le nord sur

---

[4] See *supra*, 169.—J. D.
[5] *Supra*, 168.—J. D.

une cinquantaine de milles, puis se replie sur elle-même pour se déverser vers le lac Saint-Jean; aussi croyait-on alors (comme l'a illustré Jolliet sur la carte de 1679, et comme le mentionne dans son journal, en 1792 le botaniste Michaux) que cette portion supérieure de la Nestowkanow était une rivière se jetant dans le lac Albanel. Ces renseignements sur le cours supérieur de la rivière Nestowkanow m'ont été communiqués par des Indiens dont le territoire de chasse s'étend dans ces parages. Les cartes modernes n'en font pas mention car cette région n'a pas été explorée encore. Non seulement Jolliet aurait placé une chaîne de lacs entre la rivière Mistassini et la Nestowkanow, mais il aurait tracé côte à côte la partie supérieure de la rivière Mistassini et la chaîne de lacs. En effet, lorsqu'on abandonne la Mistassini, trop rapide, il faut portager quelques milles vers l'ouest avant d'atteindre la chaîne des lacs.

4. *Jolliet est surement passé par la Péribonca.* Cette conclusion s'impose: le cours de la Péribonca, tel que représenté sur sa carte de 1679, est sensiblement le même que sur les cartes modernes, comme celle de Low, faite après 1885 et les autres qui suivent. Le tracé témoigne de connaissances cartographiques appuyées sur des observations astronomiques précises. Sur le cours de la Péribonca dessiné par Jolliet, notons les points suivants d'une remarquable vérité: a) cours inférieur allant sensiblement de l'est à l'ouest; b) dans le coude de la rivière, à une quinzaine de lieues du lac Saint-Jean (sur la carte de 1679), ce que je crois être le lac Tchitogama; c) plus haut, représentation exacte de la rivière Saint-Onge; d) puis le lac Onistagan; e) la fourche de la Péribonca et de la rivière Grande-Loutre; f) les lacs de la rivière Grande-Loutre; g) les lacs de la Témiscamie, près de la hauteur des terres; h) le cours de la Témiscamie vers l'ouest; i) puis le brusque coude de la Témiscamie vers le nord; j) ensuite le lac Albanel, dont Jolliet ne représente que le lobe nord-est, ignorant la présence d'un lobe aussi grand vers le sud-ouest, au-delà du détroit d'Opapouchka, qu'il n'a pas remarqué, d'autant plus qu'il passait nécessairement deux ou trois milles au large; k) décharge du lac Albanel, sur la carte de 1684 (représentée par une rivière et non un détroit entre deux lacs); l) enfin la baie Crespieul avec l'île de la Chasse, dans le lac Mistassini. La baie Crespieul est particulièrement dessinée sur la carte de 1684: on y distingue en effet la pointe Saint-Nicolas et la pointe Saint-Jean. C'est dans cette baie que Jolliet a construit une maison. C'est d'ailleurs au même endroit que campent toutes les personnes passant du lac Albanel au lac Mistassini ou vice versa. Ces nombreux détails rapportés par Jolliet ne peuvent avoir été basés sur des ouï-dire. Si l'on étudie le trajet à rebours, du lac Mistassini au lac Saint-Jean, il est évident que l'on ne peut envisager un passage par le sud-ouest du lac (donc par les deux routes de l'Ashouapmouchouan). La comparaison des tracés de la rivière Mistassini et de la Péribonca d'autre part ne peut qu'incliner en faveur de la dernière hypothèse.

Pour l'étude de ce problème, des cartes anciennes comme celle de Low (Labrador peninsula, Southwest sheet, N°. 585, 25 milles au pouce, Ottawa 1896) [6] sont souvent beaucoup plus révélatrices que les récentes, car elles sont dépouillées et ne comptent à peu près que les cours d'eau parcourus le plus fréquemment en canot.

5. *Passage par la rivière Shipshaw, pour rejoindre la Péribonca, et sur la rivière Saint-Onge, un affluent de la Péribonca.* Il semble bien que Jolliet est passé par la rivière Saint-Onge, un affluent du, côté ouest de la Péribonca, pour se rendre dans le lac Onistagan, car autrement il aurait noté que la Péribonca sort du centre du lac Onistagan, du côté est. Il est probable aussi, comme on l'a suggéré au père Adrien Pouliot, S.J.[7] à Chicoutimi, que Jolliet est passé par la rivière Shipshaw, après avoir laissé la région de Chicoutimi. Ce trajet lui aurait permis d'éviter les très nombreuses chutes entre 49° 30' et 50° N. Après avoir monté la Shipshaw jusqu'au 49° 38' N, il serait passé à la rivière Manouan par une série de portages bien connus, puis à la rivière à la Carpe, au lac au Sable, au lac Shipshaw (qu'il ne faut pas confondre avec un autre lac Shipshaw sur la rivière du même nom), enfin à la Péribonca tout près du 50° N. Jolliet a pu aussi monter la Péribonca depuis le lac Saint-Jean jusqu'au 49° 30' N., puis, comme décrit précédemment, s'engager dans la Manouan, la rivière à la Carpe, le lac au Sable, le lac Shipshaw et de nouveau la Péribonca vers le 50° N. Peut être a-t-il employé un trajet à l'aller et un autre au retour. L'examen seul de la carte ne permet pas de choisir entre ces hypothèses.

6. *Comment Jolliet s'est engagé dans la Rupert.* Comme il n'y a rien sur les cartes de Jolliet rappellant même de loin la baie Duhamel du Monceau, il semble évident qu'il s'est engagé directement dans la rivière Rupert au point que les Mistassini nomment Akopitoun, la décharge même du lac. Quant à la première partie de la rivière qui l'a conduit à la baie James, elle correspond plus à la rivière à la Marte qu' à la branche nord de la Rupert.

7. *Origine du nom Timagaming donné par Jolliet au lac Mistassini.* Ce nom semble une transposition de celui du lac ou de la rivière Témiscamie. Quant au nom Mistassini, Jolliet l'a attribué au lac Onistagan.

JACQUES ROUSSEAU

---

[6] A simplified version of this map is reproduced *supra*, 167.— J. D.

[7] The editor of the fourth reprint of *Louis Jolliet* by Gagnon.— J. D.

APPENDIX B

A CALENDAR OF JOLLIET DOCUMENTS

Two classes of documents have been entered in this calendar: 1) Those prior to May 4, 1700 (the date of his last known signature) which mention Jolliet, and 2) those which he himself wrote or signed. When full bibliographical data are given in the text, we have referred to them as follows: 1, n. 5, scl. Chapter 1, note 5. Unless otherwise specified, the place of origin is Quebec. The notations in parentheses indicate whether the document is a Jolliet autograph (A. D. S., or A. L. S.) or merely signed by him (D. S.) or a copy.

1645
September 21. Baptismal entry in the church register. 1, n. 5.

1662
August 10. Jolliet receives minor orders. 1, n. 9.

1665
January 1. At the Jesuit college. 1, n. 10.

1666
Mentioned in the census of this year. 1, n. 12.
May 7. Receipt. 1, n. 18. (D. S.)

1667
Mentioned in the census of this year. 1, n. 14.
Autumn. Jolliet goes to France.

1668
October 8. Sale of property to Laval. 1, n. 30. (D. S.)
October 14. Itemized account of indebtedness to Laval. 1, n. 23. (A. D. S.)
November 9. Cap-de-la-Madeleine. Louis Jolliet's autograph note signed by his brother Adrien. 1, n. 31.

1669
April 13. Adrien Jolliet gives his brother Louis power of attorney. 1, n. 32 and n. 53. (D. S.)

1671
June 4. Sault Ste Marie. Jolliet signs St. Lusson's procès-verbal. 1, n. 63. (Copy)
September 12. Jolliet's declaration. 1, n. 32 and n. 53. (D. S.)

1672
October 1. Partnership contract. 6, n. 16. (D. S.)

October 2. Statement by Jolliet concerning his brother Zacharie and Chavigny. AJQ, Greffe Rageot, no. 940. (D. S.)
October 3. Jolliet's statement regarding Pierre Moreau. 6, n. 17. (D. S.)
November 2. Frontenac to Colbert. 6, n. 1.

1674

Before July 7. Montreal. Normandin's claim against Jolliet. 7, n. 12.
July 7. Montreal. Settlement of Normandin's claim. 7, n. 12. (D. S.)
August 1. Dablon's account of the discovery of the Mississippi. 3, n. 2; other copies of this account, 3, n. 14 and n. 15; modified copies, 3, n. 20 and n. 21.
October 3. Jolliet appears before the Sovereign Council. *Jugements et délibérations du Conseil Souverain*, 3: 863 f.
October 10. Jolliet to Laval. 3, n. 15 and n. 38. (Copy)
October 25. Dablon to Pinette. 7, n. 16.
Before November 14. Jolliet's dedicatory letter to Frontenac inscribed on the map which he drew from memory. 3, n. 46; 4, n. 22. (Copy.) Other copies of the letter, 3, n. 47 and n. 48.
November 14. Frontenac to Colbert. 3, n. 50.

1675

After 1674. Paris. *Relation de la Nouvelle France.* 5, n. 1.
October 1. Marriage contract. 7, n. 23. (D. S.)
October 7. Marriage of Jolliet and Claire Bissot. 7, n. 24.

1676

1676. Paris. Bernou's questionnaire to Barrois. 5, n. 7.
January 7, 14, and 18. Jolliet appears before the Sovereign Council. 7, n. 26.
January 23. Evidence given by Jolliet. The document is in the Chicago Historical Society Library, Gunther Collection. (D. S.)
February 3, and 24. Jolliet appears before the Sovereign Council. 7, n. 26.
April 23. Partnership contract. 7, n. 27. (D. S.)
May 2. Jolliet rents Denis Guyon's ship. 7, n. 27. (D. S.)
October 20. Jolliet present at a meeting for fixing the price of beaver. 7, n. 29.
November 2. Jolliet buys La Vallière's ship. 7, n. 37. (D. S.)
December 4. Hiring of a servant. AJQ, Greffe Rageot, no. 1572. (D. S.)

1677

Paris. Bernou's memoir. 5, n. 18; answers to this memoir. 5, n. 20.
April 28. Paris. Colbert to Duchesneau. 7, n. 30.
May 1. Lease to Lalande. 7, n. 39. (D. S.)
May 12. Grants concession to Claude Maugue. 7, n. 39. (D. S.)

May 12. Paris. Dudouyt to Laval. 7, n. 36.
November 8. Partnership contract. 7, n. 40. (D. S.)

1678
Paris. Bernou's questionnaire to Daleyrac. 5, n. 13.
Map by Franquelin based on Jolliet's sketch. 7, n. 53.
Paris. Bernou's memoir. 7, n. 50.
March 5. Jolliet grants a concession to Etienne Landeron. 7, n. 41.
     (D. S.)
April 5. Hiring of a shoemaker. 7, n. 42. (D. S.)
April 21. Sale of a third share in his ship to his brother Zacharie.
     7, n. 43. (D. S.)
June 5. Jolliet buys a house in Quebec. 7, n. 44. (D. S.)
June 18. Summoned to appear before the Sovereign Council. 7, n. 45.
October 20. Jolliet assists at the "brandy parliament." 7, n. 57.
Before October 25. Dablon's "Récit des voyages et des découvertes
     du Père Jacques Marquette." 5, n. 30.
November 17. Witnesses the marriage contract of his brother Zach-
     arie. 7, n. 68. (D. S.)

1679
February 9. Jolliet hires two sailors. 7, n. 69. (D. S.)
March 10. Seven Island and Mingan are conceded to him and to his
     father-in-law. 7, no. 70.
March 11. Partnership contract. 7, 76. (Copy).
May 9. Pays for house bought on June 5, 1678. 7, n. 77. (D. S.)
[June]. Names of Jolliet's companions on his voyage to Hudson
     Bay. 8, n. 72.
October 25. Abridged narrative of Jolliet's voyage to Hudson Bay. 8,
     n. 63. (Copy).
November 8. Map illustrating his voyage to Hudson Bay. 8, n. 67.
     (A. D. S.)

1680
February 4. Sale of a house to La Chesnaye. 9, n. 2. (D. S.)
February 19. Dissolution of partnership with Gabriel Gosselin. 9,
     n. 2. (D. S.)
March. Jolliet is granted Anticosti Island in fief. 9, n. 3.
April 10. Boisseau's protest against the Anticosti grant. 9, n. 11.
April 14. Contract for sale of property in Lower Town, Quebec. The
     document is in the Chicago Historical Society Library, Gunther
     Collection. (D. S.)
April 16. Land Grant to Lalande. AJQ, Greffe Becquet, minute. (D.
     S.)
April 17. Partnership contract. AJQ, Greffe Rageot, no. 668. (D.
     S.)

1681

Boisseau's mémoire et preuve. 9, n. 21.
Mentioned in the census of this year. 9, n. 51.
April 30. Paris. Louis XIV to Frontenac. 9, n. 36.
August 23. Out of court settlement of a lawsuit. 9, n. 29. (D. S.)
November 13. Duchesneau to Seignelay. 9, n. 43.

1682

Paris. Bernou's Relation des descouvertes. 7, n. 52.

1683

February 15. Jolliet appears before the Sovereign Council. 9, n. 51.
October 10. Hiring of a man-servant. 9, n. 62. (D. S.)
November 22. Jolliet appears before the Sovereign Council. 9, n. 63.
December 1. Contract with Claude Baillif. 9, n. 64. (A. D. S.)

1684

Map dedicated to La Barre; a variant of the map of November 8,
    1679. 8, n. 69. (A. D. S.)
January 19. Receipt. 9, n. 65. (D. S.)
March 9. Settlement of partnership accounts. 9, n. 66.   (A. D. S.)
March 14. Receipt. AJQ, Greffe Genaple. (D. S.)
Summer. Jolliet at Anticosti. 7, n. 62.
September 4. Jolliet and Baillif bring the contract of December 1,
    1683, to Rageot. 9, n. 65. (D. S.)

1685

January 23. Hiring of a sailor. 9, n. 68. (D. S.)
March 2. Jolliet leases his father-in-law's share of the Mingan con-
    cession. 9, n. 70. (D. S.)
September 9. Settlement out of court for damages incurred in 1681.
    9, n. 72. (D. S.)
November 10. Jolliet to Seignelay. 9, n. 75. (A. L. S.)
November 13. Denonville to Seignelay. 9, n. 83.
November 13. Denonville to Seignelay. 9, n. 91.

1686

Memoir of Jean Deshayes. 9, n. 89.
April 5. Jolliet waives his rights to the Lauzon seignioral grant. 9,
    n. 93. (D. S.)

1687

February 25. Receipt. 9, n. 95. (D. S.)
November 5. Jolliet buys a ship from Riverin. 9, n. 96. (D. S.)
December 20. Sells a ship to Damours de Louvières. 9, n. 96. (D.
    S.)

1688

April 29.   Settlement of accounts with Charet, private deed.   9, n. 96.   (Copy)

September 3.   Lease of his Quebec house to Bénac.   9, n. 97.   (D. S.)

September 7.   Account of Jolliet's indebtedness to Riverin.   9, n. 97. (D. S.)

1691

June 9.   Indebtedness to Verneuil.   9, n. 100.   (D. S.)

June 19.   Hiring of Bouchard.   9, n. 100.   (D S.)

July 15.   Jolliet leases his Quebec house to Prat. 9, n. 100.   (A. D. S.)

September 11.   Legalization of the lease of July 15.   9, n. 100.   (D. S.)

1692

September 15.   Frontenac and Champigny to Pontchartrain.   9, n. 101.

1693

October 25.   Frontenac to Lagny. 9, n. 106.

[November].   Jolliet to (Pontchartrain).   11, n. 1.   (Copy)

November 2.   Jolliet to Lagny.   9, n. 108.   (A. L. S.)

1694

January 25.   Acts as interpreter for a Montagnais-speaking woman. 10, n. 1.

October 28.   Jolliet to [Lagny]; transmitting (A. L. S.) the journal (A. D.) of his voyage to Labrador.   10, n. 21.

November 5.   Frontenac and Champigny to Pontchartrain.   11, n. 4.

1695

June 14.   Paris.   Louis XIV to Frontenac and Champigny.   11, n. 5.

[November] Frontenac to Pontchartrain.   11, n. 11.

November 2.   Frontenac to Lagny.   11, n. 8.

November 9.   Jolliet's contract with Charles and François Bissot.   11, n. 10.   (D. S.)

November 10.   Frontenac and Champigny to Pontchartrain.   11, n. 7.

1696

Returns to Canada.   11, n. 14.

June 13.   Jolliet at Seven Islands.   11, n. 13.

October 25.   Frontenac to Lagny.   11, n. 16.

November 7.   Receipt.   11, n. 12.   (Copy)

1697

April 30. Paris.   Commission of royal hydrographer.   11, n. 18.

April 30.   Jolliet receives the Etchemin concession.   11, n. 19.

1698

Map of the Gulf of St. Lawrence. 11, n. 20. (Copy)

1699

October 23. Map of the St. Lawrence River. 11, n. 22. (A. D. S.)

1700

March 9. Receipt. 11, n. 23. (Copy)
March 15. Summoned to appear before the Sovereign Council. 11, n. 23.
March 16. Hiring of Pierre Lusson. 11, n. 23. (Copy)
May 4. Jolliet signs the cathedral register. 11, n. 24.

BIBLIOGRAPHY

The following bibliography comprises only those books and articles quoted from or referred to in the series of articles on which this book is based.

ADAMS, RANDOLPH G. *Three Americanists.* Philadelphia, 1939.

ALFONCE DE SAINTONGE, JEAN FONTENEAU *dit. La Cosmographie auec l'Espère et le Régime du Soleil et du Nord.* G. Musset, ed. Paris, 1904.

    Les Voyages auantureux dv capitaine Ian Alfonce, Saincton-geois. 2d ed., Poitiers, 1559.

ALVORD, CLARENCE W. "An Unrecognized Father Marquette Letter." *The American Historical Review,* 25 (1920): 676–680.

ARMSTRONG, PERRY A. *The Piaza or the Devil among the Indians.* Morris, Illinois, 1887.

[BARCIA CARBILLADO Y ZUNIGA, ANDRÉS GONZÁLEZ DE.] *Ensayo cronologico para la Historia general de la Florida.* Madrid, 1723.

BAYLISS, CLARA K. "The Significance of the Piasa." *Transactions* of the Illinois State Historical Society for the Year 1908. Springfield, Illinois, 1909, 114–123.

BERNARD, JEAN F., ed. *Relations de la Louisiane et du Fléuve Missis-sipi.* Amsterdam, 1720.

BIRKET-SMITH, KAJ. *The Caribou Eskimos.* 2 parts, Copenhagen, 1929.

BOLTON, HERBERT E. "The Spanish Occupation of Texas, 1519–1590." *The Southwestern Historical Quarterly,* 16 (1912): 1–26.

BRYMNER, DOUGLAS, ed. *Report on Canadian Archives 1883.* Ottawa, 1884.

    Report on Canadian Archives 1885. Ottawa, 1886.

    Report on Canadian Archives 1887. Ottawa, 1888.

CABOT, WILLIAM B. *Labrador.* Boston, 1920.

CAOUETTE, JEAN-BAPTISTE. "Documents inédits sur Claire-Françoise Bissot, veuve de Louis Jolliet." *Bulletin des recherches his-toriques,* 22 (1916): 336–340.

CARON, IVANHOE. "Prêtres séculiers et Religieux qui ont exercé le ministère au Canada (1680–1690)." *Bulletin des recherches historiques*, 47 (1941): 256–268.

ED. *Journal de l'expédition du Chevalier de Troyes à la Baye d'Hudson en 1686.* Beauceville, 1918.

CARTER, HERBERT D. *Sea of Destiny; The Story of Hudson Bay— Our Undefended Backdoor.* New York, 1940.

CHARLAND, PAUL-V. "La date de la mort de Louis Joliet." *Bulletin des recherches historiques*, 20 (1914): 267.

CHARLEVOIX, PIERRE FRANCOIS XAVIER DE. *Histoire et description generale de la Nouvelle-France, avec le Journal historique d'un Voyage fait par ordre du Roi dans l'Amérique Septentrionnalle.* 3 volumes, Paris, 1744.

CLÉMENT, PIERRE, ed. *Lettres, Instructions et Mémoires de Colbert.* 7 volumes, Paris, 1861–1873.

COLEMAN, ARTHUR P. *La partie nord-est du Labrador et le Nouveau Québec.* Ottawa, 1922.

Collection de Manuscrits contenant lettres, mémoires, et autres documents historiques relatifs à la Nouvelle-France. 4 volumes, Quebec, 1883–1885.

CORDIER, HENRI. *Mélanges Américains.* Paris, 1913.

COYNE, JAMES H., ed. *Papers and Records*, Ontario Historical Society, volume 4, part 1, Toronto, 1913.

CROUSE, NELLIS M. *Contributions of the Canadian Jesuits to the Geographical Knowledge of New France 1632–1675.* Ithaca, New York, 1924.

DELANGLEZ, JEAN. "The Authorship of the Journal of Jean Cavelier." *Mid-America*, 25 (1943): 220–223.

"A Calendar of La Salle's Travels 1643–1683." *Mid-America*, 22 (1940): 278–305.

"Claude Dablon, S.J., 1619–1697." *Mid-America*, 26 (1944): 91–110.

* "The Discovery of the Mississippi. Primary Sources." *Mid-America*, 27 (1945): 219–231.

* "The Discovery of the Mississippi. Secondary Sources." *Mid-America*, 28 (1946): 3–22.

"Franquelin, Mapmaker." *Mid-America*, 25 (1943): 29–74.

Frontenac and the Jesuits. Chicago, 1939.

Hennepin's Description of Louisiana. Chicago, 1941.

"Hennepin's Voyage to the Gulf of Mexico 1680." *Mid-America,* 21 (1939): 32–82.

* "The Jolliet Lost Map of the Mississippi." *Mid-America,* 28 (1946): 67–144.

The Journal of Jean Cavelier. The Account of a Survivor of La Salle's Texas Expedition 1684–1688. Chicago, 1938.

"La Salle's Expedition of 1682." *Mid-America,* 22 (1940): 3–37.

* "Last Voyages and Death of Louis Jolliet." *Rapport de l'Archiviste de la Province de Québec pour 1943–1944.* Quebec, 1944, 149–206.

* "Louis Jolliet. Early Years: 1645–1674." *Mid-America,* 27 (1945): 3–29.

* "Louis Jolliet. The Middle Years: 1674–1686." *Mid-America,* 27 (1945): 67–96.

* "Marquette's Autograph Map of the Mississippi River." *Mid-America,* 27 (1945): 30–53.

* "The 'Récit des voyages et des découvertes du Père Jacques Marquette'." *Mid-America,* 28 (1946): 173–194, 211–258.

El Rio del Espíritu Santo. An Essay on the Cartography of the Gulf Coast and the Adjacent Territory during the Sixteenth and Seventeenth Centuries. New York, 1945.

✓ * "The 1674 Account of the Discovery of the Mississippi." *Mid-America,* 26 (1944): 301–324.

Some La Salle Journeys. Chicago, 1938.

"The Sources of the Delisle Map of America 1703." *Mid-America,* 25 (1943): 275–298.

* "The Voyage of Louis Jolliet to Hudson Bay in 1679." *Mid-America,* 26 (1944): 221–250.

"The Voyages of Tonti in North America, 1678–1704." *Mid-America,* 26 (1944): 255–300.

DESAULNIERS, FRANCOIS L. "Le Greffe du Notaire Jean Cusson." *Revue Canadienne,* 46 (1904): 62–65.

"Le Greffe de Jean Cusson." *Bulletin des recherches historiques,* 10 (1904): 51–56.

DESJARDINS, PAUL. *Le Collège Sainte–Marie de Montréal.* Montreal, 1940.

DRAPER, LYMAN C., ed. *Collections* of the State Historical Society of Wisconsin for the years 1880, 1881, and 1882. Madison, Wisconsin, 1883.

DUNN, WILLIAM E. *Spanish and French Rivalry in the Gulf Region of the United States, 1678–1702.* Austin, Texas, 1917.

DURO, CESAREO F. *Don Diego de Peñalosa y su descubrimiento del reino de Quivira.* Madrid, 1882.

FAILLON, ÉTIENNE-M. *Histoire de la colonie française en Canada.* 3 volumes, Villemarie, 1865–1866.

FAYE, STANLEY. "Jolliet goes West." *Journal* of the Illinois State Historical Society, 27 (1934): 5–30.

FERLAND, JEAN-BAPTISTE. *Notes sur les registres de Notre-Dame de Québec.* 2d ed., Quebec, 1863.

FOX, LUKE. *North-VVest Fox, or, Fox from the North-west passage.* London, 1635.

FRÉGAULT, GUY. *Iberville le conquérant.* Montreal, 1944.

GAGNON, ERNEST. " 'Jolliet' ou 'Joliet'." *Bulletin des recherches historiques*, 12 (1906): 306–310.

Louis Jolliet. Découvreur du Missisipi et du pays des Illinois, premier seigneur de l'Ile d'Anticosti. Montreal, 1946. On the various printings of this book see Foreword.

GAGNON, PHILÉAS. "Noms propres au Canada-Français." *Bulletin des recherches historiques*, 15 (1909): 17–30, 49–61, 80–94, 112–124, 143–157, 177–186.

GARRAGHAN, GILBERT J. " 'The Jolliet-Marquette Expedition of 1673'." *Thought*, 4 (1929): 32–71.

"Some Hitherto Unpublished Marquettiana." *Mid-America*, 18 (1936): 3–14.

"Some Newly Discovered Marquette and La Salle Letters." *Archivum Historicum Societatis Jesu*, 4 (1935): 268–290.

GILBERTSON, ALBERT N. "Some Ethical Phases of Eskimo Culture." *Journal of Religious Psychology*, 6 (1913): 321–374; 7 (1914): 45–74.

GOSLING, WILLIAM G. *Labrador: its Discovery, Exploration and Development.* London, 1910.

GOSSELIN, AMÉDÉE. "A Chicoutimi et au Lac St.-Jean à la fin du XVIIⁱᵉᵐᵉ siècle. Notes tirées d'un ancien registre." *Proceed-*

ings and Transactions of the Royal Society of Canada, 3rd series, volume 11 (1917), section 1, 113–135.

L'instruction publique au Canada sous le régime français. Quebec, 1911.

"Jean Jolliet et ses enfants." *Proceedings and Transactions* of the Royal Society of Canada, 3rd series, volume 14 (1921), section 1, 65–81.

GOSSELIN, AUGUSTE. *"Encore le P. de Bonnécampts (1707–1790)."* Proceedings and Transactions of the Royal Society of Canada, 2d series, volume 3 (1898), section 1, 93–117.

Vie de Mgr de Laval, premier évêque de Québec et apôtre du Canada, 1622–1708. 2 volumes, Quebec, 1890.

GRANDBOIS, ALAIN. *Né à Québec ... Louis Jolliet.* Paris, 1933.

GRAVIER, GABRIEL. *Etude sur une Carte inconnue. La première dressée par Louis Joliet en 1674.* Paris, 1880.

GREGORY, JOHN U. *Anticosti. Its Shipwrecks.* Quebec, 1881.

GRENFELL, WILFRED T. *A Labrador Doctor.* Boston and New York, 1922.

AND OTHERS. *Labrador: The Country and the People.* New York, 1910.

HABIG, MARION. *The Franciscan Père Marquette. A Critical Biography of Father Zénobe Membré, O.F.M., La Salle's Chaplain and Missionary Companion 1645 (ca.)–1689.* New York, 1934.

HACKETT, CHARLES W. "New Light on Don Diego de Peñalosa; Proof that he never made an Expedition from Santa Fé to Quivira and the Mississippi River in 1662." *The Mississippi Valley Historical Review,* 6 (1919): 313–335.

ED. *Historical Documents relating to New Mexico, Nueva Vizcaya and Approaches thereto, to 1773.* 3 volumes, Washington, D. C., 1923–1937.

HALE, HORATIO E. *Iroquois Book of Rites.* Philadelphia, 1883.

HAMY, ALFRED. *Au Mississippi. La première exploration (1673).* Paris, 1903.

HANNA, CHARLES H. *The Wilderness Trail.* 2 volumes, New York, 1911.

HARRISSE, HENRY. *Notes pour servir à l'histoire, à la bibliographie et à la cartographie de la Nouvelle-France et des pays adjacents 1545–1700.* Paris, 1872.

HAWKES, ERNEST W. *The Labrador Eskimo.* Ottawa, 1916.

HENNEPIN, LOUIS. *Description de la Louisiane.* Paris, 1863.
Nouvelle Decouverte d'un tres grand Pays Situé dans l'Amerique. Utrecht, 1697.

HODGE, FREDERICK W., ed. *Handbook of American Indians North of Mexico.* 2 volumes, 4th printing, Washington, D. C., 1912.

HUARD, VICTOR A. *Labrador et Anticosti.* Montreal, 1897.

HUTTON, SAMUEL K. *Among the Eskimos of Labrador.* London, 1912.

JAMES, THOMAS. *The Strange and Dangerous Voyage of Captaine Thomas Iames.* London, 1633.

JENKS, ALBERT E. "The Wild Rice Gatherers of the Upper Lakes." *Nineteenth Annual Report of the Bureau of American Ethnology, 1897–1898.* Washington, D. C., 1900, pp. 1019–1137.

JONES, ARTHUR E. "The Site of Mascoutin." *Proceedings* of the State Historical Society of Wisconsin for 1906. Madison, Wisconsin, 1907, pp. 175–182.

Jugements et délibérations du Conseil Souverain de la Nouvelle France, 1663–1710. 6 volumes, Quebec, 1885-1891.

KARPINSKI, LOUIS C. *Bibliography of the Printed Maps of Michigan.* Lansing, Michigan, 1931.

KELLOGG, LOUISE P. *Early Narratives of the Northwest 1634–1699.* New York, 1917.
The French Régime in Wisconsin and the Northwest. Madison, Wisconsin, 1925.
"Marquette's Authentic Map Possibly Identified." *Proceedings* of the State Historical Society of Wisconsin for 1906. Madison, Wisconsin, 1907, pp. 183–193.

KNIGHT, ROBERT and ZEUCH, LUCIUS H. *The Location of the Chicago Portage Route of the Seventeenth Century.* Chicago, 1928.

LAFITAU, JOSEPH F. *Moeurs des sauvages ameriquains comparées aux moeurs des premiers temps.* 2 volumes, Paris, 1724.

LAHONTAN, ARMAND L. DE L'OM DARCE, BARON DE. *Nouveaux Voyages de Mr. Le Baron de Lahontan dans l'Amerique Septentrionale.* La Haye, 1703.

LA POTHERIE, CLAUDE C. LE ROY, SIEUR DE BACQUEVILLE DE. *Voyage de l'Amerique, contenant Ce qui s'est passé de plus remarquable dans l'Amerique Septentrionale depuis 1534. jusqu'à present.* 4 volumes, Amsterdam, 1723.

LAUT, AGNES C. *The Conquest of the Great Northwest.* 2 volumes, New York, 1908.

LAVERDIÈRE, CHARLES H., ed. *Oeuvres de Champlain.* 7 Tomes in 3 volumes, Quebec, 1870.

    and CASGRAIN, HENRI R., eds. *Le Journal des Jésuites.* Montreal, 1892.

LE CLERCQ, CHRESTIEN. *Premier Etablissement de la Foy dans la Nouvelle France.* 2 volumes, Paris, 1691.

LE JEUNE, LOUIS. *Dictionnaire général ... du Canada.* 2 volumes, Ottawa, 1931.

LELAND, WALDO G., ed. *Guide to Material for American History in the Libraries and Archives of Paris.* Volume I. *Libraries.* Washington, D. C., 1932.

LELAND, WALDO G., MENG, JOHN J., and DOYSIÉ, ABEL, eds. *Guide to Materials for American History in the Libraries and Archives of Paris.* Volume II. *Archives of the Ministry of Foreign Affairs.* Washington, D. C. 1943.

LE TAC, SIXTE. *Histoire chronologique de la Nouvelle France.* E. Réveillaud, ed. Paris, 1888.

LEYMARIE, A.-LÉO. *Catalogue illustré* (Exposition restrospective des colonies françaises de l'Amérique du Nord). Paris, 1929.

LORIN, HENRI. *Le Comte de Frontenac.* Paris, 1895.

MARCEL, GABRIEL. *Cartographie de la Nouvelle France. Supplément à l'ouvrage de M. Harrisse.* Paris, 1885.

    Catalogue des documents géographiques exposés à la Section des Cartes et Plans de la Bibliothèque Nationale. Paris, 1892.

    Reproductions de cartes et de globes relatifs à la découverte de l'Amérique du XVIe au XVIIe siècle. Atlas and text. Paris, 1892.

MARGRY, PIERRE. "Louis Joliet." *Revue Canadienne*, 8 (1871): 930–942; 9 (1872): 61–72, 121–138, 205–219.

ED. *Découvertes et Établissements des Français dans l'Ouest et dans le Sud de l'Amérique Septentrionale.* 6 volumes, Paris, 1876–1888.

MARIE DE L'INCARNATION. *Lettres de la Venerable Mere Marie de l'Incarnation premiere Superieure des Ursulines de la Nouvelle France,* Paris, 1681.

MARKHAM, ALBERT H., ed. *The Voyages and Works of John Davis.* London, 1880.

MASSICOTTE, EDOUARD Z., ed. *Montréal sous le régime français.* Montreal, 1919.

[MONTÉZON, FORTUNÉ DE], ed. *Relations inédites de la Nouvelle-France (1672–1679) pour faire suite aux anciennes Relations (1615–1672).* 2 volumes, Paris, 1861.

MOREAU, STANISLAS-A. "Le Capitaine Alexandre de Berthier." *Bulletin des recherches historiques,* 7 (1901): 155–157.

MORTON, ARTHUR S. *A History of the Canadian West to 1870–1871.* London, [1939].

MOTT, MILDRED. "The Relation of History Indian Tribes to Archaeological Manifestations in Iowa." *The Iowa Journal of History and Politics,* 36 (1938): 227–314.

MYRAND, ERNEST. *Frontenac et ses amis.* Quebec, 1902.
Sir William Phips devant Québec. Quebec, 1893.

NEVILLE, A. C. "Some Historic Sites about Green Bay." *Proceedings of the Wisconsin Historical Society for 1905.* Madison, Wisconsin, 1906, pp. 143–156.

NUTE, GRACE L. *Caesars of the Wilderness.* New York, 1943.
Lake Superior. New York and Indianapolis. 1944.

O'CALLAGHAN, EDMUND B., ed. *Documents relative to the Colonial History of the State of New York.* Volume 9, Albany, New York, 1855.

OLDMIXON, JOHN. "The History of Hudson's Bay," in *The British Empire in America.* London, 1708.

PACKARD, ALPHEUS S. *The Labrador Coast.* New York, 1891.

PARKMAN, FRANCIS. *La Salle and the Discovery of the Great West.* 11th ed., Boston, 1907.

PEASE, THEODORE C. and WERNER, RAYMOND W., eds. *The French Foundations.* Collections of the Illinois State Historical Library, volume 23, French Series, volume 1, Springfield, Illinois, 1934.

PERROT, NICOLAS. *Memoire sur les Moeurs, Coustumes et Relligion des Sauvages de l'Amerique Septentrionale par Nicolas Perrot.* Jules Tailhan, ed., Paris, Leipzig and 1864.

PINART, ALPHONSE L., ed. *Recueil de Cartes, Plans et Vues relatifs aux États-Unis et au Canada, New York, Boston, Montréai, Québec, Louisbourg (1651–1731).* Paris, 1893.

POULIOT, ADRIEN and GIROUX, T.-EDMOND. "Où est né Louis Jolliet?" *Bulletin des recherches historiques,* 51 (1945): 334–346; 359–363; 374.

POTVIN, DAMASE. *En Zigzag. Sur la Côte et dans l'Ile.* Quebec, 1929.

REPPLIER, AGNES. *Père Marquette.* Garden City, New York, 1929.

RICH, EDWIN E., ed. *Minutes of the Hudson's Bay Company 1671–1674.* Toronto, 1942.

RICHARD, EDOUARD, ed. *Supplement to Dr. Brymner's Report on Canadian Archives 1899.* Ottawa, 1901.

ROBSON, JOSEPH. *An Account of six years residence in Hudson's Bay, 1733–1736, 1744–1747.* London, 1752.

ROCHEMONTEIX, CAMILLE DE. *Les Jésuites et la Nouvelle-France au XVIIe siècle.* 3 volumes, Paris, 1895–1896.

ED. *Relation par lettres de l'Amerique Septentrionalle (années 1709 et 1710).* Paris, 1904.

ROUILLARD, EUGENE. *La Côte Nord du Saint-Laurent et le Labrador Canadien.* Quebec, 1908.

ROY, ANTOINE, ed. *Inventaire des Greffes des Notaires du Régime Français.* 7 volumes, Quebec, 1942–1946.

ROY, JOSEPH-E. "Le Baron de Lahontan." *Proceedings and Transactions* of the Royal Society of Canada, 1st series, volume 12 (1895), section 1, 63–192.

Histoire de la seigneurie de Lauzon. 5 volumes, Lévis, 1897–1904.

"Jean Bourdon et la baie d'Hudson." *Bulletin des recherches historiques,* 2 (1896): 2–9, 21–23.

Rapport sur les Archives de France relatives à l'histoire du Canada. Ottawa, 1911.

Roy, Pierre-G. *Les cimetières de Québec.* Lévis, 1943.

  La Famille Vianney Pachot. Lévis, 1915.

"Jean Péré et Pierre Moreau dit La Taupine." *Bulletin des recherches historiques,* 10 (1905): 213–221.

Les petites choses de notre histoire. Sixième série. Lévis, 1931.

Toutes petites choses du Régime Français. Première série. Quebec, 1944.

ED. *Inventaire de Pièces sur la côte de Labrador.* 2 volumes, Quebec, 1940–1942.

ED. *Inventaire des Insinuations de la Prévôté de Québec.* 3 volumes, Quebec, 1936.

ED. *Inventaire d'une collection de pièces ... conservées aux Archives judiciaires de Québec.* 2 volumes, Beauceville, 1917.

ED. *Rapport de l'Archiviste de la Province de Québec pour 1921–1922* (Quebec, 1922); *pour 1922–1923* (Quebec, 1923); *pour 1924–1925* (Quebec, 1925); *pour 1925–1926* (Quebec, 1926); *pour 1926–1927* (Quebec, 1927); *pour 1927–1928* (Quebec, 1928); *pour 1928–1929* (Quebec, 1929); *pour 1930–1931* (Quebec, 1931); *pour 1935–1936.* Quebec, 1936.

Roy, Régis and Malchelosse, Gérard. *Le Régiment de Carignan.* Montreal, 1925.

Schmitt, Joseph. *Monographie de l'Ile d'Anticosti.* Paris, 1904.

Scott, Henri-A. *Nos Anciens Historiographes.* Lévis, 1930.

Shea, John G. *Discovery and Exploration of the Mississippi Valley.* Redfield, 1852.

ED. *Relation de ce qui s'est passé de plus remarquable aux Missions des Peres de la Compagnie de Jesus en la Nouvelle France.* New York, 1861.

ED. and transl. *The Expedition of Don Diego de Peñalosa, Governor of New Mexico, from Santa Fé to the River Mischipi and Quivira in 1662, as described by Father Nicholas de Freytas, O.S.F.* New York, 1882.

ED. and transl. *First Establishment of the Faith in New France. By Father Christian Le Clercq, Recollect Missionary.* 2 volumes, New York, 1881.

ED. and transl. *History and General Description of New France. By the Rev. P. F. X. de Charlevoix, S.J.* 6 volumes, New York, 1866–1872.

SMITH, CLARA S. *Manuscript Maps in the Edward E. Ayer Collection.* Planographed, Chicago, 1927.

SPARKS, JARED. "Father Marquette." *The Library of American Biography.* 2d ed., 10 volumes, New York, 1848, volume 10: 265-299.

STEARNS, WINFRID A. *Labrador.* Boston, 1884.

STECK, FRANCIS B. *Father Garraghan and "The Jolliet-Marquette Expedition, 1673."* [St. Louis, 1930].

The Jolliet-Marquette Expedition, 1673. Quincy, Illinois, 1928.

SULTE, BENJAMIN. "Les Français dans l'Ouest en 1671." *Proceedings and Transactions* of the Royal Society of Canada, 3rd series, volume 12 (1918), section 1, 1-32.

Histoire des Canadiens-Français. 8 volumes, Montreal, 1882-1884.

Mélanges historiques. G. Malchelosse, ed. Volume 8, Montreal, 1922.

"Le Régiment de Carignan." *Proceedings and Transactions* of the Royal Society of Canada, 2d series, volume 8 (1902), section 1, 25-95.

TANGUAY, CYPRIEN. *A Travers les Registres.* Montreal, 1886.

Dictionnaire généalogique des familles canadiennes. Volume 1, Montreal, 1871.

THÉVENOT, MELCHISSÉDECH, ed. *Recueil de voyages de Mᵣ Thevenot.* Paris, 1681.

THWAITES, REUBEN G. *Historic Waterways.* Chicago, 1888.

ED. *The Jesuit Relations and Allied Documents.* 73 volumes, Cleveland, 1896-1901.

ED. *A New Discovery of a Vast Country in America.* By Father Louis Hennepin. 2 volumes, Chicago, 1903.

TUCKER, SARA J. *Indian Villages of the Illinois Country.* Volume II, Scientific Papers, Illinois State Museum, Part I, *Atlas.* Springfield, Illinois, 1942.

TYRRELL, JOSEPH B., ed. *Documents Relating to the Early History of Hudson Bay.* Toronto, 1931.

UNITED STATES HYDROGRAPHIC OFFICE. *Sailing Directions for the Gulf and River St. Lawrence.* Washington, D. C., 1934.

VERWYST, CHRYSOSTOM. "Geographical Names in Wisconsin, Minnesota and Michigan Having a Chippewa Origin." *Collections of the State Historical Society of Wisconsin.* Volume 12, Madison, Wisconsin, 1892, pp. 390–398.

VILLIERS DU TERRAGE, MARC DE. *La Louisiane. Histoire de son nom et de ses frontières successives (1681–1819).* Paris, 1929.

ED. *Les Raretés des Indes.* "Codex Canadiensis." *Album manuscrit de la fin du XVIIe siècle contenant 180 dessins concernant les indigènes, leurs coutumes, tatouages, la faune et la flore de la Nouvelle France, plus deux cartes.* Paris, 1930.

WELD, LAENAS G. "Joliet and Marquette in Iowa." *The Iowa Journal of History and Politics,* 1 (1903): 3–16.

WINSOR, JUSTIN. *Cartier to Frontenac.* Boston and New York, 1894.

ED. *Narrative and Critical History of America.* 8 volumes, Boston and New York, 1884–1889.

WOOD, J. J. "The Mascoutin Village." *Proceedings* of the State Historical Society of Wisconsin for 1906. Madison, Wisconsin, 1907, pp. 167–174.

INDEX

ABBREVIATIONS

B.— Bay
C.— Cape
G.— Gulf
I.— Island

Is.— Islands
L.—Lake
R.— River

Abancourt, Marie d', 1, 6
Acadia, 86, 88
Action Catholique (Quebec), 17, 190
Aganalt (Aganahi, Aganatchi), 122
Akansea, 64; see Arkansas
Akansea (Indians), 118; village, 119
Akansea, former name of Ohio R., 113
Albanel, Charles, 151, 158; to Hudson Bay, 34, 43, 102, 149, 161 ff; second voyage to Hudson Bay, 164 f
Albanel, L., 170
Albany R., 169; English post on, 165
Alienak, Eskimo chief, 231
Alim8ec, 19
Allemand, Pierre, 207; map of Labrador coast, 205
Allouez, Claude, first western voyage, 27; second western voyage, 23; brings samples of copper ore, 9; first mention of Mississippi by name, 23 f, 109; to Mascoutens village, 77; and Sea of the North, 161; journal of 1669–1670; report of 1674; letter of, 93 f; map of Lake Superior, 35
Amaillouk, Eskimo chief, 231 f
André, Louis, on Lake Huron, 34; with Jolliet to Anticosti, 143
Annapolis, N. S., 84
Anticosti Corporation, 178
Anticosti I., 193, 241; size, 178; granted in fief to Jolliet, 78,

141, 177, 246; location of Jolliet's first house on, 189 ff; on Jolliet's maps of 1679 and 1684, 170; chaplain at, 143
Anville, Jean Baptiste Bourguignon d', map, 205
Archives du Service Hydrographique, ms in, 52 f, 82
Ashwapmuchuan R., 168 f
Assiniboin (Assinipoüalac), country, 32; Indians, 35, 175
Arkansas, country, 120; Indians, 118; river, 53, 67, 112 f, 117; villages, 112; see Quapaw
Atlantic Ocean, 41
Avaugour, Pierre Dubois baron d', 159; permit to Couture, 151, 154 f
Aviktok (Eskimo B.), 203

Baffin I., 169
Bailiff, Claude, 191
Baillargé, Antoine, 16
Balsamon, see Belles Amours
Barcia Carbillado y Zunigo, A. G. de, 250
Barrois, Jacques, 83, 85
Basset, Bénigne, 131
Baudrand, Michel A., 41
Bayly, Charles, 152; takes possession of Port Nelson, 164; ships Albanel to England, 165; letter of Jolliet to, 172 f; meets Jolliet, 182
Bazire, Charles, 134, 139
Beauharnois, Charles de la Boische, marquis de, and Hocquart,

Chouart, C., 205, 207
"Codex Canadiensis," 75
Colbert, Jean Baptiste, 11, 78, 141; to Talon, 10, 136; Frontenac to, 44, 58, 130, 134; to Talon, 14; notified of Jolliet's return, 105 f; given a map of the Great Lakes, 89 f; petitioned by Jolliet, 135; denies Jolliet's petition, 144; interview with Dudouyt, 144
Colbertie, 84
Collège Sainte-Marie, archives, 46 f, 62, 94
Columbus, Christopher, 157
Compagnie de la Baie du Nord, 152 f
Compagnie de la Nouvelle-France, 1, 146
Compagnie de Richelieu, 146
Compagnie des Habitants, 146 f
Compagnie des Indes Occidentales, 146
Compagnie du Nord, 195
Comporté, Philippe Gaultier de, 180, 186
Conception, mission, 126, 129
Conception, R. (Mississippi), 64 f, 109, 123 f
Conestoga, 8
Corda, Jérôme, 240
Cormorant, C., 243
Corossol, the, 236
Corte Reals, the, 202
Côte du Nord, 202 f
Couillard, Marie, 147 f, 243
Courcelle, Daniel de Rémy, sieur de, 33; to Lake Ontario, 35, 39
Couture, Guillaume, voyage to Lake Nemiskau, 151, 154; testimony of, 159 f
Cree (Guilistinons), 28
Cumberland G., 169
Cumberland R., 22

Dablon, Claude, 56, 63, 85, 158, 164; report on western geo-graphy, 27 ff; route to Vermilion Sea, 57; to Lake Nikabau, 26, 151, 155, 159; and Sea of the North, 161; certificate, 153 ff; on death of Ménard, 27; goes to the West, 23; to Mascoutens village, 34, 38, 125; and map of Lake Superior, 35; rector of Jesuit College of Quebec, 34; Relation of 1670–1671, 76 f; letter transmitting Relation of 1671–1672, 43, 102; orders Marquette to accompany Jolliet, 107; interviews Jolliet, 45, 77; letter of August 1, 1674, 82, 89 f, 95, 103 f, 121 f, 130, 133, 136, 248; mss, 45 ff; title of, 59 f, 106; and map of voyage of 1673, 107 f; to Boucher, 92, 97; author of the Récit, 95 ff, 100; concept of history, 98
Dagneau, Georges H., 17
Daleyrac, Jean, 85
Davis, John, on Labrador coast, 203 f, 207
Davis Strait, 169
Delisle, Claude, 90; maps of 1700 and 1703, 205
Denis, sieur de Saint-Simon, Paul, voyage to Hudson Bay, 101, 149, 161; testimony, 162 f
Denonville, Jacques René de Brisay, marquis de, 158, 190; sends expedition to Hudson Bay, 153; to Seignelay, 195 ff
De Pere, Wis., 63, 108
De Quen, Jean, discovers Lake St. John, 150
Deshayes, Jean, 196 f, 209
Des Plaines R., 52, 89, 126
Detroit R., 13
Divine, R. de la, 84, 89
Dodier, Jeanne, 12, 16, 131
Dollier de Casson, François, 7 ff;

instructions to discoverers, 163 f; sends A. Jolliet to locate copper mine, 8; sends St. Lusson to the West, 36 f; sends Jolliet to discover the Sea of the South, 18, 58, 100, 105 f; sends Paul Denis to Hudson Bay, 101; to Colbert, 11; Colbert to, 136

Tamaroa, village, 112

Tanguay, Cyprien, 242, 245

Tartary, 39

Theguayo, conquest of, 86 ff

Thévenot, Melchissédec, publishes map of Mississippi, 61, 72 f, 122; publishes Récit, 95, 194, 248

Thiberge, Jean, 96, 103 ff

Three Rivers, 12, 169, 172

Thwaites, Reuben G., on Relation of 1672–1673, 46 ff; reprints Dablon's letter of August 1, 1674, 54; publishes Récit, 95; on Shea's facsimile of Marquette's map, 62

Tinawatawa, 8 f

Tokyo, 25

Tongigua, village, 117

Tonti, Henri, 112

Tourima, village, 117

Tracy, Alexandre de Prouville, marquis de, 4

Traite de Tadoussac, 46 f, 170, 177, 184

Tyrrell, Joseph B., 165

Ungava B., 169

Uzutiuhi, village, 117

Vermilion Sea (Mar Vermejo, Mer Vermeille), 22, 24 f, 38 f, 41 f, 58, 60, 89, 106, 122; route to, 57; see Gulf of California

Vimont, Barthélemy, 1

Virginia, 40, 122, 150; coast, 21, 23

Voyage of 1673, cartographical evidence, 61 ff; Marquette's journal of, 118, 120, 129; references in Bernou's papers, 83 ff; in Thévenot, 194; maps illustrating the, 61 ff; nomenclature, 78 f; narrative, 100 ff; personnel, 103 ff; equipment, 107; objective, 106; route from Michilimackinac to Prairie du Chien, 108 f; arrival at mouth of the Wisconsin River, 123; date of arrival at the Peoria village, 110; halt at the Peoria village, 113; terminus, 58 f, 75, 97, 112 ff, 117, 248 f; reasons for returning, 121; date of departure from Quapaw, 124; meeting with Monsopelea, 123 f; at the Kaskaskia village, 126; portage at Sturgeon Bay, 127; date of arrival at St. Francis Xavier mission, 128

Wabash R., 111

Washimeska R., 168

Waymouth, George, on Labrador coast, 204

West, Sea of the, 25, 29 f, 31 f, 34 ff, 39

White R., 67, 117

Whittle, C., 203

Winnebago, 28, 193

Wisconsin R., 33, 64, 70, 72, 89, 97; mouth of, 109, 113, 121, 123

Wolf R., 63

Wolstenholme, C., 29, 169

Yonge or Young, Sir Thomas, 150

Zoar, 203, 207, 209